Native Memoirs from the War of 1812

Johns Hopkins Books on the War of 1812

Donald R. Hickey, Series Editor

Also in the Series

Ralph E. Eshelman, *The War of 1812 in the Chesapeake:
A Reference Guide to Historic Sites in Maryland, Virginia,
and the District of Columbia*

Ralph E. Eshelman, *A Travel Guide to the War of 1812 in the Chesapeake:
Eighteen Tours in Maryland, Virginia, and the District of Columbia*

Donald R. Hickey and Connie D. Clark, *The Rockets' Red Glare:
An Illustrated History of the War of 1812*

Donald G. Shomette, Foreword by Fred W. Hopkins, Jr.,
*Flotilla: The Patuxent Naval Campaign
in the War of 1812*

Native Memoirs from the War of 1812

Black Hawk and William Apess

CARL BENN

Johns Hopkins University Press
Baltimore

Johns Hopkins University Press
2715 North Charles Street
Baltimore, Maryland 21218-4363
www.press.jhu.edu

Library of Congress Cataloging-in-Publication Data

Native memoirs from the War of 1812 : Black Hawk and William Apess
/ Carl Benn.
pages cm.—(Johns Hopkins books on the War of 1812)
Includes bibliographical references and index.
ISBN-13: 978-1-4214-1218-4 (hardcover : alk. paper)
ISBN-13: 978-1-4214-1219-1 (pbk. : alk. paper)
ISBN-13: 978-1-4214-1220-7 (electronic)
ISBN-10: 1-4214-1218-7 (hardcover : alk. paper)
ISBN-10: 1-4214-1219-5 (pbk. : alk. paper)
ISBN-10: 1-4214-1220-9 (electronic)
1. United States—History—War of 1812—Participation, Indian.
2. United States—History—War of 1812—Personal narratives.
3. Black Hawk, Sauk chief, 1767–1838.   4. Apess, William, 1798–1839.
5. Sauk Indians—Biography.   6. Pequot Indians—Biography.
I. Benn, Carl, 1953–   II. Black Hawk, Sauk chief, 1767–1838. Life of
Ma-ka-tai-me-she-kia-kiak or Black Hawk Selections.   III. Apess,
William, 1798–1839. Son of the forest Selections.
E359.9.I63N38 2014
973.5'20897—dc23
2013016721

A catalog record for this book is available from the British Library.

*Special discounts are available for bulk purchases of this book. For more
information, please contact Special Sales at 410-516-6936 or
specialsales@press.jhu.edu.*

For my family

Contents

Illustrations follow page 78.

Preface

In the War of 1812 Great Britain and the United States fought the last great military confrontation in eastern North America, and the First Nations who lived around the Great Lakes and along the upper Mississippi River played major roles in that struggle. Most who took up arms allied with Britain: those who lived south of the Canadian-American border and west of Lake Erie typically felt threatened by white settlers as the Republic expanded, while many natives to the north feared an American conquest of the British colonies because its aftermath could lead to the loss of their territories and freedoms. Nevertheless, a significant number of indigenous people, primarily in Ohio, New York, and other regions with large white populations, fought alongside the Americans, largely because they believed their interests could be preserved best by aligning with the dominant society. Many others chose neutrality over belligerency, hoping to protect their communities and their families through maintaining peaceful relations with the opposing powers. Beyond geopolitical reasons for going to war, other factors motivated individuals, ranging from the warrior tradition that encouraged men to demonstrate their prowess in combat, to the use of violence to avenge deaths suffered by members of their societies, to a range of other personal and cultural concerns.

Indigenous voices from the war survive in the historical records from the period, although they tend to do so in imperfect and modest forms. They appear in the minutes of councils held between First Nations and Euro-Americans or among the tribes, and in letters and other documents, written either by small numbers of literate native people or, more commonly, by outsiders who recorded their thoughts as they heard them from individuals they met. Their voices also live on in oral traditions and in recorded postwar interviews with those who witnessed the events of 1812–15. Beyond these sources, there are four extensive autobiographies by indigenous combatants from the northern fronts which preserve extended discussions of their involvement in the conflict: those of Sauk war chief Black Hawk from the upper Mississippi, Pequot teenager William Apess from Connecticut, Mohawk military and diplomatic leader John Norton from modern-day Ontario, and the enigmatic Mohawk Eleazer Williams from today's Quebec. This book presents those portions of the memoirs related to the war by the two indigenous men who lived in the United States: Black Hawk, who fought against the Americans at the head of traditional war parties, and William Apess, who served the Republic within the ranks of two of its artillery formations. (In a separate publication I plan to explore John Norton's experiences; but I will leave Eleazer Williams alone because I believe his memoirs are so unreliable and exaggerated that they do not warrant the kind of close study presented in the pages below.)

My objective in presenting the autobiographies of Black Hawk and William Apess is to encourage readers to explore the thoughts and experiences recorded by these indigenous participants through their own words. Their stories present fascinating insights into native perspectives and involvement in the conflict in their own right. They also are two of the best memoirs produced by any of the war's veterans and thus possess significance for understanding the period beyond the obvious desire to hear important First Nations voices. While each text stands up well by itself, combining them in one book enhances opportunities to appreciate the diversities of aboriginal experiences, which arose in part because of differences in tribal affiliations, religious beliefs, personal histories, and geographical settings. Despite the dissimilarities between the authors and their exceptional status as the creators of extended autobiographies within native societies of their time, they shared deep indigenous identities, affirmed aboriginal cultures and nationalisms with vigor, and possessed an intense commitment to protecting First Nations interests. Accordingly, their memoirs serve as vibrant links to the lives and views of indigenous people at an important watershed in North American history, speaking to us in the twenty-first century with a vitality that commands our attention.

Rather than present the autobiographies on their own with only a minimum amount of introductory material, I deployed my skills as a historian to research, introduce, and annotate them in some detail in order to place these veterans of the War of 1812 in their historical contexts, address salient issues, and clarify their words where necessary, as well as present new information and interpretations to refine our appreciation of these men and their texts. I used Black Hawk's original 1833 edition of his *Life of Ma-ka-tai-me-she-kia-kiak or Black Hawk* and William Apess's 1831 (second) edition of *A Son of the Forest* as the base documents for this book. The originals are longer than the presentations below because they contain materials focused beyond the authors' participation in the War of 1812. Quotations and references to parts of their memoirs that fall outside the sections included in this book are drawn from Barry O'Connell's 1992 important compilation of Apess's writings and Donald Jackson's excellent modern edition of Black Hawk's autobiography (first published in 1955 but which exists in a newer version).[1]

Within the portions of the autobiographies covering Black Hawk's and William Apess's participation in the war, I did not cut or add words (except to insert the occasional clarifying word in square brackets), although sometimes I corrected word or verb errors silently where it seemed appropriate to do so. To facilitate understanding of these texts and the other historical documents cited, I regularized spelling, punctuation, numbering, and capitalization, and I wrote out abbreviations in full. For the sake of clarity, I also corrected proper names when they were misspelled and when the original presentation did not align with today's common usage. I left grammatically incorrect sentences unchanged where they could not be mended through adjusting the punctuation or by adding a word in square brackets. In the case of Black Hawk's memoirs, the original nineteenth-century editor used exclamation points and italicized words extensively when he prepared the document for print, even for the time period when such devices were common (but reduced their numbers in a later edition of the book). As other scholars have noted, most of these elements imposed a tone or emphasis that probably was not authentic to Black Hawk's voice, while undermining the narrative force of his autobiography and adding an unfortunate quaintness that might inhibit readers from recognizing the maturity of Black Hawk's words.[2] Therefore, I converted the majority of exclamation points to more modest punctuation and the bulk of italicized type to roman type, and, to a lesser degree, I did the same in William Apess's memoirs where it seemed fitting to do so. I changed sentence and paragraph breaks when such adjustments enhanced clarity or made better sense of the chronological sequencing. A few of the changes might appear to have altered the meaning of sentences, but where this has occurred I believe the modifications captured the authors' intentions better than the earlier versions of the texts did. (Anyone wishing to examine the originals without these intrusions may do so easily by consulting other editions listed in the bibliography.) I split Black Hawk's undivided autobiography into sections to accommodate introductions to the discrete components of his narrative but left Apess's preexisting chapter divisions in place. Dates have been added as subheadings to help readers navigate the sequencing of events, which can be confusing in Black Hawk's memoirs because they are less chronological than Apess's.

As there is some disagreement today on how native people ought to be addressed in print, an explanation of my approach in those parts of the book which present my words rather than those of the indigenous authors seems appropriate. First, I employed speech patterns when describing First Nations which are the same as those I use for European nations in order to affirm equality. Thus, I used the common English word for a people (e.g., "Mohawks") rather than the nation's own word, as I would do for Europeans (e.g., "Germans"). As English is an evolving language, some aboriginal terms have become common in conventional parlance and thus entered my prose, such as "Kahnawake," which has replaced "Caughnawaga" in my lifetime, just as "Beijing" has replaced "Peking." I used "First Nations" as an equivalent to "European." I did this not only because the other common term, "Indian," has fallen out of use in much of North America (especially in Canada, where I live), but because it often conjures up unfortunate images due to the legacy of how "Indians" have been misrepresented in history, literature, and popular culture. I did not use "Native American," despite the term's common acceptance in the United States, because it sounds tinny to Canadian ears and because its structure subtly implies that aboriginal populations do not have a distinct place in North America from, say, Swedish Americans or Chinese Canadians; and I did not use "Amerindian" as it does not seem to have taken root as a common word despite attempts to introduce it over the past several decades.

I used collective confederacy names equally (e.g., "Iroquois" and "British"), as I did national and community names (e.g., "Shawnees" and "Americans," or "Saukenuk" and "Detroit"). The words "native," "indigenous," and "aboriginal" seem limiting because of intermarriage, cross-cultural migration, and other such factors among both natives and newcomers of the early nineteenth century, despite their utility, so I did not capitalize them, as I did not capitalize the equivalently limited but functional words "white" and "black." (Using lowercase also appeals to me because of our growing rejection of race as a legitimate division among peoples.) Today, some people object to the term "aboriginal," often associating it with words like "abnormal," but its etymology from the Latin *ab* simply means "from," while *origine* conveys the idea of "beginning" or "origin," and hence "aboriginal" is an appropriate term because it means "from the beginning" in reference to a people's occupancy of a region. I used the word "tribe" interchangeably with "nation," as was common in the early 1800s, and which respects the freer nature of the political structures of indigenous nations at the time in a nonjudgmental way, much as "constitutional monarchy" and "republic" should be read as descriptive rather than value-laden terms.

In many instances, it did not seem possible to be precise in listing statistical information in my annotations, such as the exact numbers of people engaged in battles; therefore, I generally rounded figures from what I believed were the most credible available sources. In an effort to keep citations manageable in a work where descriptive notes form a large part of the text, I tried to limit source citations to items that were particularly germane to the main stories of Black Hawk and William Apess, choosing not to provide references to lesser factual points or to those that enjoy widespread acceptance among scholars or can be checked easily through recourse to standard reference works. As well, the old custom of providing only short citations in notes from the first instance which was common a century ago has begun to be used again, and accordingly this book follows that practice, but of course the bibliography offers readers full data on the publications and other documents used.

Many people and organizations helped me in researching and writing this book. In particular I want to acknowledge my most sincere appreciation for the encouragement, advice, and support I received from the series editor of the Johns Hopkins Books on the War of 1812, Donald Hickey, and from Bob Brugger, senior editor at the press. In addition, I would like to express my gratitude to fellow historians John Grodzinski at the Royal Military College of Canada, Timothy Willig of Indiana University, Heriberto Dixon, Laurence M. Hauptman, Donald Graves, and Robert Malcomson, all of whom were particularly generous in sharing research and providing guidance. As always, I thank Ann Joan Procyk for her excellent editorial advice. I am grateful to Michael Morrish, a geography student at Ryerson University, for creating the maps in this book. My appreciation goes to David Hudson, who undertook research on my behalf in Iowa to assist with the Black Hawk section of this publication. Likewise, I must recognize my debts to people who took time to comment on parts of the manuscript and thereby helped me create a stronger work: Daniel Colbert of the Old Fort Madison Research Committee, Michael Dickey at the Arrow Rock State Historic Site, Robert Owens of Wichita State University, Karim Tiro at Xavier University, Roald Tweet of Augustana College, William Whittaker of the University of Iowa, along with Dave Bennett, Richard Barbuto, Michael Harris, Catherine Molnar, Gerry Neilands, and Stuart Sutherland.

The following individuals helped through sharing ideas and research: Phyllis Airhart at the University of Toronto, Rosemary Burns and Nancy Soderberg of the Mashpee Historical Commission and Archives, Brian Leigh Dunnigan at the William L. Clements Library, as well as Alan Finlayson, Peter Gibbons, Robert Henderson, Jon Jouppien, Laurie Leclair, Roger Sharpe, and Mike Sherfy. I also would like to acknowledge my gratitude to the efficient staff at the Ryerson University and the University of Toronto libraries, and to the people at similar institutions who cooperated with them in providing interlibrary loan services. In addition, I thank the following for their assistance: Joan Avant of the Mashpee Historical Society, Betsy Caldwell at the Indiana Historical Society, Beth Carvey of the Hauberg Museum, Diane Denyes-Wenn at Macaulay Heritage Park, Prudence Doherty of the University of Vermont Library, Pam Galbraith at the Cragin Memorial Library, Allison Gifford of the Mashpee Public Library, Kara Jackman at the Boston University School of Theology Library, Ara Kaye of the State Historical Society of Missouri, Harry Miller at the Wisconsin Historical Society, Scott W. Nickerson of the Barnstable Superior Court, Trudy Nicks at the Royal Ontario Museum, Dennis Northcott of the Missouri Historical Society, Eunice Schlichting at the Putnam Museum of History and Natural Science, Antonia Stephens of the Sturgis Library, along with the staff at the Archives of Ontario, Library and Archives Canada, the McCord Museum, and the Davenport Public Library for access to their documentary collections, and all the people at the institutions credited elsewhere in these pages who provided evocative illustrations for this book. Finally, I would like to recognize that over the years many people from within and beyond the First Nations world contributed to my formation as a historian, either in direct conversation or through the texts they wrote, and the pages below reflect their impact on my development.

I began writing this book before moving into full-time academia from the museum field, and so I did not have access to much of the funding normally available for such projects. Once I came to Ryerson University, however, I did benefit from my generous start-up research fund and other resources provided by the Faculty of Arts in completing this work, for which I am most grateful.

Finally, I wish to acknowledge my gratitude to other people who worked on creating an attractive and accessible book at Johns Hopkins University Press—Melissa Solarz, Martha Sewall, Julie McCarthy, and Kimberly Johnson—as well as Julie Burris for her excellent design work and Jeremy Horsefield for his professionally elegant copyediting. Thanks also to the anonymous reviewer of the manuscript for his or her generous comments and valuable suggestions.

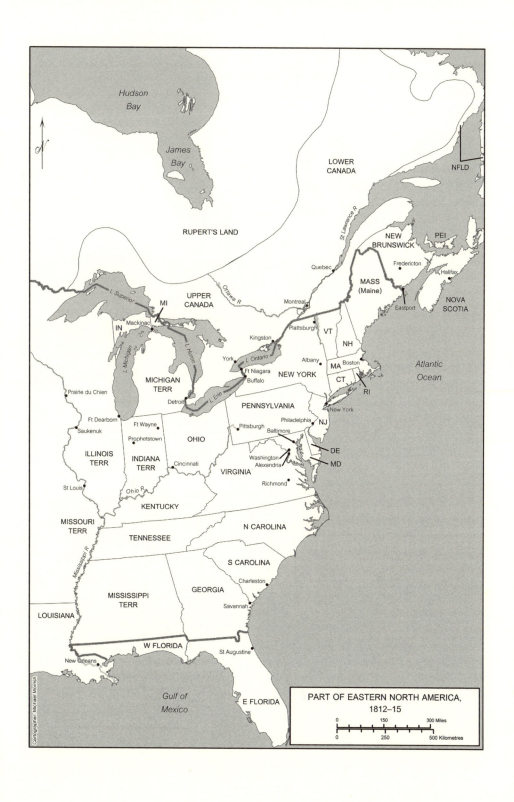

PART OF EASTERN NORTH AMERICA,
1812–15

Hudson
Bay

James
Bay

NFLD

LOWER
CANADA

RUPERT'S LAND

St Lawrence R

NEW
BRUNSWICK

PEI

Fredericton

Halifax

MASS
(Maine)

NOVA
SCOTIA

Quebec

L Superior

MI

UPPER
CANADA

Ottawa R

Montreal

Plattsburgh

Eastport

Mackinac

IN

VT

Kingston

L Michigan

L Huron

York

L Ontario

NH

Atlantic
Ocean

MICHIGAN
TERR

Ft Niagara

Albany

MA

Boston

Prairie du Chien

NEW YORK

Buffalo

CT

RI

Detroit

L Erie

Ft Dearborn

Ft Wayne

PENNSYLVANIA

New York

Saukenuk

Prophetstown

OHIO

Pittsburgh

Philadelphia

NJ

ILLINOIS
TERR

INDIANA
TERR

Cincinnati

Baltimore

DE

Washington

MD

St Louis

Ohio R

VIRGINIA

Alexandria

Richmond

KENTUCKY

MISSOURI
TERR

Mississippi R

TENNESSEE

N CAROLINA

S CAROLINA

Charleston

MISSISSIPPI
TERR

GEORGIA

Savannah

LOUISIANA

W FLORIDA

St Augustine

New Orleans

Gulf of
Mexico

E FLORIDA

Cartographer: Michael Morrish

0   150   300 Miles

0   250   500 Kilometres

FIRST NATIONS OF THE OLD NORTHWEST
AND ADJOINING REGIONS, 1812–15

OJIBWA Dominant native group in a region

Alienated First Nations land (often disputed)
with the relevant treaty dates

Note: aboriginal communities often were mixed culturally and ethnically at this
time, and people other than the dominant nation frequently lived within an area

0   90   180 Miles

0 150 300 Kilometres

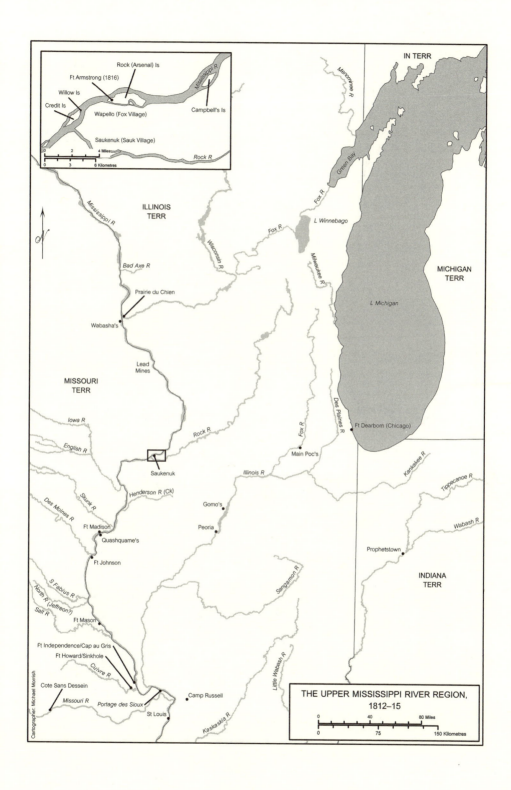

Inset map labels:

Rock (Arsenal) Is
Ft Armstrong (1816)
Willow Is
Credit Is
Wapello (Fox Village)
Saukenuk (Sauk Village)
Campbell's Is
Mississippi R
Rock R

0   2   4 Miles
0   3   6 Kilometres

Main map labels:

IN TERR
Menominee R
Green Bay
Fox R
L Winnebago
Fox R
MICHIGAN TERR
Milwaukee R
L Michigan
Des Plaines R
Ft Dearborn (Chicago)
Karkakee R
Tippecanoe R
Wabash R

ILLINOIS TERR
Mississippi R
Wisconsin R
Bad Axe R
Prairie du Chien
Wabasha's
Lead Mines

MISSOURI TERR
Iowa R
English R
Rock R
Fox R
Main Poc's
Illinois R
Saukenuk

Des Moines R
Skunk R
Henderson R (Ck)
Gomo's
Peoria
Sangamon R
Prophetstown

Ft Madison
Quashquame's
Ft Johnson
S Fabius R
North R (Jeffreon?)
Salt R
Ft Mason

INDIANA TERR

Ft Independence/Cap au Gris
Ft Howard/Sinkhole
Cuivre R
Cote Sans Dessein
Missouri R
Portage des Sioux
St Louis
Camp Russell
Little Wabash R
Kaskaskia R

Cartographer: Michael Morish

THE UPPER MISSISSIPPI RIVER REGION, 1812–15

0   40   80 Miles
0   75   150 Kilometres

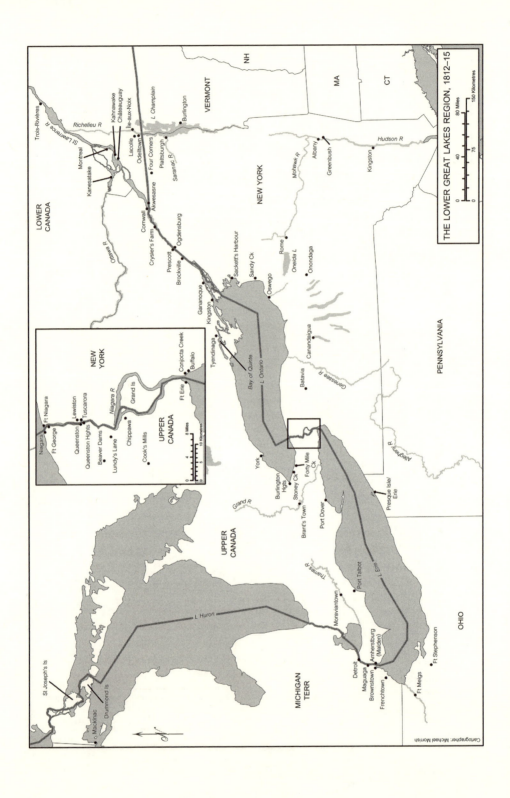

THE LOWER GREAT LAKES REGION, 1812–15

80 Miles
40 75
0 150 Kilometres
0

NH

VERMONT

MA

CT

Trois-Rivières

Richelieu R

Kahnawake
Chateauguay
Ile-aux-Noix

LOWER
CANADA

Montreal

Lacolle
Odelltown
Four Corners
Plattsburgh
L. Champlain
Burlington

Saranac R
Kanesatake

Ottawa R

Cornwall
Akwesasne

Crysler's Farm
Ogdensburg

Prescott
Brockville

Gananoque

Kingston

Tyendinaga

Bay of Quinte

Hudson R

Albany
Greenbush

Mohawk R

Kingston

NEW YORK

Sackett's Harbour

Sandy Ck

Oswego

Rome
Oneida L
Onondaga

L. Ontario

Batavia

Canandaigua

Genesee R

PENNSYLVANIA

NEW
YORK

Niagara
Ft Niagara
Lewiston
Tuscarora
Queenston
Queenston Hights

Beaver Dams
Lundy's Lane
Chippawa

Cook's Mills

Conjocta Creek
Buffalo

Niagara R

Grand Is

Ft Erie

UPPER
CANADA

8 Miles
10 Kilometres

York

Burlington
Hghts
Stoney Ck
Forty Mile
Ck

Grand R

Brant's Town

Port Dover

Presque Isle/
Erie

Allegheny R

UPPER CANADA

L Huron

Thames R

Moraviantown

Port Talbot

L Erie

OHIO

St Joseph's Is

Mackinac
Drummond Is

MICHIGAN
TERR

Detroit
Maguaga
Brownstown
Frenchtown
Amherstburg
(Malden)

Ft Meigs
Ft Stephenson

Cartographer: Michael Morrish

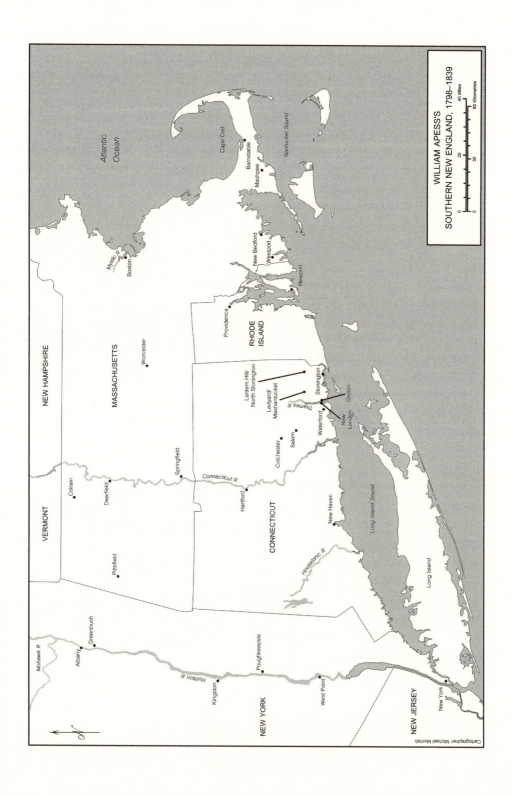

WILLIAM APESS'S
SOUTHERN NEW ENGLAND, 1798–1839

Cartographer: Michael Morrish

Native Memoirs from the War of 1812

Chronological Overview

This summary charts the course of the War of 1812 to place the general story of native participation and both Black Hawk's and William Apess's memoirs within their broad historical contexts, provide an introduction to readers unfamiliar with the details of the conflict, and serve as an aide-mémoire to individuals possessing expertise in the period. The initials BH and WA with italicized entries in the tables signify the presence of Black Hawk or William Apess in combat or at a series of skirmishes. Asterisks indicate the approximate size of the aboriginal contingent that participated *actively* on at least one side of a military confrontation. At some (such as the attack on Fort Stephenson), the number of warriors present was large, but their contributions to the fighting were modest; at others (such as the Battle of Crysler's Farm), natives numbered less than 5 percent of the combatants on one of the two sides but played important roles. Most land actions in the Great Lakes and upper Mississippi River regions saw some natives taking part, but their presence often cannot be verified with confidence below the 5 percent level; hence, there is no notation for this more limited threshold:

*	5–25 percent
**	26–50 percent
***	51–75 percent
****	76–100 percent.[1]

1803–11

In 1803, at a time of war in Europe, Napoleon Bonaparte's France sold its vast Louisiana colony west of the Mississippi River to the United States, in part to help finance hostilities against Great Britain. The changes brought on by that transfer attracted Euro-American settlers from the East to regions where the American presence previously had been limited. A year later, Black Hawk's Sauks (and their Fox allies) lost an enormous amount of land in the modern states of Missouri, Illinois, and Wisconsin in a deeply problematic treaty signed at St. Louis. In the late eighteenth and early nineteenth centuries, Americans worked aggressively to alienate native territories in order to open them for white settlement, assert government control over the tribes, and, in the process, undermine indigenous ways of life, compelling aboriginal populations either to assimilate into the dominant society or to move beyond the regions that newcomers wanted to acquire at the time. Alarmed by these threats, some Sauks attempted to form a pan-tribal alliance to protect their cultural integrity and remaining lands, although little came of those efforts. In 1805, two Shawnee half brothers, Tecumseh, a diplomatic and political leader, and Tenskwatawa, a religious prophet, began to form their famous Western Tribal Confederacy in the easterly portions of America's Old Northwest (largely north of the Ohio River in the lower and western Great Lakes region).[2] The Shawnees, Potawatomis, Ottawas, Wyandots, Ojibwas, Mingos, and others who listened to Tecumseh and Tenskwatawa, like the Sauks, hoped to protect their people from the degradations associated with exploitive treaties and trade practices, escalating newcomer intrusions into their lives, and other pressures exerted by the government and citizens of the United States. Part of their vision called for the creation of an independent aboriginal homeland where native communities might evolve on their own terms and in their own time with enough territory to ensure their social stability and economic viability.

While the American Republic expanded westward at the expense of indigenous populations, it also sought to increase its share of international trade with Europe, the West Indies, and other parts of the globe, but it did so in a world full of danger and uncertainty. Great Britain fought wars with revolutionary and Napoleonic France from 1793 to 1802, from 1803 to 1814, and again briefly in 1815 to preserve its independence and prevent the French from using force to dominate the multiplicity of states that made up the European continent. With a comparatively small army, the British relied on the Royal Navy to carry much of the burden of the struggle, partly by blockading ports controlled by France and enforcing various regulations that affected the world's trading nations. The French retaliated with their own decrees and endeavors, hoping to cripple the economy of the United Kingdom, which not only paid for its own defense but provided crucial subsidies to its allies. In the process both powers curtailed preexisting American trade, restrained the United States from gaining access to new markets, and seized hundreds of commercial vessels that violated their restrictions (although many merchants found ways to overcome these challenges and profit by opportunities generated by the European war). The British also experienced tremendous difficulty in maintaining the strength of their ships' companies, while the French rebuilt their fleet to rival Britain's after suffering a disastrous defeat at the Battle of Trafalgar in 1805. The Royal Navy, therefore, stopped commercial vessels on the world's oceans and forcibly conscripted, or "impressed," seamen who were British subjects, as well as captured deserters from its naval service, including Americans and other foreigners. At times its officers seized innocent citizens, although officials in the United States then and historians since have exaggerated the number of people affected, while British attempts to resolve tensions with the Americans over impressment largely have been overlooked, both then and in subsequent interpretations of the slide toward war in 1812. Nevertheless, people in the United States had justifiable reasons for expressing frustration and anger toward Britain (and France), which, like many major powers through the centuries, often disregarded the aspirations, rights, and dignity of smaller nations when they conflicted with their own. American distress turned to outrage in 1807 after the captain of HMS *Leopard* ordered his crew to fire not a warning shot across the bow of a merchant ship but a deadly broadside into a warship, the USS *Chesapeake*, when its captain refused to allow the British to search for deserters on his vessel. Although the government of the United Kingdom repudiated the action and made amends, relations between the two countries degenerated sharply afterward. The administration in the American capital of Washington responded by escalating efforts to force Britain and France to respect the country's rights and accommodate its interests, using a range of measures, based mainly on the imposition of trade restrictions. These initiatives did not work against Great Britain, in part because its North American colonies filled much of the void through their own exports and by serving as conduits for Americans to smuggle their goods across the ocean to evade Washington's prohibitions. For instance, shipments of pine from these provinces increased 556 percent between 1807 and 1811 to meet growing demands in the mother country, some of which originated in the neighboring Republic.

Nevertheless, the government at the imperial center in London wanted to maintain peace with the United States and therefore offered concessions that might have prevented hostilities had the Federalists (the party of George Washington and John Adams which had governed from 1789 to 1801) formed the administration rather than the Democratic-Republican (or Republican) party of Thomas Jefferson and James Madison, which directed the nation's affairs from 1801 to 1817 (and beyond). For instance, in 1806, Britain tried to renew a treaty signed during Washington's presidency in an effort to resolve Anglo-American tensions, but which the Jefferson administration refused to countenance or use as a step toward addressing additional problems not covered by the document. Later, to encourage peace, the British government offered the United States half of the ten thousand licenses it granted annually for merchants to trade into enemy ports (which the Napoleonic regime allowed where the practice met its needs), but again the Americans did not respond favorably or utilize the gesture as a basis for rapprochement. Then, among other efforts before learning of the American declaration of war in 1812, the ministry, led by Prime Minister Lord Liverpool (Robert Jenkinson), revoked the most offensive of its trade regulations, a series of orders-in-council that had been approved between 1806 and 1809, but again this had no impact on American policy. These were major concessions from the United Kingdom, which, in Napoleon Bonaparte, faced the gravest threat to its freedom since the Spanish Armada in the 1580s and had no choice but to ensure that it did not undermine its war effort against the French by conceding too much to the Americans.

Despite these attempts to preserve peace, Crown officials recognized that the situation was dangerous and that, should a rupture occur, the United States could deploy more powerful forces against British North America than the United Kingdom could send to protect the colonies. Consequently, they strengthened their long-standing relationships with the tribes of the Great Lakes and upper Mississippi River regions—including people who lived within the Old Northwest beyond the Canadian border—to garner aboriginal military assistance in the event of war. These initiatives required them to balance the difficult tasks of mustering support from the First Nations should hostilities erupt while discouraging aboriginal belligerency in an attempt to defuse tensions that might spill over into an Anglo-American confrontation. Inspired by twin-headed anti-British and anti-native prejudices formed during the War of Independence and the conflict for the Ohio Country (west of the Appalachian Mountains and south of Lake Erie) which followed between the 1780s and the 1790s, many people in the United States assumed that the king's officials encouraged indigenous violence in order to oppose westward expansion and undermine the Republic's growth.[3] At the same time, Americans overlooked their own culpability in provoking aboriginal resistance and failed to recognize the fact that native communities usually made decisions for their own reasons in relations with foreigners regardless of the pleas of outsiders to take up arms or sit quietly at home. (Black Hawk's Sauks, as we shall see, were exceptions, bowing to external pressures once the War of 1812 broke out in terms of how they deployed their forces.) Some politically prominent

Americans, such as William Henry Harrison, who oversaw much of the treaty process at the time, including the alienation of Sauk and Fox lands, recognized that British agents were working defensively but harnessed popular misconceptions to encourage indignation and generate support for war with the United Kingdom.[4] There was logic to such a stance on the part of those who looked to northern expansion beyond America's borders, but not for people content to coerce native peoples to relinquish land within a region Euro-American powers recognized as part of the sovereign territory of the United States: hostilities with Britain were not needed to accomplish that goal, as the history of the 1780s and 1790s had demonstrated. Then, the Federalist administration of George Washington had waged a successful war of conquest in the Ohio Country while maintaining a tenuous peace with Great Britain despite an aggressive stance by its officials in Canada to support the tribes in their struggles with the United States. At the height of the crisis, the British even had deployed troops on American soil and garrisoned a formerly abandoned post south of Detroit at the center of aboriginal resistance, both of which were gestures that went far beyond anything the Crown's servants contemplated between 1807 and 1812 as they tried to defuse tensions with the American Republic. (As well as the Federalists' success on their frontier regions, they had their naval forces cooperate with those of the British subsequently during America's Quasi-War with France between 1798 and 1800 when Washington and Adams directed foreign relations with more sophistication than the Republicans would under Jefferson and Madison.)

In the years before the outbreak of the War of 1812, many aboriginal people who lived outside the areas where Tecumseh and Tenskwatawa exerted their influence, such as the Sauks of the upper Mississippi, sympathized with the aspirations and growing militancy of the western tribes but stood back from joining the emerging confederacy. Some nevertheless embraced a bellicose attitude toward the Americans, including a faction within the Sauks that gathered around Black Hawk. Elsewhere, indigenous people who lived in heavily Europeanized parts of the United States, such as the Iroquois (or Haudenosaunee) in New York, also watched events unfold, often with empathy for the aspirations of the western tribes. Nevertheless, they usually adopted a neutralist stance, primarily to protect their communities at a time when the conditions of their lives within a white-dominated world made other options impractical. Across the border, First Nations in Upper and Lower Canada (now the southern portions of Ontario and Quebec) typically expressed sympathy and support for the efforts of Tecumseh and Tenskwatawa to assert native independence, but they generally assumed they would not take up arms in an Anglo-American confrontation, in large part be-

cause they felt that aligning with the British would be futile, given the comparative strength of the Americans in the region, since the United States ultimately
would punish any indigenous community that opposed the Republic in battle.
Beyond geopolitical concerns for not fighting, some natives held pacifist views
for religious reasons, such as Seneca and other Iroquois followers of the prophet
Handsome Lake, or a portion of the Delawares who adhered to the antiwar Christianity of the Moravian Church.

After an escalation of low-level violence between whites and natives in the
Old Northwest, large-scale fighting between the United States and the Western
Tribal Confederacy erupted in Indiana in 1811. William Henry Harrison wanted
to strike a blow against Tecumseh and Tenskwatawa before their alliance grew in
strength and influence. So with the consent of the administration in Washington,
he marched against the multinational indigenous community of Prophetstown,
which the two Shawnees had established near the confluence of the Tippecanoe
and Wabash Rivers. In the ensuing Battle of Tippecanoe (at which Tecumseh
was not present but his half brother was), the Americans held the field and then
burned Prophetstown, but at the cost of hardening aboriginal resolve to oppose
white expansion. That confrontation occurred seven months before the outbreak
of the War of 1812, reminding us that the struggle for the Old Northwest within
the United States in many ways was a parallel conflict to the Anglo-American
war, and that it likely would have occurred even had the two white powers managed to preserve peace between themselves.

1762	Spain acquired the French colony of Louisiana (but retro-ceded it in 1800)
1767	Kneebingkemewoin gave birth to Black Hawk at Sauke-nuk (today's Rock Island, Illinois); his father was Pyesa
1775–83	The United States won independence from Great Britain in the American Revolution, with a border established between the new Republic and the remaining portion of eastern British North America
1787–95	Americans won control of the Ohio Country in a war with the First Nations
1793–1802	Great Britain fought France as part of the larger French Revolutionary Wars of 1792–1802
1798	William Apess was born near Colrain, Massachusetts,

	possibly to Candace Apes(s); William Apes(s) Sr. was his father
1798–1800	Americans fought the French in the Quasi-War (mainly through naval and privateering actions)
1803	The Anglo-French war of 1793–1802 resumed after a short peace
1803	The United States purchased France's immense Louisiana territories
1804	A treaty signed at St. Louis on the Mississippi River alienated vast tracts of Sauk and Fox land as part of larger American efforts to acquire indigenous territories
1805	Tecumseh and Tenskwatawa's confederacy began to form in the Old Northwest
1807	Anglo-American relations degenerated sharply due to the *Chesapeake* Affair
1808	Tecumseh and Tenskwatawa founded Prophetstown in the Indiana Territory
1808–15	*Low-level aboriginal-white violence afflicted the Old Northwest and the Louisiana Territory (renamed the Missouri Territory in 1812), marked partly by the murder of non-combatants on both sides and the burning of villages and settlements (BH)*****
1809	*Natives harassed the American garrison at Fort Bellevue (Madison) on the Mississippi in the Louisiana Territory (BH)*****
1811	Fearful white and indigenous peoples in the Old Northwest moved away from each other
1811	Aboriginal and American forces clashed at Tippecanoe in the Indiana Territory on November 7****

1812

While President James Madison thought a successful military campaign against British Canada would weaken the western tribes and facilitate expansion into their lands when Congress voted for war in June 1812, he was much more concerned to make radical changes to the international situation across the Atlantic world. Fundamentally, he hoped to coerce Britain to open international trade both in preexisting areas closed by the European war and into new regions beyond those London was willing to concede, as well as to make concessions that would respect American neutrality and sailors' rights. The best way of achieving these goals in Madison's mind was to conquer Canada to deny the United Kingdom access to North American goods outside of Washington's control and thereby either force the British to respect the Republic's desires or face economic ruin, or compel them to negotiate a treaty to meet American demands in order to reclaim their lost possessions.[5] Winning support for war required the president to gather a coalition of interests among people who favored hostilities, including those who wanted to annex the colonies on America's northern border for other purposes, which likely would have made it difficult for his government to return territory to the United Kingdom should the Americans defeat the British. These included desires to realize popular dreams of seizing King George III's North American dominions for nationalistic and ideological reasons, and to acquire territories with enormous potential for the prosperity, power, and grandeur of their country (which only the naive would claim Madison did not recognize as well). Thus, for a complex range of motives related to international affairs and American expansionary desires during a period marked by several decades of territorial growth for the United States at the expense of other peoples, the conquest of Canada became the chief (if officially unstated) military objective of the administration. Other issues helped bring on hostilities, including Madison's desire to keep the White House from challengers within his own party who accused him of weakness in prewar diplomacy, Republican desires to destroy the pro-British Federalists as a political force in the country, and hopes that an Anglo-American war could advance the Republic's efforts to expand its southern borders into the Spanish colonies of East and West Florida. (The United States annexed part of West Florida in 1810 and 1812 and acquired East Florida through a treaty with Spain in 1819 outside of the context of the War of 1812.) In contrast, the war aims of the Tory government in Great Britain headed by Lord Liverpool, which had hoped to avoid an armed confrontation altogether, were more modest, essentially consisting of preserving the status quo through defending its North American territories and refusing to make concessions beyond those it already had offered before learning of the outbreak of hostilities.

Britain was a major power in 1812, being wealthier and stronger than the United States, but the greater part of its land and naval resources had to be deployed in Europe against Napoleon Bonaparte, who seemed ready to expand his control over most of the continent, while other components of its military had to be directed to fight the French elsewhere across the world. Thus, few soldiers and sailors could be sent thousands of miles across the Atlantic Ocean to defend its possessions. The dangerous situation in Europe consequently made the United States the greater power within North America with ostensibly little to fear from the island kingdom at that moment. For many of the Republic's citizens, if war was to be waged against the British Empire, the time to do so had come. Given the state of international affairs in the early summer of 1812, when news of Washington's decision to fight spread out from the capital, many people—whichever side they supported—naturally would have agreed with Thomas Jefferson's expectation that "the acquisition of Canada this year as far as the neighborhood of Quebec, will be a mere matter of marching, and will give us experience for the attack of Halifax the next, and the final expulsion of England from the American continent." (The retired president also assumed that the European war would see Britain lose access to the Baltic ports in northern Europe which supplied some of the same important materials, such as timber for shipbuilding, that it obtained from North America, which would be followed by the fall of the established order in the United Kingdom, possibly into revolution, which would drive its most creative subjects across the Atlantic to benefit his own nation.)[6] In retrospect, conquering extensive British territories with the limited resources Washington could or would deploy between 1812 and 1815 seems improbable, beyond the potential seizure of Upper Canada and perhaps the neighboring lower province. Yet, for someone like Jefferson, the situation in 1812 looked very different. He recognized that Britain's prospects in Europe were indeed grim and realized how little London could do to preserve its North American possessions, and he knew that the Republic enjoyed other advantages over the British colonies. For instance, the United States, with a population of 7.7 million, would call out 450,000 militiamen during the conflict, a number only fifty thousand less than the entire population of British North America. Furthermore, the history of the Western Hemisphere up to that time had presented numerous instances of relatively modest military resources being deployed to effect immense political change, such as during the Seven Years' War in the 1750s–60s, the American War of Independence of the 1770s–80s, and the Frontier War of the 1780s–90s. As well, diplomatic initiatives, such as the Louisiana Purchase and the one-sided treaties forced upon indigenous peoples, had produced stunning changes that benefitted the rapidly growing United States. In that light, conquest did not seem like a fantastic idea. Perhaps there would be difficulties in acquiring the vast northern interior of Rupert's Land under the control of the Hudson's Bay Company, as well as the poorly understood Pacific and Arctic regions, but in 1812 those territories did not compete with the United States in terms of North American exports the way the easterly border provinces did. The eventual acquisition of these remote lands by the Republic, however, would have seemed to be a logical probability should at least a good part of Upper and Lower Canada, New Brunswick, Nova Scotia, Prince Edward Island, and Newfoundland fall into America's grasp.

Despite Jefferson's expectations of an easy victory in 1812, British and Canadian regulars and militia, strengthened by First Nations warriors, turned back American thrusts aimed at southwestern Upper Canada near Detroit, the Niagara Peninsula between Lakes Erie and Ontario, and the Montreal region, and even acquired control over Michigan. Part of the reason for the lack of American success was the inability of the United States to manage its military affairs competently or concentrate its strength under effective leadership to take advantage of the Republic's numerical and other advantages. Beyond the major campaigns of the war's first year, the combatants raided each other's posts, captured ships and smaller vessels, and otherwise tried to undermine their opponent's capabilities or secure local strategic advantages. Toward the end of the year, on America's Eastern Seaboard, the Royal Navy established its first blockades with the small number of warships at its disposal in the western Atlantic to limit access by the Republic's navy and privateers to the world's oceans in order to protect British commerce, and to undermine the Republic's international commerce, which also would have a negative impact on American government revenues. Over the three years of the conflict, each side's navy, along with privateers and other privately owned vessels, seized well over a thousand of the other's merchant ships and schooners on the high seas and in coastal waters. (The British and American merchant fleets were the largest and second largest in the world, respectively, but the Republic's losses represented a far larger percentage of its shipping than that of the Empire). Privateering, however, generally was inefficient: most vessels failed to take a prize, and at least one-third of those acquired by the Americans were recaptured. The British also seized or sank significant numbers of the Republic's privateers, while the Americans defeated few of the Empire's in return. The Royal and United States Navies each won half of the twenty-six saltwater actions between their forces in which one side captured or sank the other's warship or warships, but the overall toll on the American navy was higher due to British attacks on ports and other actions, and the Republic also lost additional government vessels beyond those deployed by its navy.

In the Old Northwest, combat between the Americans and the tribes escalated with the coming of the War of 1812 as the opposing sides fought for control over the future of the region. Elsewhere, other native people also took up arms, as represented by Black Hawk's decision to join an attempt to capture Fort Madison on the Mississippi River to the west of the lands dominated by Tecumseh and Tenskwatawa's alliance. Naturally, many tribespeople hoped to obtain British help to realize their dream of creating independent homelands, but they were suspicious of Britain's intentions and its ability to act decisively because of its weakness in North America compared to the United States. A large number of aboriginal individuals also remembered how their ally had failed to protect indigenous welfare when it conflicted with Britain's interests during peace negotiations with the rebellious colonies which had ended the American Revolutionary War in 1783 and in the ensuing conflict between the now-independent United States and the aboriginal peoples for the Ohio Country, which together saw the First Nations lose control over much of their territory south of the lower Great Lakes which otherwise might have been preserved. Even with these doubts, however, the western tribes and other indigenous groups proved to be valuable allies of the British in the opening weeks of the War of 1812. As well, many natives who had been uncertain as to how they might act if war came, or even had planned to be neutral (such as a large percentage of the population in Upper Canada), also took up arms alongside the British once the king's soldiers and the warriors already aligned to them achieved several signal victories and once the outbreak of hostilities clarified the threat the Americans posed to their well-being. In contrast, smaller numbers of Iroquois and other aboriginal people in New York and parts of Ohio, who had favored neutrality before June 1812, joined the Americans over the course of the war, in part because they came to identify their interests with those of the Republic, or hoped that displays of support for the government would help protect their people from the pressures being exerted by the larger white society to give up land and assimilate. At the same time, many individuals on both sides of the border continued to follow their prewar decision to stay out of the conflict. (Of the sixty thousand natives who lived in the Great Lakes and upper Mississippi regions, twelve thousand were men of military age. Given the divisions within these communities, the Americans might expect the support of eighteen hundred warriors, while the majority of the rest aligned with the British, but only a fraction of their number on either side ever could assemble for a campaign at once.)[7] Beyond these broad alliance decisions, other factors influenced the way indigenous people reacted to the outbreak of war. On one level, the different villages of specific nations often chose separate ways of addressing their external relations, often based on considerations related to their proximity to other aboriginal peoples and concentrations of white settlers. On another level, indigenous societies gave their members the freedom to follow their consciences; thus, while many people accepted the consensus developed within their communities, either to embrace neutrality or to take up arms alongside one of the white belligerents, some individuals rejected the decision or limited their commitment to it to token levels of support.

January–December	Native-white violence continued on the American–First Nations frontier****
June 4/17	President James Madison's war bill passed the two houses of Congress
June 18	Madison signed the war bill, bringing on hostilities with Britain
June 23	News of the outbreak of hostilities reached Albany, New York
June 23	Unaware of the declaration of war, Britain revoked the orders-in-council in hopes of defusing Anglo-American tensions and improving trade (while later that year, upon news of this concession crossing the ocean, local commanders arranged a truce assuming that diplomacy could bring hostilities to a close, but Washington decided to continue fighting)
June 25	News of the outbreak reached Quebec, Lower Canada, and other Canadian communities
July 12	American forces invaded Upper Canada from Detroit; some skirmishing occurred**
July 17	Americans surrendered Fort Mackinac at the head of Lake Michigan in the Michigan Territory***
July 30	News of the outbreak of war reached London, England
August 5/9	Near Detroit, Americans suffered defeat at Brownstown and failed to open communications to the south at Maguaga**
August 7–11	The American army that invaded Canada on July 12 withdrew to Michigan

August 15	Natives defeated the Americans outside Fort Dearborn (Chicago)****
August 16	Americans capitulated at Detroit; surrendered Michigan**
September 5–8	*First Nations forces failed to capture the American post of Fort Madison on the Mississippi (BH)****
September 5–12	Americans withstood a native siege at Fort Wayne in Indiana****
October	The Royal Navy blockaded part of the American Atlantic coast (and earlier had instituted a convoy system to protect the British Empire's merchant vessels)
October 13	Americans were routed at Queenston Heights on the Niagara River in Upper Canada*
October 13	Britain authorized "reprisals" in response to the American declaration of war after diplomacy had failed to bring the conflict to an early end
November 20	An American thrust to capture Montreal, Lower Canada, collapsed south of the city at the Battle of Lacolle River
November 28	The British repelled an American crossing of the Niagara near Fort Erie*

1813

The fighting escalated in the second year of hostilities as the belligerents increased their commitments to the war effort, although Great Britain continued to experience serious constraints in its ability to reinforce Canada because of the ongoing struggle against Napoleonic France, while political constraints, bureaucratic ineptitude, and poor strategic thinking in the Madison administration continued to limit the effectiveness of the Republic's initiatives into 1813. The Royal Navy, with the transfer of more vessels to the western Atlantic, extended its blockade to a larger portion of the American East Coast and cooperated with the army in launching numerous small-scale and largely successful raids against seaboard communities. As before, the First Nations, British, and Americans engaged in operations to secure local advantages in the Great Lakes and upper Mississippi regions beyond the fighting that occurred during the larger campaigns.

The Americans enjoyed early successes, capturing York (Toronto) on Lake

Ontario and Fort George at the mouth of the Niagara River, and then threatened to take control of Upper Canada while, at the same time, repulsing a counterattack on their main Lake Ontario naval base at Sackett's Harbour in northern New York. Their invasion, however, disintegrated that summer, and by the end of the year the British regained control of their side of the Niagara Peninsula and captured the important American post of Fort Niagara in New York opposite Fort George (which they retained until the return of peace). Additionally, the largest American push of the war, a two-pronged, eleven-thousand-man attempt against Montreal, ended when the British won the crucial battles of Châteauguay south of the city (at which William Apess fought within the ranks of the American army) and Crysler's Farm on the St. Lawrence River. On the Detroit front, American forces endured setbacks early in the year but withstood sieges at Fort Meigs and Fort Stephenson in the spring and summer (with Black Hawk present). They then reasserted the control they had lost a year earlier by winning the Battle of Lake Erie and defeating a combined British and native force at Moraviantown in Upper Canada. At the latter, Tecumseh died in combat. With his passing and American ascendancy in the eastern portions of the Old Northwest, the Western Tribal Confederacy began to disintegrate as some members made peace with the United States and as Tenskwatawa's influence fell into decline. (Some warriors, however, retreated to the Niagara region with their families to continue fighting into 1814, while others returned to their homelands and engaged in hostilities south of the western Great Lakes.) After these victories, the Americans held southwestern Upper Canada until the return of peace in their only productive campaign against the British provinces during the conflict. Despite this, the rest of British North America survived the second year of the war.

January 18	Americans repulsed British and aboriginal forces at Frenchtown (Monroe) in Michigan***
January 22	Americans suffered defeat at Frenchtown***
February–onward	The British expanded their naval blockade and began raiding along the Atlantic coast
February 7/22	On the St. Lawrence River, Americans raided Brockville, Upper Canada; the British raided Ogdensburg, New York
March–October	High levels of American–First Nations frontier violence occurred****
April 19	William Apess joined the United States Army in New York City

April 27	American forces captured and then briefly occupied York (Toronto), Upper Canada*
April 27–May 9	*Americans withstood the first siege of Fort Meigs (Perrysburg) in Ohio (BH)***
May 27	American forces captured Fort George in Upper Canada at the mouth of the Niagara River*
May 28	The British evacuated Fort Erie, Upper Canada, and other posts along the Niagara, and then retired to Burlington Heights (Hamilton), Upper Canada
May 29	Americans drove off an assault on Sackett's Harbour on Lake Ontario in New York
June 5–6	British forces halted an American thrust into Upper Canada's Niagara region at Stoney Creek, forcing the invaders back to Forty Mile Creek
June 8	Americans experienced defeat at Forty Mile Creek near Stoney Creek*
June 9	The British reoccupied Fort Erie
June	Americans retreated from Forty Mile Creek to Fort George pursued by the British and natives**
June–October	British forces blockaded the Americans in Fort George; numerous skirmishes occurred**
June 24	Americans endured defeat at Beaver Dams on the Niagara Peninsula****
July	Opposing forces raided each side of the Niagara River*
July 21–28	*Americans withstood a second siege at Fort Meigs in Ohio (BH)****
July 31–August 3	The British raided communities on Lake Champlain in New York and Vermont
August 1–2	*Americans defended Fort Stephenson (Fremont) in Ohio (BH)***
September 10	The United States Navy defeated the Royal Navy on Lake Erie
September 27	British and First Nations forces evacuated the Detroit border region

September 27	Americans entered Detroit as well as Amherstburg in Upper Canada; some tribespeople made peace with the United States at about the same time
September 28	The inconclusive "Battle" of Burlington Races on Lake Ontario favored the British
October 5	*American forces emerged victorious at Moraviantown (Thames), Upper Canada; Tecumseh fell (BH?)***[8]
October–December	After Tecumseh's death, more natives made peace with the Americans
October–onward	The Western Tribal Confederacy dissolved, but some people who had rallied around Tecumseh and Tenskwatawa continued to resist the Americans
October 26	*Americans suffered defeat south of Montreal on the Châteauguay River in Lower Canada (WA)**
November 4	The American garrison abandoned Fort Madison after months of aboriginal harassment****[9]
November 11	Americans were defeated at Crysler's Farm (Morrisburg) on the St. Lawrence River in Upper Canada
December 10–11	American forces evacuated Fort George and destroyed the Canadian towns of Niagara and Queenston on the Niagara River
December 12/19	The British reoccupied Fort George and then captured Fort Niagara at the mouth of the Niagara in New York
December 19–30	British and indigenous forces burned villages on the American side of the Niagara River in retaliation for the destruction of Niagara and Queenston**

1814

In 1814, both sides continued to engage in small actions to achieve local advantages, with the British concentrating some of their efforts along the St. Lawrence region of New York, while the Americans focused their raids in southwestern Upper Canada. The Republic's military forces attempted but failed to seize Montreal in Lower Canada (with William Apess present) and retake Mackinac at the head of Lake Michigan. They also lost a campaign along the upper Mississippi (in which Black Hawk played a leading role) where native resistance continued even though the Western Tribal Confederacy farther east had collapsed as most of its supporters negotiated peace with the United States during 1814. The American military's main invasion of Canada that year occurred along the Niagara Peninsula, starting with the capture of Fort Erie, followed by a victory at Chippawa near Niagara Falls at which hundreds of aboriginal warriors fought alongside both opposing armies. Despite these successes, the British checked the Americans at Lundy's Lane nearby. Subsequently, British forces, assisted by small numbers of warriors, pushed their enemy back along the Niagara River to Fort Erie, although the Americans repelled attempts to retake that foothold, holding the post until the end of the year when they destroyed the fort and retired to Buffalo, New York.

Earlier in 1814, notwithstanding American hopes and British fears in 1812, Great Britain won its war with Napoleonic France and thus could dispatch reinforcements both to secure Canada and to attack the United States in expectation of bringing the War of 1812 to a close. At the pinnacle of operations in 1814, each belligerent deployed over forty thousand regular soldiers across eastern North America, exclusive of militia, volunteers, and others, along with sailors and marines in fresh- and saltwater contexts. Yet the war remained small by European standards. For instance, the Duke of Wellington's army, assembled in a few farm fields for the Battle of Waterloo (after the continental war resumed for a brief period in 1815), was 50 percent larger than the entire British regular army in North America in the war's last year. Reinforced in 1814, the Royal Navy blockaded the entire American Eastern Seaboard with far more warships than had been available in 1812. The consequences of the blockade were devastating, even though few shots were fired: most of the United States Navy's ships could not get out to sea, the Republic's international trade fell by 90 percent from prewar levels (while that of the British Empire expanded considerably), and people engaged in America's internal trade had to abandon coastal waters and use costly and slow land routes because of the Royal Navy's patrols. Washington's finances crumbled into crisis to the point where the government defaulted on its loan payments, and in November 1814 the army ran out of money. Toward the end of the conflict, a quasi-secessionist movement emerged in New England among people who opposed both the war and James Madison's administration. Meanwhile, the British occupied much of today's Maine and undertook many small-scale, overwhelmingly successful raids along the Atlantic coast against fortifications, naval forces, commercial shipping, and towns. They also launched several raids in strength (commonly misinterpreted as invasions), which failed against Plattsburgh in northern New York and Baltimore in Maryland but succeeded against Washington, DC, and nearby Alexandria, Virginia, on the Potomac River. While the war raged on the western side of the Atlantic Ocean, Anglo-American peace negotiators met in Ghent (in today's Belgium) to work on ending the conflict, arriving at a settlement on Christmas Eve, 1814.

Winter	British forces raided into the St. Lawrence River districts of New York
March 30	*Americans were defeated at Odelltown near Montreal in Lower Canada at the Battle of Lacolle Mill (WA)**
April	Napoleon abdicated and went into exile, freeing a portion of British military resources for redeployment to the American war
April–May	The Royal Navy blockaded the entire American Atlantic coast; coastal raids recommenced
May 5–6	British forces captured Oswego, New York, on Lake Ontario
May–November	Americans destroyed Upper Canadian settlements along the north shore of Lake Erie*
May 30	The British experienced defeat at Sandy Creek in northern New York by a combined American and aboriginal force**
June 2	Americans seized Prairie du Chien in the Illinois Territory on the Mississippi**
July 3	American forces captured Fort Erie
July 5	Americans and their indigenous allies defeated the British and natives at Chippawa north of Fort Erie*
July 11	The British captured Eastport as the first step in occupying much of modern Maine
July 17–20	Native and British forces besieged and recaptured Prairie du Chien***
July 21	*Indigenous warriors defeated the Americans at Campbell Island in the Illinois Territory on the Mississippi (BH)*****

July 25	The British halted the American invasion of the Niagara Peninsula at Lundy's Lane, Upper Canada
August 3	Americans stopped a British thrust on the New York side of the Niagara River at Conjocta Creek intended to destroy supply depots in the Buffalo area
August 4	American forces failed to retake Mackinac***
August–September	The British and their aboriginal allies kept the Americans confined in Fort Erie but failed to recapture the post
August 8	Peace negotiations began in Ghent
August 24–29	Washington, DC, and Alexandria, Virginia, fell to large-scale British raids
September	British forces won control of the upper Great Lakes after several small actions between July and September*
September	The Royal Navy won the "shipbuilder's war" on Lake Ontario, securing control of the waterway for the rest of the conflict
September 5	*Natives defeated the Americans at Credit Island on the Mississippi in the Missouri Territory (BH)****
September 11	*The United States Navy won control of Lake Champlain; the British consequently cancelled a land attack on Plattsburgh, New York (WA)*
September 12–14	British forces failed to capture Baltimore, Maryland
October 19	Americans were turned back at Cook's Mill, Upper Canada, near Fort Erie
November 5	Americans evacuated and destroyed Fort Erie and then retired to Buffalo
December 14	British sailors seized the American Lake Borgne squadron near New Orleans, Louisiana
December 23–28	Small actions outside New Orleans favored the British
December 24	Treaty negotiations concluded in Ghent
December 27	Great Britain ratified the Treaty of Ghent

1815–17

Although diplomats had concluded negotiations for a peace treaty at the end of 1814, the war did not come to an official end until mid-February 1815, when the American government ratified the agreement. Owing to the period's slow communications, some fighting continued during this twilight period, most notably when the British attacked New Orleans deep in the American south as part of their campaign to bring the war to the United States and speed peace negotiations, but they were defeated in the Republic's greatest victory of the conflict. (The American commander, Andrew Jackson, also had fought indigenous peoples in the Creek War of 1813–14, mainly in the Mississippi Territory, in a clash that raged in parallel to the War of 1812 but which was separate from the Anglo-American, Old Northwest, and upper Mississippi conflicts that had engulfed natives elsewhere.) In addition, some skirmishing between the Americans and First Nations occurred along the upper Mississippi River beyond the official end of the Euro-American war.

The peace treaty between the two white powers reestablished the status quo of 1811 and returned captured territories to their prewar owners, as well as made provisions for more discussions to resolve other issues in subsequent years. The outcome of the war fulfilled Great Britain's primary war aim of retaining its North American possessions, an achievement that probably would not have been possible without the support received from its First Nations allies, especially in 1812 and 1813. In effect, Britain had fought a successful defensive war, which is a very different thing from the old platitude that the two sides had fought each other to a standstill (although the British abandoned a secondary desire that had emerged during the conflict to redraw the Canadian-American border to improve colonial security, largely because London wanted to restore peace as quickly as possible). Additionally, Prime Minister Lord Liverpool's government did not make any concessions on other prewar Anglo-American disputes, such as over trade restrictions and impressment, which might have undermined its ability to wage war effectively on the world's oceans in the future, thus fulfilling its other primary war aims in relation to commercial, maritime, and naval issues. (To a large degree, tensions over impressment and trade had been relieved because of the British and allied victory over France and the return to peace in Europe.) The Liverpool ministry also did not give into demands that the Madison administration introduced during peace negotiations beyond the American government's primary and unfulfilled war aims. As well, the United States agreed to join Great Britain in suppressing the Atlantic slave trade. The important and ostensible reason for Washington's declaration of war, Britain's orders-in-council, which had disrupted and harmed American trade before 1812, had been withdrawn by London before learning of the declaration of war, and thus the conflict had no effect on their termination.

King George III's First Nations allies in the Old Northwest and upper Mississippi River theaters of operations did not achieve their main war aim of establishing an independent aboriginal homeland. While Black Hawk's Sauks and other tribespeople (with some support from white allies) dominated in the west, in effect winning their military campaign against the Americans, the Republic's forces controlled much of the easterly portion of the region at the end of the conflict. Tecumseh and Tenskwatawa's confederacy had collapsed, and many of its members had made peace with the United States before the conclusion of negotiations for the Treaty of Ghent. (The aboriginal treaties not only highlight the independent nature of First Nations diplomacy in relation to the desires of white allies but underscore the profound regional nature of native affairs in recognizing how different the situation was for distinct groups of indigenous peoples.) Despite the weak state of aboriginal affairs in 1814 on the Detroit front, Lord Liverpool had considered continuing hostilities to try to compel the United States to cede some land for a separate indigenous home. Yet, with uncertainty over the stability of Europe and concern to protect Britain's interests on the continent, along with weariness following two decades of war with France, the tremendous drain the continental conflict had imposed on public finances, widespread desires to reestablish prosperity through trade, and a view that national dignity had to be maintained for the two powers to achieve a lasting peace, the prime minister decided that it was not in the best interests of either the United Kingdom or its Canadian provinces to continue fighting over indigenous aspirations within the borders of the United States in what might be a doubtful campaign. Article IX of the Treaty of Ghent, however, required the white powers to end hostilities with the First Nations and restore the possessions, rights, and privileges that the aboriginal peoples had enjoyed in 1811 within the larger treaty principle of reestablishing the prewar status quo. Naturally, this provision was more important in the United States than in Canada because of the widespread hostility of natives within the Republic's boundaries to the nation's government and citizens. Thus, while Britain achieved its objectives with the American Republic and the Madison administration failed to realize its ambitions with the United Kingdom in its conflict, the war between the First Nations and the United States within the Old Northwest and upper Mississippi region ended essentially in a diplomatic stalemate, irrespective of native defeat in the eastern portion and aboriginal victory in the western section. Consequently, the various First Nations, including Black

Hawk's Sauks, signed treaties with their white adversaries between 1815 and 1817 (along with formulating peace agreements between indigenous groups that had fought against each other).

Yet, in the war's aftermath, Americans simply resumed their aggressive efforts to acquire native territories, impose control over indigenous populations, and drive people west; thus, the events of 1812–15 only provided a temporary setback in the Republic's expansionary desire to obtain aboriginal lands and open them for white settlement. People in Canada viewed those developments with alarm, in part because they doubted that the peace would last and worried that in a future conflict they would continue to need native support (at least until the 1830s, when the influx of Euro-American immigrants shifted the demographic situation so greatly that First Nations forces no longer were large enough to play decisive roles). Sorrowfully, even people who had sided with the Americans during the war, such as the Iroquois in New York, found themselves more or less equally persecuted by the dominant society as it made them cede territory and move away once peace had returned. For the indigenous population in Canada, in contrast, there was satisfaction to be found in participating in the successful struggle to prevent the United States from conquering the colonies and imposing its oppressive policies on native peoples. Yet there was sadness too for aboriginal peoples within British North America—beyond the grief all communities that had lost loved ones felt in the war's aftermath. One source of pain lay in the knowledge that their brethren south of the border continued to suffer after the conclusion of hostilities from American greed for their lands. Another emerged in the decades after 1815 when they too faced pressures to assimilate into the dominant society and surrender land to make way for the growing numbers of immigrants from Britain, although the weight of this strain was lighter north of the international border than it was in the United States owing to smaller aboriginal and settler populations and the different economic and environmental contexts in which relations between European and First Nations people unfolded in Canada.

Although natives within the British provinces experienced unwanted assimilationist pressures, aboriginal contributions to the defense of the colonies always formed part of the larger public consciousness in Canada, whereas the citizens of the United States generally forgot that some indigenous communities had joined them in their war against the United Kingdom. At the same time, while people in Britain largely overlooked the war in their history, primarily because the great struggles in Europe of the period were so much larger and more important to the kingdom, and while the war for Americans became half-forgotten and relegated to minor status in light of the other great conflicts of the nineteenth century, such as the Mexican and Civil Wars, the War of 1812 maintained currency in the Canadian imagination, shared with the First Nations, as a defining moment in the evolution of the distinct society north of the border with the United States.

January 1–8, 1815	American forces defeated the British at New Orleans in Louisiana
January 2	Naval vessels departed England for the United States with the Treaty of Ghent, ratified by the Prince Regent on behalf of King George
February 16	The United States ratified the Treaty of Ghent, ending the War of 1812
February 17	British and American officials exchanged ratifications in Washington
Late winter/spring	*American-aboriginal skirmishing continued along the upper Mississippi and in the Old Northwest (BH)*****
March 1	News of the peace reached British headquarters in Quebec, Lower Canada
March or later	William Apess left the American army in or near Plattsburgh
March–June	Napoleon returned to Paris; the European war resumed
March 28	The British government learned of the American ratification of the treaty
April 16	News of the peace reached the British at Prairie du Chien on the Mississippi from American sources, but they did not receive official word from their superiors until May 24
May 24	*Natives and Americans skirmished at Fort Howard (Sinkhole) beside the Mississippi in the Missouri Territory (BH)*****
May 25	American and British forces began withdrawing from occupied territories
June 18	The British and their allies defeated Napoleon at Waterloo near Brussels
June 24	Napoleon again abdicated and subsequently went into exile as a British prisoner; peace returned to Europe afterward

1815–17	Indigenous peace treaties were signed with tribes still at war as of the ratification of the Treaty of Ghent
1838	Black Hawk died at his home along the Des Moines River on October 3
1839	William Apess died in a New York City boardinghouse on April 10

BLACK HAWK
(SAUK)

Introduction to Black Hawk

The more famous of the memoirs in this book is that of the Sauk military leader Black Hawk. He led war parties on the upper Mississippi and Detroit fronts between 1812 and 1815, played a leading role in defeating future American president Zachary Taylor in action in 1814, and went on to fight in the last native-newcomer war of the Great Lakes region in 1832 in a conflict that bears his name. In its entirety, his autobiography summarizes Sauk history as he had heard it from his elders and recounts his own life from his birth in the 1760s to the aftermath of the hostilities of the 1830s. Published in Cincinnati by Illinois newspaperman John B. Patterson in 1833 as the *Life of Ma-ka-tai-me-she-kia-kiak or Black Hawk*, the text remains in print today.[1] The *Life*, however, is problematic because Black Hawk did not write it himself; rather, he dictated his story in the Sauk language to an interpreter, who translated it into English for a newspaper publisher, who edited it for a Euro-American audience. While the translator and editor affirmed that they strove for accuracy, the creation of extensive memoirs through such a process naturally raises questions about how reliably they preserved Black Hawk's views and voice. Some observers, such as an early governor of Illinois, Thomas Ford, even claimed that the autobiography was a hoax. In 1854, he declared that "Black Hawk knew little, if anything, about it" and that the work "was never intended for anything but a catchpenny publication."[2] In a land claims dispute in the 1950s, the United States government argued that the *Life* was a fabrication, a position taken in order to undermine the Sauks and Foxes who used materials in the text to support their cause, although the tribunal that heard the case accepted Black Hawk's life story as historically valid.[3] Even knowledgeable readers who accept the autobiography as authentic cannot help noticing some simplifications and a few suspicious turns of phrase that suggest they were the creations of a Euro-American mind.[4] Nevertheless, scholars overwhelmingly accept the text as

a genuine presentation of Black Hawk's memories and opinions, while also recognizing that it is a mediated one. They do this either implicitly, through treating
it as an important primary source, or explicitly, after studying the work for the
express purpose of determining its authenticity.[5] As this introduction and the
annotations below demonstrate, we can read the autobiography with confidence
as an important firsthand Sauk document from the early nineteenth century,
although we must do so with some discernment.

Black Hawk (or Black Sparrow Hawk or Sparrow Hawk) was born in 1767 at
Saukenuk on the Rock River, close to the Mississippi River (in today's Rock Island, Illinois). His father was Pyesa, a member of the Eagle clan, his mother
was Kneebingkemewoin, and he had at least one sibling, a younger brother. The
Sauks belonged to the Algonquian language group, whose culture was related to
that of the neighboring Kickapoos and Foxes (or Mesquakies).[6] The Sauks and
Foxes were close allies in Black Hawk's time, as they had been for decades, but
did not form a united tribe as some people have affirmed. Before moving to the
Mississippi, the Sauks had lived in present-day Wisconsin from the second quarter of the seventeenth century after settling there as refugees from more easterly
regions (likely east of Lake Michigan) during the upheavals that had terrorized
the Great Lakes when the Iroquois Confederacy had expanded outward from its
homelands south of Lake Ontario in the mid-1600s. In a series of southward
movements in the eighteenth century, the Sauks competed for lands with other
indigenous populations in modern Illinois, Iowa, and Missouri. By Black Hawk's
time, Sauk and Fox villages generally sat alongside the Mississippi, mainly from
a point in the area near Prairie du Chien in the north to the country just below
the Des Moines River in the south. The two nations had separate villages, but
intermarriage, personal preference, and other reasons led members of both
tribes to live together. Sauk and Fox territories as a whole encompassed more
land than their dozen or so villages occupied, as was normal for indigenous
peoples who utilized extensive hinterlands for hunting and other subsistence
activities. Although other tribes contested their ownership of the land or were
allowed to share territory with them, the Sauks and Foxes claimed the region
between approximately the Missouri River in the south and the Wisconsin River
to the north, and from the Illinois River in the east to much of the area of the Des
Moines–Missouri watersheds in the west.

The Sauks supported themselves primarily through a seasonal round of activities that enabled them to use the environment's resources effectively. For part of
each year, for instance, people in Saukenuk occupied a hundred or more large

bark- and mat-covered lodges along the rich bottomlands of the Rock River, where they cultivated extensive fields of corn, beans, squash, pumpkins, melons, and tobacco, and where they pastured their horses on adjoining grasslands. At other periods, they divided into small groups to pursue various activities, primarily gathering, hunting, and trapping, but also including fishing, trading, receiving gifts from allies, and taking spoils from enemies. The main animals they hunted were bison, deer, raccoon, beaver, and muskrat, along with diverse kinds of water-fowl. In return for Euro-American goods, they exchanged corn, furs, hides, deer tallow, beeswax, feathers, and maple sugar. They also mined and smelted lead from surface deposits, which they traded for European goods or cast into bullets for their own use.

There were three thousand or more Sauks in the early 1800s along with up-ward of two thousand Foxes. One contemporary American observer, Thomas Forsyth, believed the two tribes collectively had between twelve hundred and fif-teen hundred fighting men, while the British thought there were twelve hundred Sauk and Fox warriors.[7] The Sauks were divided into two moieties and twelve clans, which, with their subgroups, governed family affairs along with ritualistic and spiritual matters. Traditionally, there was a paramount chief, drawn from the Sturgeon clan, while lesser hereditary chiefs came from the others. These men and their assistants, the runners and criers, took the lead in civil affairs; how-ever, their authority was constrained because the Sauks embraced broad debate and tried to resolve disputes through establishing a wide consensus on the issues they faced. Decisions could be enforced at certain levels, such as by deploying men to guard villages in order to stop families from returning early from hunt-ing and digging up other people's food stores; yet Sauk communities lacked the means to impose their will over larger dissenting groups (such as occurred when Black Hawk's followers occasionally separated themselves from collective resolu-tions, as we shall see below). Separate military leaders attended to warfare and sometimes foreign affairs. By the early nineteenth century, these men gained their status mainly through recognition of their skills and experience, for the Sauks increasingly accepted people who rose on their own merits as leaders, rather than those who assumed leadership roles through hereditary succession. Black Hawk was one such talented individual, as was his primary rival, Keokuk, both of whom exerted substantial influence in the nation's affairs and sometimes overshadowed civil chiefs.

Around 1781, in his fifteenth year, Black Hawk took up the ways of the war-rior (which never was a full-time occupation among native peoples), wounding his first enemy in combat. Shortly afterward, he joined his father in a campaign against the Osages, who lived to the southwest. In the ensuing battle, he remembered being "proud to have an opportunity to prove" to his father that he "was not an unworthy son" but "had courage and bravery." He fought by his father's side and watched the older man kill and scalp an enemy warrior. Excited with "valor and ambition," Black Hawk recalled that he "rushed furiously upon another, smote him to the earth" with his tomahawk, ran his lance through his body, and took his scalp. His father watched, said nothing, but "looked pleased." Upon returning home in triumph, Black Hawk joined other veterans in his first scalp dance to celebrate their prowess and recognize their victims, whose spiritual strength, concentrated in the scalp, enhanced the powers of the victors.[8]

Black Hawk became a military leader and continued to fight Sauk enemies to protect tribal access to hunting lands from other aboriginal challengers and to avenge the killing or capture of members of his nation by outsiders. About the year 1786, for example, he led two hundred men against a comparable number of Osages in an engagement where his warriors destroyed half their opponents while losing only nineteen of their own. Black Hawk remembered killing five men and one woman himself on that occasion. This victory led the Osages to leave the Sauks and Foxes in peace for a while, which allowed his people to turn their attention to another enemy, the Cherokees, who they also fought successfully. Around 1790, Black Hawk's father fell mortally wounded in combat. Black Hawk returned to his village in sorrow, blackened his face, fasted regularly, and prayed for five years. That was an unusually long period of mourning by Sauk standards and may have symbolized a particularly zealous adherence to his people's cultural traditions, as well as the place that these customs held in the formation of his own identity. He then went to war again in response to renewed Osage challenges and also battled Cherokees, Ojibwas, and Kaskaskias from the mid-1790s to about 1802, when there appears to have been a respite from hostilities for a time. Through victory in those conflicts, the Sauks and Foxes largely secured their hunting territories from outsiders, although fighting native enemies continued to consume some of their energies until well into the nineteenth century.

New and forceful challenges emerged for the Sauks and Foxes when American officials assumed control of the fur trade center of St. Louis on the Mississippi River following the acquisition by the United States of 828,000 square miles of territory on the west side of the Mississippi in the Louisiana Purchase of 1803. A year later, the newcomers coerced some native leaders to sign a treaty—widely regarded as fraudulent—that sold land in today's Missouri, Illinois, and Wisconsin as a condition for avoiding war with Euro-Americans after an outbreak of small-scale violence between natives and whites. The tribespeople, however, retained the right to live in the ceded territory until white authorities subsequently sold the land to newcomers. The impending loss to their homes, along with intercultural tensions and threats to aboriginal society arising from increasing Euro-American settlement, had a profound impact on Black Hawk. In response, he maintained friendly relations with British subjects to the north along the frontiers with Canada in hopes of gaining their help if it were needed to preserve Sauk independence. Then, in the War of 1812, he allied with the British, although the decision was not unequivocal because the Sauks and British had competing objectives in the conflict. The Sauks had fought against the British in the Seven Years' War and Pontiac's War in the 1750s–60s, but some had aligned with the Crown during the War of Independence and had suffered the torching of Saukenuk at the hands of revolutionary forces in 1780 when Black Hawk was about thirteen. Like most villagers, he had escaped before the attack, although one tradition asserts that his mother, who was too sick to leave, perished in the flames.[9] The Sauks rebuilt their town, and after the war they maintained their ties to British officials, traded with people from Canada on the upper Mississippi, and participated in a modest way in the war for the Ohio Country in the 1780s–90s as part of a pan-tribal confederacy that opposed American expansion into that more easterly region.

In contrast to Black Hawk's supporters, who became known as the "British band," another group of Sauks, the "peace band," chose a neutralist path in 1812. They did this partly in response to growing white social and economic influences following the American occupation of St. Louis and subsequent settlement along the Mississippi, and partly because they did not believe they could oppose the newcomers successfully. As it was, some Sauk leaders before the War of 1812 seem to have accepted the hated 1804 treaty as a fait accompli in order to avoid hostilities with Americans, although they worked to mitigate its consequences in post-treaty negotiations with white officials.[10] Other Sauks participated in an unsuccessful attempt to create a pan-tribal confederacy with such peoples as the Foxes, Dakota Sioux, and Potawatomis to resist the Americans independently of the formation of the better-known (and more easterly) alliance of the Shawnee half brothers, Tecumseh and Tenskwatawa. The Sauks failed, however, because of divisions among the First Nations and because British officials, trying to pre-vent an Anglo-American war by restraining indigenous militancy, would not give them the support they desired.[11] Even though the Sauks were divided on how to deal with the Americans, they continued to cooperate with one another, such as occurred when the men of Black Hawk's band went on campaign while their de-pendents took shelter with a party of neutralists. Nevertheless, the separation of the nation into opposing groups in meeting external challenges was significant and ought to be remembered while reading Black Hawk's memoirs because he focused his story on his party's actions, and thus the narrative does not represent the perspectives of the entire nation. Black Hawk held a minority position within the tribe, but he believed his actions were faithful to Sauk traditions and needs, while his ambitions to gain distinction as a leader in combat against American troops venerated tribal customs and values that esteemed military prowess.[12]

Sauks and Foxes who were hostile to the United States, like other native people on the western frontiers of the Republic, engaged in small-scale but serious fighting with whites before the coming of the War of 1812. Once conflict broke out between Great Britain and the United States, Black Hawk resisted American efforts to establish control along the upper Mississippi by participating in an attack on Fort Madison in 1812. He journeyed east early in 1813 to fight on the Detroit front beside British and other native forces, and then he returned west to lead his followers into battle in his homeland in 1814. He continued to fight into 1815 and did not sign a peace treaty with the United States until 1816, a year after other Sauks had terminated hostilities with the Republic. Those treaties not only ended the tribe's conflict with the Americans but affirmed native acceptance of the 1804 land surrender, although, as we shall see, Black Hawk and other Sauks said that they did not know that the postwar agreements included such a disturbing provision.

After 1815, strains between Black Hawk and Keokuk that had emerged during the conflict escalated sharply. While the former rejected the treaty of 1804 and tried to ignore or oppose it, Keokuk believed the Sauks could not withstand American power and therefore had to make the best accommodation they could, relying on cooperation and goodwill to encourage the United States to protect tribal interests. Yet aboriginal concerns were held in contempt when they clashed with those of white officials and settlers. The postwar influx of Euro-American immigrants aggravated the already tense situation as the tribespeople came under growing pressure to abandon their homes and move west to avoid a succession of abuses and losses that undermined their abilities to support themselves. Black Hawk recorded an example of this oppression when he recalled the story of a friend who cultivated his crops on an island in the Rock River: "He planted his corn; it came up well, but the white man saw it. He wanted the island and took his teams over, plowed up the corn, and replanted it for himself. The old man shed tears, not for himself, but the distress his family would be in if they raised no corn."[13] During those depressing years, Black Hawk and other Sauks traveled to Canada periodically to obtain advice about the tribe's rights in negotiating with the Americans, to maintain their British alliance, and to receive presents from the Crown. Along with explaining their legal status to tribal emissaries, the king's representatives encouraged them to seek peaceful solutions to their problems, telling them, as Black Hawk said, that "there never would be war between England and America again."[14] Nevertheless, these visits generated suspicion in the United States, which were intensified by aboriginal acts of defiance to the new order, such as pulling surveyors' stakes out of the ground, theft, acts of violence, and threats of war.

Many Sauk leaders bowed to American pressure to relocate west of the Mississippi among their Fox allies. Black Hawk belonged to a minority, perhaps one-fifth of the nation, that opposed such a move. Usually he refused to acknowledge the legality of the 1804 sale, although he sometimes claimed that its provisions permitted the tribe to remain in place until the government sold the land to settlers, which had not yet occurred at the time his fellow Sauks were leaving their homes. Even with impending sales, he assumed that at least the important village of Saukenuk could be preserved for his nation. He found the events of the 1820s to be deeply frustrating on a personal level when settlers victimized him along with other members of the tribe. For instance, in 1827, when the Sauks were away from home on a hunt, American newcomers burned Saukenuk, forcing the tribespeople to rebuild their lodges when they returned. Over the winter of 1828–29, when Black Hawk was away again on a hunt, squatters moved into his lodge, destroyed property, and plowed through graves that stood in the way of their plans to lay out a Euro-American settlement. In 1830, American officials told the Sauks that the land had been sold in and around Saukenuk and ordered them to leave; however, Black Hawk was one of a number of leaders who tried to remain. If necessary he was willing to kill those responsible for the loss, including not only settlers and government officials but also Keokuk, who had advocated moving west after failing to get the Americans to secure the tribe's possession of the village. Nevertheless, those who remained at Saukenuk did not take hostile action apart from some minor brawling with squatters. In the end, the Americans forced the Sauks from the town at a time of escalating native-white tensions generated not only by the purchase of land at Saukenuk by some whites but also because of intertribal violence involving residents of the village who fought indigenous people to the west, which threatened a general aboriginal war independent of the white-native crisis. In June 1831, regular troops and volunteer militia surrounded Saukenuk, opened fire with artillery, and then moved in. The village, however, was empty: its residents had fled across the Mississippi in advance of the assault. The Americans set fire to people's homes, seized property, and destroyed crops. Then, not content to evict the living, they opened graves and burned or scattered the remains of the dead across the ground, perhaps knowing how much importance the Sauks placed on sites associated with the spiritual world of their ancestors. This desecration occurred only a short while after Black Hawk had declared, "I am a Sauk; my fathers were great men, and I wish to remain where the bones of my fathers are laid. I desire to be buried with my fathers. Why then should I leave their fields?"[15]

A few days after the attack on Saukenuk, an intimidated Black Hawk and other leaders met with American officials. The natives agreed to stay west of the Mississippi, keep the peace, affirm the 1804 treaty, and submit to other conditions. In return, the Americans promised to give them corn and other presents because the tribespeople had been compelled to abandon their crops before they could harvest them. The distribution of these gifts served as a face-saving gesture allowing Black Hawk's people to accept the new situation. Yet when the Americans did not deliver enough supplies and when they opened fire on Sauks who reentered their fields to gather food to relieve their hunger, Black Hawk and other leaders seem to have decided that the principled course was to return home, thinking they would receive help from other tribes and from the British if they did so. Accordingly, Black Hawk, with about one thousand Sauk, Fox, Kickapoo, and Winnebago men, women, and children, came back to Illinois in April 1832. They were prepared to defend themselves if attacked but hoped to proceed peacefully. As white forces mustered to oppose them and as few other natives offered encouragement, they realized that the assumption that they would receive assistance was wrong and that their move had been a mistake. They decided to retire back across the Mississippi, and in May they sent a small party of men to open negotiations with the Americans and thereby avoid a confrontation. Tragically, when the emissaries approached some militiamen, the whites opened fire, killing some of them. The survivors fled with their enemies in pursuit. Realizing what had happened, Black Hawk set an ambush and defeated the Americans in a minor engagement. Thus began the Black Hawk War, a tragic series of horrors that brutalized the native-white frontier for a few months despite at least two more attempts by the natives to surrender. The last actions occurred when remnants of the band attempted to swim across the Mississippi near the Bad Axe River in today's Wisconsin in August, where a large number of them were shot by American and white-allied native forces or drowned during the confusion and terror of the action. Many of those who escaped the massacre subsequently encountered death or capture at the hands of the Sioux, who had emerged as a significant enemy once the Sauks competed with them for hunting lands in the west to replace the territory they had lost to settlers in the east. Soon afterward, with more than half of his followers dead, Black Hawk and a party of supporters gave themselves up to a group of American-allied Winnebagos, who turned them over to white authorities at Prairie du Chien.

Black Hawk's captors interned him and a number of other people at Jefferson Barracks outside St. Louis until the spring of 1833. Then they released the less important men but sent Black Hawk and five others east to meet President Andrew Jackson and be imprisoned far from their homeland. The government, however, changed its plan, deciding instead to release them into Keokuk's care in an effort to strengthen the friendly leader's power among the Sauks and Foxes. Prior to their return, Black Hawk and his compatriots were taken on a long tour through eastern cities. Ostensibly American officials wanted to impress upon them the power and might of the United States and the futility of further resistance. The tour also gave the Jackson administration an opportunity to put some recently hostile aboriginal leaders on display as trophies to help justify its ruthless Indian Removal Act of 1830 and other oppressive measures directed against the indigenous peoples who lived east of the Mississippi.[16] During his visits to cities along the Eastern Seaboard, Black Hawk realized just how bad the imbalance was between the tribes and the Americans when he noted that "I had no idea that the white people had such large villages and so many people."[17] After viewing the sights and experiencing the attention of curious crowds, he returned home through Buffalo, Detroit, and Prairie du Chien.

Following the Black Hawk War, Sauk and Fox society suffered from the decline of game animals, internal divisions, population losses, ongoing warfare with neighboring tribes, and increased social problems due in large part to the alcohol trade and growing contact with unscrupulous and exploitive settlers. Most Sauks and Foxes bowed to mounting pressures and moved west into modern Iowa and then to today's Kansas in the 1830s and 1840s, although many had to be forced to do so by the American military. Then in the 1860s and the 1880s most found themselves compelled to relocate again, to present-day Oklahoma. Some, mainly Foxes, managed to stay in, or return to, Iowa in spite of white opposition and were allowed to purchase some land in the 1850s, while others maintained homes in Missouri. Today there are three Sauk and Fox reservations recognized by the American federal government: the Sac and Fox Nation in Oklahoma, the Sac and Fox Tribe of the Mississippi in Iowa, and the Sac and Fox Nation of Missouri in Kansas and Nebraska. They serve as homes for thousands of people, while many other members of these communities pursue their lives elsewhere in the country and beyond, as is common among the First Nations of modern North America.

Black Hawk did not live to move to Kansas, although he realized that it would not be long before his people would be forced to leave their Iowa homes. He passed most of his remaining years quietly in his neatly kept bark lodge with his wife and children, first near the Iowa River and then on the Des Moines. Throughout this final period of his life, Black Hawk was overshadowed by Keokuk's leadership, as he had been told by American officials to follow his old rival's much-resented direction. Then, on October 3, 1838, after a short illness, Black Hawk passed away. His family buried him in the traditional sitting position in a small log mausoleum with some of his possessions, dressed in a uniform he had received from President Jackson. Within the year, a white man broke into his grave and stole first his head and then the rest of his remains. Black Hawk's bones later were recovered, but rather than being reinterred, they were placed in a museum in Burlington, Iowa. In 1855, they were lost in a fire.[18]

During Black Hawk's famous eastern tour, he found that he had not been able to express his thoughts as clearly as he had wished. As he noted, "My opinions were asked on different subjects but for want of a good interpreter, were very seldom given."[19] To add to his frustration, he knew that many people's views of him were inaccurate and hostile. At the same time, his months of incarceration and travel through strange environments provided an unusual opportunity to meditate on his own behavior, its place within Sauk history, and the problems his people had experienced with the Americans, and then organize his thoughts for what would become a carefully constructed presentation that would lead to the publication of his autobiography. He also likely learned enough about white society to recognize the potential of promoting indigenous interests to a large audience through converting a native speech into print, in contrast to the now-impossible option of going to war to protect his people's honor, rights, and freedoms.[20] Once he returned home, where he continued to suffer from insult and criticism for his militancy, he called upon Antoine LeClair (or LeClaire), the government interpreter to the Sauk and Fox nations, to help him produce his apologia out of a sense of "duty" to "lay the most important" of his views "before the public," where he assumed his thoughts would be found "acceptable."[21] Furthermore, Black Hawk stated that, as he contemplated the approaching "journey to the land of my fathers, I have determined to give my motives and reasons for my former hostilities to the whites, and to vindicate my character from misrepresentation."[22]

LeClair, a man of Potawatomi and French Canadian ancestry who had grown up in the Great Lakes and upper Mississippi regions, recorded that Black Hawk visited him in August 1833 to "express a great desire to have a history of his life written and published, in order . . . that the people of the United States . . . might know the *causes* that had impelled him to act as he had done, and the *principles* by which he was governed."[23] LeClair, a talented linguist, translated the dictated words from Sauk into written English, being "particularly cautious," as he wrote, "to understand distinctly the narrative of Black Hawk throughout."[24] John Barton Patterson, an Illinois newspaperman, edited the text for publication, as he said, "according to the dictation of Black Hawk, through the United States interpreter." He claimed that he presented Black Hawk's words so faithfully that he felt the need to absolve himself of responsibility "for any of the facts, or views, contained" in the finished work.[25] Before the text went to press, LeClair examined Patterson's typeset proofs and expressed "no hesitation" in pronouncing them "strictly correct" in all their "particulars."[26] As well, Black Hawk apparently had the English-language document translated back to him for his approval, and he verified its legitimacy to other people afterward.[27] Despite these assertions of authenticity, there are some challenges with the *Life of Ma-ka-tai-me-she-kia-kiak* that remind readers that it is the product of cultural mediation: a Sauk dictated his memoirs in his own language in order to educate a white audience; a person of mixed ancestry employed by the government translated and wrote it down in English; and an anglophone newspaperman edited it for publication in what one scholar, Arnold Krupat, described as "an original bicultural composite composition."[28]

One problem with the text is that some of the English-language words and phrases used to represent Sauk concepts seem like poor choices that LeClair or Patterson may have made in order to meet the expectations of Jacksonian-era readers of what natives sounded like. The printed book also may have been intended to give Black Hawk's autobiography a simplified or romantic hue to soften his pointed condemnations of the United States—especially when Indian Removal lay at the forefront of public discussion in the country—but which may have robbed Black Hawk of some of the vitality and nuance of his own speech patterns. Yet with the limited amount of surviving documentation surrounding the production of the text, we cannot do much more than use our intellectual skills to recognize that this problem likely exists, try to identify places where Black Hawk's ideas may have been paraphrased inadequately, and then attempt to appreciate the underlying indigenous views with more accuracy. For instance, the book, even with its pointed condemnation of white society for the injustices inflicted on the Sauks, possesses a somewhat calmer tone than do Black Hawk's words preserved in council negotiations, although a comparison between these sources shows fundamental consistencies in content and expression, despite being translated by a range of people for different audiences and purposes, and at varying points in Black Hawk's life in relation to his age and condition.[29] Notwithstanding this concern with the autobiography, Black Hawk's perspective clearly remains strong and much or most of the nuance and character of his original presentation seems to have been preserved fairly well in English. For instance, the document includes stories that were meaningful to Black Hawk on several levels, but their details would have eluded white audiences in the 1830s, yet neither LeClair nor Patterson evidently asked him to explain them more clearly or added a gloss that would have enriched the account for readers. An excellent example of this is his tale of a Sioux man shot by a British firing squad, which we will read in section 2, and which has been explicated in detail in the notes below for the first time so that we can understand the underlying context in Black Hawk's thoughts about that incident in a text focused heavily on the themes of betrayal and oppression. In some ways, Black Hawk undermined his objectives in dictating his autobiography by not saying more or by not expressing himself with greater clarity. We must remember, however, that the dictation of his memoirs was a new and strange thing for him to undertake, and that he did it for an audience he did not understand completely. As well, he presumably framed his presentation within native cultural principles that valued reserve and discretion in speech, and in a context where he likely found it difficult to balance his primary focus on Sauk-American problems with a wish to say more about his people and their world.

An additional difficulty with the text is that some sentences seem to reflect the views of either LeClair or Patterson more than Black Hawk; nevertheless, the number of these interventions seems to be small, and they are clumsy enough that they seem easy to recognize (and have been identified where they occur below, such as a comparison of British and American musketry that is inaccurate but which fed into the self-perceptions of the Republic's citizens). Another problem is that Patterson's decision to use italics and exclamation marks freely (even by the standards of the 1830s) seems to distort Black Hawk's voice, but the presentation of the *Life* below changes most of these elements to a conventional presentation, which should help modern audiences hear Black Hawk with greater clarity. (Furthermore, when comparing native speeches preserved in council minutes, where exclamation points and italics appear far less frequently than they do in the 1833 edition of the *Life*, it seems unlikely that these forms of emphasis would have been captured in the translation process from Black Hawk to LeClair, and thus they presumably were Patterson's rather than LeClair's interventions.) Although

LeClair and Patterson apparently did not ask Black Hawk to explain his points when they may have been unclear, we do know that they attempted to shape the content of the document by posing questions for Black Hawk to answer on things that concerned them. While we do not know how forthcoming Black Hawk was, we have an indication that he was not very cooperative and consequently seems to have preserved the shape of his narrative as he intended to give it. Many years after publishing the autobiography, Patterson remembered that "in regard to Tecumseh, Black Hawk seemed averse to talk about him. All that I could get from him appears in my book. The interpreter, when talking to him about Tecumseh, tried to induce him to tell all he knew, but he gave *his reasons* for not saying anything more." Regrettably, Patterson did not say what the reasons were (if he ever knew), although he and LeClair thought the Shawnee leader had offended Black Hawk because he had not treated him with adequate deference and had not invited him to join his inner circle of counselors.[30] Another interpretation for Black Hawk's reticence to speak about Tecumseh can be found in his own words below, which indicated a sorrowful sense of missed opportunity because the Sauks had been reluctant to join Tecumseh's confederacy, which he thought may have deprived the alliance of some of the strength it needed to counter the white threat to native independence. Alternatively, details about Tecumseh simply may have been peripheral to Black Hawk's purposes in narrating the story of his own life and concerns. Outside of the problems with translation, another challenge lies with Black Hawk's decision to not present his story chronologically. Some lapses may have been accidental, but others appear to have been deliberate, such as infelicities in the sequencing of events which seem to have been done to make particular points to his readers (and which have been identified below).

The autobiography as a whole is a self-vindication narrative based on a traditional speech genre common in nonliterate societies. Despite some potential softening by LeClair and Patterson, it is full of antagonism, defiance, and indigenous thought that exist in fundamental distinction to Euro-American perspectives and that speak to the authenticity of the text. At heart, it asserts the values and goodness of Sauk society while describing the causes of the strife faced by Black Hawk's people with the Americans (centered on the crises initiated by the 1804 treaty but also addressing other problems), and it affirms the principles that drove Black Hawk to defend his nation's interests.[31] He wanted to mark how American treatment of the Sauks had been unjust and deceitful, and how his response was sound and honorable within his people's customs and mores. Furthermore, Black Hawk affirmed the superiority of native customs compared to those of whites, an assertion made not within the context of Eurocentric dis-

course, such as that of the "noble savage," but from within the cultural heart of
the Sauk worldview, one that must have seemed alien to his white readers in the
1830s.[32] In short, this text is a profound act of resistance, albeit one by a defeated
older man who no longer could turn to customary forms of confrontation when
he believed his people were endangered and wronged. From a literary perspective, readers familiar with native speeches preserved in council minutes from
the eighteenth and nineteenth centuries will notice similarities between those
documents and this text. Some of the shared characteristics include a simplified
rehearsal of history designed to gain acceptance of the speaker's point of view,
along with the use of irony, emphasizing narrative over accusation to attack white
behavior, posing questions for Euro-Americans to reflect upon (and feel shame)
in relation to how they had treated native people, and outwardly unsophisticated
statements employed to express pointed and complex views that a white audience
would have had difficulty refuting with good grace.

It might be easy to be diverted by the textual problems of the *Life* from the
fundamental reality that this culturally mediated document presents us with a
rare opportunity for hearing a Sauk voice from the early nineteenth century. Yet
this cross-cultural interaction among Black Hawk, Antoine LeClair, and J. B. Patterson, while unusual in producing a text, is representative of much of what was
normal in Black Hawk's life in an era when people of diverse origins competed,
cooperated, and intermingled with each other on the upper Mississippi frontier.
Ultimately, the access the autobiography provides into the thoughts and life of a
Sauk man and all he represented simply would not have been possible had the
collaboration not taken place. Thus, the *Life of Ma-ka-tai-me-she-kia-kiak* is one of
the most fascinating published First Nations texts from the nineteenth century
and, despite its problems, is a rich and complex document by a significant aboriginal participant in the history of native-newcomer relations.

In the pages below, the sections covering the years from c. 1803 to 1816 have been
reproduced from the first edition of Black Hawk's 1833 autobiography from a
copy of the book in the collection of the University of Alberta, between pages 25
and 71 of the original 155-page work.[33]

1. Crisis on the Upper Mississippi Frontier, 1803?–12

*Black Hawk's autobiography prior to our entry into his story recounts Sauk history and
explores the events of his life up to about 1803, with an emphasis on fighting aboriginal*

enemies. The narrative below begins during a period of reduced intertribal conflict and greater hopefulness, but just before new challenges emerged in the region. It starts with Black Hawk's visit to St. Louis, a community of two hundred houses beside the Mississippi, located over two hundred miles south of his home in Saukenuk. The purpose of the visit was to see his "Spanish father," Charles de Hault Delassus, the governor of Upper Louisiana, who had maintained good relations with the Sauks from the time of his arrival in 1799.

Spain had acquired Louisiana from France in the 1760s but retroceded it in 1800. The French emperor, Napoleon Bonaparte, then sold that vast territory to the United States in 1803, but Delassus remained in office to represent French interests and oversee the transfer to American authority. By Euro-American standards, Washington already possessed an unenforced dominion over, but not ownership of, Sauk lands east of the Mississippi River, and the Louisiana Purchase extended the American Republic's control over the territories of the closely allied Fox nation concentrated on the west bank. The sale pulled settlers westward both to the old American east side of the river and into the newly acquired areas. This heralded the beginning of a period of despondency for the indigenous peoples who had experienced only limited contact with the Republic's citizens up to that point. For Black Hawk, the newcomers became a grave menace as natives and settlers clashed over crime, as government officials imposed a draconian treaty on the Sauks and Foxes in 1804 that deprived them of an enormous amount of land, as the newcomers favored other tribes over his own, as the Americans established a military presence in his homeland, and as the growing numbers of settlers assaulted his sense of aboriginal rights and sovereignty.

As the likelihood of an Anglo-American war grew by 1811–12, the Sauks disagreed on what they should do. Many were antagonistic to the United States, but only a portion of even this group wanted to fight. Others thought an accommodation with the Republic would serve their well-being better. At the same time, representatives of the British, the Americans, and Tecumseh and Tenskwatawa's Western Tribal Confederacy worked to draw the Sauks into their respective orbits.

[1803?]

We generally paid a visit to St. Louis every summer; but in consequence of the protracted war in which we had been engaged, I had not been there for some years. Our difficulties having all been settled, I concluded to take a small party that summer and go down to see our Spanish father.[34] We went, and on our arrival put up our lodges where the market house now stands. After painting and dressing, we called to see our Spanish father and were well received. He gave us a variety of presents and plenty of provisions. We danced through the town as usual, and its inhabitants all seemed to be well pleased. They appeared to us like brothers and always gave us good advice.[35]

[1804]

On my next and last visit to my Spanish father, I discovered on landing that all was not right. Every countenance seemed sad and gloomy. I inquired the cause and was informed that the Americans were coming to take possession of the town and country, and that we should then lose our Spanish father! This news made myself and band sad because we had always heard bad accounts of the Americans from Indians who had lived near them, and we were sorry to lose our Spanish father who had always treated us with great friendship. A few days afterward the Americans arrived.[36] I took my band and went to take leave for the last time of our father. The Americans came to see him also. Seeing them approach, we passed out at one door as they entered another, and immediately started, in canoes, for our village on Rock River, not liking the change any more than our friends appeared to at St. Louis.[37] On arriving at our village we gave the news that strange people had taken St. Louis and that we should never see our Spanish father again. This information made all our people sorry.

[1805]

Some time afterward a boat came up the river with a young American chief [Lieutenant (afterward General) Pike] and a small party of soldiers.[38] We heard of him (by runners) soon after he had passed Salt River. Some of our young braves watched him every day to see what sort of people he had on board. The boat at length arrived at Rock River, and the young chief came on shore with his interpreter, made a speech, and gave us some presents. We, in return, presented him with meat and such provisions as we could spare. We were all well pleased with the speech of the young chief. He gave us good advice [and] said our American father would treat us well. He presented us an American flag, which was hoisted. He then requested us to pull down our British flags and give him our British medals, promising to send us others on his return to St. Louis. This we declined, as we wished to have *two fathers*.[39] When the young chief started, we sent runners to the Fox village some miles distant to direct them to treat him well as he passed, which they did. He went to the head of the Mississippi and then returned to St. Louis.[40] We did not see any Americans again for some time, being supplied with goods by British traders. We were fortunate in not giving up our medals, for we learned afterward from our traders that the chiefs high up on the Mississippi who gave theirs never received any in exchange for them.[41] But the fault was not with the young American chief; he was a good man and a great brave, and died in his country's service.[42]

[1804–5]

Some moons after this young chief descended the Mississippi, one of our people killed an American and was confined in the prison at St. Louis for the offense.[43] We held a council at our village to see what could be done for him, which determined that Quashquame, Pashepaho, Ouchequaka, and Hashequarhiqua should go down to St. Louis to see our American father and do all they could to have our friend released by paying for the person killed, thus "covering" the blood and satisfying the relations of the man murdered (this being the only means with us of saving a person who had killed another, and we *then* thought it was the same way with the whites).[44] The party started with the good wishes of the whole nation, hoping they would accomplish the object of their mission. The relatives of the prisoner blacked their faces and fasted, hoping the Great Spirit would take pity on them and return the husband and father to his wife and children.

Quashquame and party remained a long time absent. They at length returned and encamped a short distance below the village but did not come up that day, nor did any person approach their camp. They appeared to be dressed in fine coats and had medals. From these circumstances we were in hopes that they had brought good news. Early the next morning, the council lodge was crowded. Quashquame and party came up and gave us the following account of their mission. On their arrival at St. Louis, they met their American father and explained to him their business and urged the release of their friend.[45] The American chief told them he wanted land, and they had agreed to give him some on the west side of the Mississippi and some on the Illinois side opposite the Jeffreon.[46] When the business was all arranged they expected to have their friend released to come home with them; but about the time they were ready to start, their friend was let out of prison, who ran a short distance and was *shot dead!*[47] This was all they could recollect of what was said and done. They had been drunk the greater part of the time they were in St. Louis. This is all myself or nation knew of the treaty of 1804. It has been explained to me since. I find by that treaty all our country east of the Mississippi and south of the Jeffreon was ceded to the United States for *one thousand dollars* a year! I will leave it to the people of the United States to say whether our nation was properly represented in this treaty or whether we received a fair compensation for the extent of country ceded by those *four* individuals. I could say much about this treaty but I will not at this time. It has been the origin of all our difficulties.[48]

[1808]

Some time after this treaty was made, a war chief with a party of soldiers came up in keel boats and encamped a short distance above the head of the Des Moines Rapids, and commenced cutting timber and building houses [Fort Bellevue, later Fort Madison]. The news of their arrival was soon carried to all the villages when council after council was held.[49] We could not understand the intention or reason why the Americans wanted to build houses at that place, but were told that they were a party of soldiers who had brought *great guns* with them and looked like a *war party* of whites. A number of our people immediately went down to see what was doing, myself among them. On our arrival we found they were building a fort! The soldiers were busily engaged in cutting timber; and I observed that they took their arms with them when they went to the woods, and the whole party acted as they would do in an enemy's country. The chiefs held a council with the officers, or headmen, of the party, which I did not attend but understood from them that the war chief had said that they were building houses for a trader, who was coming there to live and would sell us goods very cheap, and that these soldiers were to remain to keep him company.[50] We were pleased at this information and hoped it was all true, but we could not believe that all these buildings were intended merely for the accommodation of a trader. Being distrustful of their intentions, we were anxious for them to leave off building and go down the river again.

[1809]

By this time, a considerable number of Indians had arrived to see what was doing. I discovered that the whites were alarmed. Some of our young men watched a party of soldiers who went out to work carrying their arms, which were laid aside before they commenced. Having stolen up quietly to the spot, they seized the guns and gave a yell. The party threw down their axes and ran for their arms but found them gone and themselves surrounded. Our men laughed at them and returned them their guns. When this party came to the fort, they reported what had been done, and the war chief made a serious affair of it.[51] He called our chiefs to council inside of his fort. This created considerable excitement in our camp. Everyone wanted to know what was going to be done, and the picketing which had been put up being low, every Indian crowded round the fort and got upon blocks of wood and old barrels that they might see what was going on inside. Some were armed with guns and others with bows and arrows. We used this precaution, seeing that the soldiers had their guns loaded and having seen them load their big gun that morning.[52]

A party of our braves commenced dancing and proceeded up to the gate with an intention of going in but was stopped. The council immediately broke up. The soldiers, with their arms in their hands, rushed out of their rooms where they had been concealed. The cannon was hauled in front of the gateway and a soldier came running with fire in his hand ready to apply the match. Our braves gave way and all retired to the camp. There was no preconcerted plan to attack the whites at that time, but I am of opinion now, had our party got into the fort, all the whites would have been killed, as the British soldiers had been at Mackinac many years before.[53] We broke up our camp and returned to Rock River. A short time afterward the fort party received a reinforcement, among whom we observed some of our old friends from St. Louis.[54]

[1810–12]

Soon after our return from Fort Madison, runners came to our village from the Shawnee prophet (whilst others were dispatched by him to the villages of the Winnebagos) with invitations for us to meet him on the Wabash.[55] Accordingly, a party went from each village.[56] All of our party returned, among whom came a prophet, who explained to us the bad treatment the different nations of Indians had received from the Americans by giving them a few presents and taking their land from them. I remember well his saying, "If you do not join your friends on the Wabash, the Americans will take this very village from you!" I little thought then that his words would come true! Supposing that he used these arguments merely to encourage us to join him, we agreed that we would not.[57] He then returned to the Wabash where a party of Winnebagos had arrived and preparations were making for war! A battle soon ensued in which several Winnebagos were killed.[58] As soon as their nation heard of this battle and that some of their people had been killed, they started war parties in different directions, one to the mining country, one to Prairie du Chien, and another to Fort Madison. This last returned by our village and exhibited several scalps which they had taken.[59]

[1812]

Their success induced several other parties to go against the fort. Myself and several of my band joined the last party, and were determined to take the fort.[60] We arrived in the vicinity during the night. The spies that we had sent out several days before, to watch the movements of those at the garrison and ascertain their numbers, came to us and gave the following information: that a keel boat had arrived from below that evening with seventeen men, that there were about fifty men in the fort, and that they marched out every morning at sunrise to exercise. It was immediately determined that we should take a position as near as we could to conceal ourselves to the place where the soldiers would come, and when the signal was given, each man [was] to fire and then rush into the fort.

I dug a hole with my knife deep enough (by placing a few weeds around it) to conceal myself. I was so near to the fort that I could hear the sentinel walking. By daybreak I had finished my work and was anxiously awaiting the rising of the sun. The drum beat.[61] I examined the priming of my gun and eagerly watched for the gate to open. It did open but instead of the troops marching out, a young man came alone. The gate closed after him. He passed close by me—so near that I could have killed him with my knife—but I let him pass. He kept the path toward the river, and had he went one step out of it, he must have come upon us and would have been killed. He returned immediately and entered the gate. I would now have rushed for the gate and entered it with him, but I feared that our party was not prepared to follow me. The gate opened again, four men came out, and went down to the river after wood. Whilst they were gone another man came out and walked toward the river, was fired upon, and killed by a Winnebago. The others immediately ran for the fort, and two of them were killed.[62]

We then took shelter under the bank, out of reach of fire from the fort. The firing now commenced from both parties and continued all day. I advised our party to set fire to the fort and commenced preparing arrows for that purpose. At night we made the attempt and succeeded to fire the buildings several times but without effect as the fire was almost instantly extinguished.[63] The next day I took my rifle and shot in two the cord by which they hoisted their flag and prevented them from raising it again.[64] We continued firing until all our ammunition was expended, and finding that we could not take the fort, returned home, having had one Winnebago killed and one wounded during the siege. I have since learned that the trader who lived in the fort wounded the Winnebago when he was scalping the first man that was killed. The Winnebago recovered, is now living, and is very friendly disposed toward the trader, believing him to be a great brave.[65]

2. Joining the British on the Detroit Front, 1812–13

With the coming of the Anglo-American war, Black Hawk favored hostilities within the confines of traditional campaigns against local enemies to fulfill Sauk objectives in affirming and maintaining independence from American control, as demonstrated by his presence at the attack on Fort Madison. Other Sauks preferred to remain neutral, in part because of pledges from the American government that it would meet the tribe's needs for trade at the fort. That offer held out the prospect for many that they might be able to pursue their livelihood, at least for the immediate future, without having to gamble on the fortunes of war and without fear of the consequences of losing trading opportunities with British subjects should they not ally with King George III. Black Hawk, however, recorded that the people of Saukenuk felt compelled to take up arms by late 1812 when the Republic's officials betrayed the promise of friendly trade at the same time that the British took advantage of the situation to encourage the Sauks to assist them on the Detroit front. Black Hawk subsequently led a large contingent against the Americans in 1813, and the narrative below discusses his presence at the sieges of Fort Meigs and Fort Stephenson between April and August of that year. His participation in the fighting at Fort Madison in 1812, described above, fundamentally seems to have been a private act of war (as represented by the small number of warriors who followed him), which he took in opposition to a wider consensus by the Sauks to remain at peace at that point in the Anglo-American conflict (as native society regularly allowed people to deviate from important collective decisions out of respect for individual rights and the inability to force compliance on those who opposed a course of action). In contrast, his conduct in 1813, given the size of the war party he led, suggests that his endeavors fell within a communal (if not unanimous) decision to participate in a campaign alongside the British who wanted warriors from the upper Mississippi to bolster native and white forces campaigning farther east.

There are several features of Black Hawk's text in this part of his autobiography that should be noted. First, by changing the chronological sequencing of events through dividing his attack on Fort Madison from the story of the American promise of friendly trade, Black Hawk's memoirs effectively separated his actions from those of the rest of his community without indicating clearly that his conduct at the fort conflicted with the wider consensus. Second, he included a chronologically misplaced description of the execution of a native man by a British firing squad in 1815 in this part of the narrative where readers logically would assume it had occurred early in the war. Black Hawk may have told the story at this point, close to the account of Sauk interactions with the white powers, to stress the pressures and intrusions the Sauks experienced from both of them, even though he preferred the British over the Americans. Third, while Black

Hawk used the description of the execution to indicate that relations with the Crown could be difficult, his discussion of the negotiations with the king's representatives that led him to take men to the Detroit front does not reveal just how tense Anglo-Sauk affairs were. At the time, white officials threatened to send allied natives to attack the tribe if it did not participate in the wider war effort rather than focus Sauk energies on regional objectives. Presumably the problems of his people's diplomacy with the British were not important to the thrust of his memoirs and in fact may have undermined his damnation of the Americans if he discussed them at length. Fourth, his story at this point expressed people's happiness with the Americans at the time he opposed the dominant opinion. We do not know what Black Hawk intended by this. It is possible he meant to be ironic or cynical, although he also might have structured his narrative this way in order to emphasize the sense of betrayal that followed, or he might have been willing to follow the community consensus of that moment, at least outwardly, while expecting that subsequent events would show it to have been misguided, as was not uncommon in First Nations politics when proponents of one view deferred to the advocates of another while awaiting a change in circumstances that would enable their opinions to become popular.

[1812]

Soon after our return home, news reached us that a war was going to take place between the British and the Americans.[66] Runners continued to arrive from different tribes, all confirming the report of the expected war. The British agent, Colonel Dickson, was holding talks with, and making presents to, the different tribes.[67] I had not made up my mind whether to join the British or remain neutral. I had not discovered one good trait in the character of the Americans who had come to the country. They made fair promises but never fulfilled them, whilst the British made but few but we could always rely upon their word.[68]

[1814–15]

One of our people having killed a Frenchman at Prairie du Chien, the British took him prisoner and said they would shoot him the next day! His family was encamped a short distance below the mouth of the Wisconsin. He begged for permission to go and see them that night as he was to die the next day. They permitted him to go, after promising to return the next morning by sunrise. He visited his family, which consisted of a wife and six children. I cannot describe their meeting and parting to be understood by the whites as it appears that their feelings are acted upon by certain rules laid down by their preachers, whilst ours are governed only by the monitor within us. He parted from his wife and children, hurried through the prairie to the fort, and arrived in time. The soldiers were ready, and immediately marched out and shot him down! I visited his family, and by hunting and fishing provided for them until they reached their relations. Why did the Great Spirit ever send the whites to this island, to drive us from our homes, and introduce among us poisonous liquors, disease, and death? They should have remained on the island where the Great Spirit first placed them.[69]

But I will proceed with my story. My memory, however, is not very good since my late visit to the white people. I have still a buzzing in my ears from the noise, and may give some parts of my story out of place, but I will endeavor to be correct.[70]

[1812]

Several of our chiefs and headmen were called upon to go to Washington to see their great father.[71] They started, and during their absence I went to Peoria on the Illinois River to see an old friend, a trader, to get his advice. He was a man who always told us the truth and knew everything that was going on. When I arrived at Peoria, he was not there but had gone to Chicago.[72] I visited the Potawatomi villages [in the Illinois River region] and then returned to Rock River, soon after which our friends returned from their visit to our great father and related what had been said and done. Their great father, they said, wished us, in the event of a war taking place with England, not to interfere on either side but to remain neutral. He did not want our help but wished us to hunt and support our families and live in peace.[73] He said that British traders would not be permitted to come on the Mississippi to furnish us with goods, but we would be well supplied by an American trader. Our chiefs then told him that the British traders always gave us credits in the fall for guns, powder, and goods to enable us to hunt and clothe our families. He replied that the trader at Fort Madison would have plenty of goods, that we should go there in the fall and he would supply us on credit as the British traders had done.[74] The party gave a good account of what they had seen and the kind treatment they received.

This information pleased us all very much. We all agreed to follow our great father's advice and not interfere with the war. Our women were much pleased at this good news. Everything went on cheerfully in our village. We resumed our pastimes of playing ball, horse racing, and dancing, which had been laid aside when this great war was first talked about. We had fine crops of corn, which were now ripe, and our women were engaged in gathering it and making caches to contain it.[75] In a short time we were ready to start to Fort Madison to get our supply of goods (that we might proceed to our hunting grounds). We passed merrily down the river all in high spirits. I had determined to spend the winter in my old favorite hunting ground on [the] Skunk River, and left part of my corn and meat at its mouth to take up when I returned. Others did the same. Next morning we arrived at the fort and made our encampment. Myself and [the] principal men paid a visit to the war chief at the fort. He received us kindly and gave us some tobacco, pipes, and provisions.[76] The trader came in and we all rose and shook hands with him, for on him all our dependence was placed to enable us to hunt and thereby support our families. We waited a long time, expecting the trader would tell us that he had orders from our great father to supply us with goods, but he said nothing on the subject. I got up and told him in a short speech what we had come for, and hoped he had plenty of goods to supply us, and told him that he should be well paid in the spring, and concluded by informing him that we had determined to follow our great father's advice and not go to war.[77] He said that he was happy to hear that we intended to remain at peace, that he had a large quantity of goods, that if we made a good hunt, we would be well supplied, but remarked that he had received no instructions to furnish us anything on credit, nor could he give us any without receiving the pay for them on the spot! We informed him what our great father had told our chiefs at Washington and contended that he could supply us if he would, believing that our great father always spoke the truth; but the war chief said that the trader could not furnish us on credit and that he had received no instructions from our great father at Washington. We left the fort dissatisfied and went to our camp. What was now to be done we knew not. We questioned the party that brought us the news from our great father that we would get credit for our winter's supplies at this place. They still told the same story and insisted upon its truth. Few of us slept that night. All was gloom and discontent.[78]

In the morning, a canoe was seen descending the river. It soon arrived bearing an express who brought intelligence that La Gouthrie, a British trader, had landed at Rock Island with two boats loaded with goods and requested us to come up immediately because he had good news for us and a variety of presents. The express presented us with tobacco, pipes, and wampum. The news ran through our camp like fire in the prairie. Our lodges were soon taken down and all started for Rock Island. Here ended all hopes of our remaining at peace, having been forced into WAR by being DECEIVED![79]

[1812–13][80]

Our party was not long in getting to Rock Island. When we came in sight and saw tents pitched, we yelled, fired our guns, and commenced beating our drums. Guns were immediately fired at the island, returning our salute, and a British flag hoisted! We landed and were cordially received by La Gouthrie, and then smoked the pipe with him, after which he made a speech to us that had been sent by Colonel Dickson, and gave us a number of handsome presents, a large silk flag, and a keg of rum, and told us to retire, take some refreshments, and rest ourselves as he would have more to say to us on the next day.[81]

We accordingly retired to our lodges (which had been put up in the meantime) and spent the night. The next morning we called upon him and told him that we wanted his two boats' load of goods to divide among our people, for which he should be well paid in the spring with furs and peltries. He consented [and] told us to take them and do as we pleased with them.[82] Whilst our people were dividing the goods he took me aside and informed me that Colonel Dickson was at Green Bay with twelve boats loaded with goods, guns, and ammunition, and wished me to raise a party immediately to go to him.[83] He said that our friend, the trader at Peoria [Thomas Forsyth], was collecting the Potawatomis and would be there before us.[84] I communicated this information to my braves, and a party of two hundred warriors was soon collected and ready to depart.

I paid a visit to the lodge of an old friend, who had been the comrade of my youth and had been in many war parties with me, but was now crippled and no longer able to travel. He had a son whom I had adopted as my own who had hunted with me the two preceding winters. I wished my old friend to let him go with me. He objected, saying that he could not get his support if his son left him, that I (who had always provided for him since he got lame) would be gone, and he had no other dependence than his son. I offered to leave my son in his place, but he still refused. He said he did not like the war. He had been down the river and had been well treated by the Americans and could not fight against them. He had promised to winter near a white settler above Salt River and must take his son with him. We parted.[85]

[1813]

I soon concluded my arrangements and started with my party to Green Bay. On our arrival there we found a large encampment and were well received by

Dickson and the war chiefs that were with him. He gave us plenty of provisions, tobacco, and pipes, and said he would hold a council with us the next day. In the encampment, I found a large number of Potawatomis, Kickapoos, Ottawas, and Winnebagos. I visited all their camps and found them in high spirits. They had all received new guns, ammunition, and a variety of clothing.[86]

In the evening a messenger came to me to visit Colonel Dickson. I went to his tent, in which were two other war chiefs and an interpreter. He received me with a hearty shake of the hand and presented me to the other chiefs, who shook my hand cordially and seemed much pleased to see me. After I was seated, Colonel Dickson said, "General Black Hawk, I sent for you to explain to you what we are going to do and the reasons that have brought us here. Our friend, La Gouthrie, informs us in the letter you brought from him what has lately taken place. You will now have to hold us fast by the hand. Your English father has found out that the Americans want to take your country from you, and has sent me and his braves to drive them back to their own country. He has, likewise, sent a large quantity of arms and ammunition; and we want all your warriors to join us." He then placed a medal around my neck, and gave me a paper (which I lost in the late war) and a silk flag, saying, "You are to command all the braves that will leave here the day after tomorrow to join our braves near Detroit."[87]

I told him that I was very much disappointed, as I wanted to descend the Mississippi and make war upon the settlements. He said he had been ordered to lay the country waste around St. Louis [but] that he had been a trader on the Mississippi many years, had always been kindly treated, and could not consent to send brave men to murder women and children, [and] that there were no soldiers there to fight; but where he was going to send us there were a number of soldiers, and if we defeated them, the Mississippi country should be ours. I was pleased with this speech; it was spoken by a brave.[88]

I inquired about my old friend, the trader at Peoria, and observed that I expected he would have been here before me. He shook his head and said he had sent express after express to him and had offered him large sums of money to come and bring all the Potawatomis and Kickapoos with him but he refused, saying, "'Your British father had not money enough to induce him to join us!' I have now laid a trap for him; I have sent Gomo and a party of Indians to take him prisoner and bring him here alive. I expect him in a few days."[89]

The next day, arms and ammunition, tomahawks, knives, and clothing were given to my band. We had a great feast in the evening, and the morning following I started with about five hundred braves to join the British army. The British war chief accompanied us.[90] We passed Chicago. The fort had been evacuated by the American soldiers who had marched for Fort Wayne. They were attacked a short distance from the fort and defeated. They had a considerable quantity of powder in the fort at Chicago, which they had promised to the Indians; but the night before they marched, they destroyed it. (I think it was thrown into the well.) If they had fulfilled their word to the Indians, I think they would have gone safe.[91] On our arrival I found that the Indians had several prisoners. I advised them to treat them well.[92]

We continued our march and joined the British army below Detroit, and soon after had a fight. The Americans fought well and drove us with considerable loss! I was surprised at this, as I had been told that the Americans could not fight. Our next movement was against a fortified place [Fort Meigs]. I was stationed with my braves to prevent any person going to, or coming from, the fort. I found two men taking care of cattle and took them prisoners. I would not kill them but delivered them to the British war chief. Soon after, several boats came down the river, full of American soldiers. They landed on the opposite side, took the British batteries, and pursued the soldiers that had left them. They went too far without knowing the forces of the British and were defeated. I hurried across the river, anxious for an opportunity to show the courage of my braves, but before we reached the ground, all was over. The British had taken many prisoners, *and the Indians were killing them*! I immediately put a stop to it, as I never thought it was brave, but cowardly, to kill an unarmed and helpless enemy.[93]

We remained here some time. I cannot detail what took place, as I was stationed with my braves in the woods. It appeared, however, that the British could not take this fort, for we were marched to another [Fort Stephenson] some distance off.[94] When we approached it, I found it a small stockade and concluded that there were not many in it. The British war chief sent a flag (Colonel Dickson carried it) and returned.[95] He said a young war chief commanded, and would not give up without fighting.[96] Dickson came to me and said, "You will see tomorrow how easily we will take that fort!" I was of opinion that they would take it, but when the morning came I was disappointed. The British advanced, commenced an attack, and fought like braves, but by braves in the fort were defeated and a great number killed.[97]

The British army was making preparations to retreat.[98] I was now tired of being with them (our success being bad and having got no plunder). I determined on leaving them and returning to Rock River to see what had become of my wife and children, as I had not heard from them since I started.[99] That night, I took about twenty of my braves and left the British camp for home.[100]

3. Return Home, Keokuk's Rise, and Private War, 1814–15

The 1813 Detroit campaign ended with success flowing to the Americans, who, in addition to their defense of Fort Meigs and Fort Stephenson, counterattacked by defeating the Royal Navy on Lake Erie, invading British territory, winning an important victory at Moraviantown, and occupying the southwestern corner of Upper Canada (until returning it to British control as part of the treaty requirements that ended the war). Those successes led some of the tribes who had opposed the United States to make peace with the former enemy in 1813 and 1814 while the Anglo-American conflict continued. Meanwhile, farther west, along the Mississippi River and in neighboring regions, the Americans fortified their settlements, raided aboriginal villages, and contested control of the frontier with the First Nations while the natives fought back with their own attacks and defensive actions. When Black Hawk returned home to Saukenuk late in 1813 or early in 1814, he heard sobering testimony that his leadership of so many men on the Detroit front had precipitated a crisis in which one individual, Keokuk, advanced his ambitions at Black Hawk's expense. This must have been galling for Black Hawk because he had made the journey eastward at the behest of the British and in conflict to his own desires to fight in defense of Sauk lands on the upper Mississippi. Furthermore, he seems to have gone east in order to protect his people from British retribution for not supporting the efforts of their troops and Tecumseh's followers in the Detroit area, and thus his presence there served as an indirect attempt to safeguard his home country from the Sauks' ostensible friends, the British and some of the tribes that had allied with them.

Aside from the story of Keokuk's challenge, this part of the autobiography focuses on events in 1814–15 that Black Hawk presented mainly as private acts of war, in distinction from the section that follows, which largely addresses the same period but within a framework of community or national war. The text below describes the murder of the son of one of Black Hawk's closest friends and the subsequent campaign to avenge his death, which culminated in a skirmish that history grandly calls the "Battle" of the Sinkhole, an event that occurred on May 24, 1815, outside Fort Howard (near today's Old Monroe, Missouri). It took place, controversially, after the return of the Anglo-American peace, allowing authorities in the United States to interpret the clash as evidence of ongoing Sauk belligerency in order to facilitate their attempts to exert control over the tribe in the postwar period. Black Hawk's narrative decision to separate his ostensibly private behavior from the larger activities of his community in the next two sections of his autobiography parallels the way he divided the events at Fort Madison from those on the Detroit front and seems to represent an important aspect of his memoirs that perhaps he intended his readers to understand, although this point seems to have escaped attention until now. As we shall see in the notes to this section, however, there is reason to think that the events that led to the Sinkhole were not entirely driven by private concerns, but reflected a larger Sauk desire to continue fighting in 1815 in order to defend their interests against the Americans.

[1813?–14]

We met no person on our journey until we reached the Illinois River. Here we found two lodges of Potawatomis. They received us very friendly and gave us something to eat and inquired about their friends who were with the British. They said there had been some fighting on the Illinois and that my old friend, the trader at Peoria, had been taken prisoner. "By Gomo and his party?" I immediately inquired. They said, "No, but by the *Americans*, who came up with two boats. They took him and the French settlers and then burnt the village of Peoria."[101] They could give us no news respecting our people [at Saukenuk] on Rock River.

In three days more, we were in the vicinity of our village when I discovered a smoke ascending from a hollow in the bluffs. I directed my party to proceed to the village, as I wished to go alone to the place from whence the smoke proceeded to see who was there. I approached the spot, and when I came in view of the fire, saw a mat stretched and an old man sitting under it in sorrow. At any other time I would have turned away without disturbing him, knowing that he had come there to be alone to humble himself before the Great Spirit that he might take pity on him. I approached and seated myself beside him. He gave one look at me and then fixed his eyes on the ground. It was my old friend! I anxiously inquired for his son, my adopted child, and what had befallen our people. My old comrade seemed scarcely alive. He must have fasted a long time. I lighted my pipe and put it in his mouth. He eagerly drew a few puffs, cast up his eyes, which met mine, and recognized me. His eyes were glassy. He would again have fallen off into forgetfulness had I not given him some water, which revived him. I again inquired, "What has befallen our people, and what has become of our son?"[102]

In a feeble voice, he said, "Soon after your departure to join the British, I descended the river with a small party to winter at the place I told you the white man had requested me to come to. When we arrived, I found a fort built, and the white family that had invited me to come and hunt near them had removed to it.[103] I then paid a visit to the fort to tell the white people that myself and little band were friendly and that we wished to hunt in the vicinity of their fort. The war chief who commanded it told me that we might hunt on the Illinois side of the Mississippi and no person would trouble us (that the horsemen only ranged on the Missouri side) and he had directed them not to cross the river.[104] I was pleased with this assurance of safety and immediately crossed over and made my winter's camp. Game was plenty, we lived happy and often talked of you. My boy regretted your absence and the hardships you would have to undergo."

"We had been here about two moons when my boy went out as usual to hunt. Night came on and he did not return. I was alarmed for his safety and passed a sleepless night. In the morning, my old woman went to the other lodges and gave the alarm, and all turned out in pursuit. There being snow on the ground, they soon came upon his track, and after pursuing it some distance found he was on the trail of a deer that led toward the river. They soon came to the place where he had stood and fired, and found a deer hanging upon the branch of a tree, which had been skinned. But here were found the tracks of white men! They had taken my boy prisoner. Their tracks led across the river and then down toward the fort. My friends followed them, and soon found my boy lying dead! He had been most cruelly murdered. His face was shot to pieces, his body stabbed in several places, and his head scalped! His arms were tied behind him!"[105]

The old man paused for some time, and then told me that his wife had died on her way up the Mississippi. I took the hand of my old friend in mine and pledged myself to avenge the death of his son. It was now dark. A terrible storm commenced raging, with heavy torrents of rain, thunder, and lightning. I had taken my blanket off and wrapped it around the old man. When the storm abated I kindled a fire and took hold of my old friend to remove him near to it, but he was dead. I remained with him the balance of the night. Some of my party came early in the morning to look for me and assisted me in burying him on the peak of the bluff. I then returned to the village with my friends. I visited the grave of my old friend the last time as I ascended the Rock River.[106]

On my arrival at the village, I was met by the chiefs and braves and conducted to a lodge that had been prepared to receive me. After eating, I gave an account of what I had seen and done. I explained to them the manner the British and Americans fought. Instead of stealing upon each other and taking every advantage to kill the enemy and save their own people as we do (which with us is considered good policy in a war chief), they marched out in open daylight and fight regardless of the number of warriors they may lose. After the battle is over they retire to feast and drink wine as if nothing had happened, after which they make a statement in writing of what they have done, each party claiming the victory and neither giving an account of half the number that have been killed on their own side. They all fought like braves but would not do to lead a war party with us. Our maxim is "to kill the enemy and save our own men." Those chiefs would do to *paddle* a canoe but not to *steer* it. The Americans shoot better than the British, but their soldiers are not so well clothed or provided for.[107]

The village chief informed me that after I started with my braves and the parties who followed, the nation was reduced to so small a party of fighting men that they would have been unable to defend themselves if the Americans had attacked them; that all the women and children and old men belonging to the warriors who had joined the British were left with them to provide for; and that a council was held which agreed that Quashquame, the Lance, and other chiefs, with the old men, women, and children, and such others as chose to accompany them, should descend the Mississippi and go to St. Louis and place themselves under the protection of the American chief stationed there. They accordingly went down to St. Louis, and were received as the friendly band of our nation, sent up the Missouri, and provided for whilst their friends were assisting the British.[108]

Keokuk was then introduced to me as the war chief of the braves then in the village.[109] I inquired how he had become a chief. They said that a large armed force was seen by their spies going toward Peoria; that fears were entertained that they would come upon and attack our village; and that a council had been convened to decide upon the best course to be adopted, which concluded upon leaving the village and going on the west side of the Mississippi to get out of the way. Keokuk, during the sitting of the council, had been standing at the door of the lodge (not being allowed to enter, having never killed an enemy), where he remained until old Wacome came out.[110] He then told him that he had heard what they had decided upon, and was anxious to be permitted to go in and speak before the council adjourned. Wacome returned and asked leave for Keokuk to come in and make a speech. His request was granted. Keokuk entered and addressed the chiefs. He said, "I have heard with sorrow that you are determined to leave our village and cross the Mississippi merely because you have been told that the Americans were seen coming in this direction! Would you leave our village, desert our homes, and fly *before* an enemy approaches? Would you leave all—even the graves of our fathers—to the mercy of an enemy without *trying* to defend them? Give me charge of your warriors. I'll defend the village, and you may sleep in safety!" The council consented that Keokuk should be a war chief. He marshaled his braves, sent out spies, and advanced with a party himself on the trail leading to Peoria. They returned without seeing an enemy. The Americans did not come by our village. All were well satisfied with the appointment of Keokuk. He used every precaution that our people should not be surprised. This is the manner in which, and the cause of, his receiving the appointment.[111] I was satisfied, and then started to visit my wife and children. I found them well and my boys were growing finely. It is not customary for us to say much about our women, as they generally perform their part cheerfully and never interfere with business belonging to the men. This is the only wife I ever had or ever will have. She is a good woman and teaches my boys to be brave.

[1815]

Here I would have rested myself and enjoyed the comforts of my lodge, but I could not. I had promised to avenge the death of my adopted son. I immediately collected a party of thirty braves and explained to them my object in making this war party, it being to avenge the death of my adopted son who had been cruelly and wantonly murdered by the whites.[112] I explained to them the pledge I had made [to] his father and told them that they were the last words that he had heard spoken! All were willing to go with me to fulfill my word.[113]

We started in canoes and descended the Mississippi until we arrived near the place where Fort Madison had stood. It had been abandoned by the whites and burnt; nothing remained but the chimneys.[114] We were pleased to see that the white people had retired from our country. We proceeded down the river again.[115] I landed with one brave near Cap au Gris; the remainder of the party went to the mouth of the Cuivre. I hurried across to the trail that led from the mouth of the Cuivre to a fort [Howard] and soon after heard firing at the mouth of the creek.[116] Myself and [the] brave concealed ourselves on the side of the road. We had not remained here long before two men riding one horse came in full speed from the direction of the sound of the firing. When they came sufficiently near, we fired, the horse jumped, and both men fell. We rushed toward them. One rose and ran. I followed him and was gaining on him when he ran over a pile of rails that had lately been made, seized a stick, and struck me. I now had an opportunity to see his face. I knew him. He had been at Quashquame's village to learn his people how to plow. We looked upon him as a good man. I did not wish to kill him, and pursued him no further.[117]

I returned and met my brave. He said he had killed the other man and had his scalp in his hand. We had not proceeded far before we met the man supposed to be killed, coming up the road staggering like a drunken man all covered with blood![118] This was the most terrible sight I had ever seen. I told my comrade to kill him to put him out of his misery. I could not look at him. I passed on and heard a rustling in the bushes and distinctly saw two little boys concealing themselves. I thought of my own children, and passed on without noticing them.[119] My comrade here joined me, and in a little while we met the balance of our party. I told them that we would be pursued and directed them to follow me. We crossed the creek and formed ourselves in the timber.

We had not been here long before a party of mounted men rushed at full speed upon us. I took deliberate aim and shot the man leading the party. He fell from his horse lifeless![120] All my people fired but without effect. The enemy rushed upon us without giving us time to reload. They surrounded us and forced us to run into a deep sinkhole, at the bottom of which there were some bushes.[121] We loaded our guns and awaited the approach of the enemy. They rushed to the edge of the hole and fired, killing one of our men. We returned the fire instantly and killed one of their party. We reloaded and commenced digging holes in the side of the bank to protect ourselves whilst a party watched the movements of the enemy, expecting that their whole force would be upon us immediately. Some of my warriors commenced singing their death songs![122] I heard the whites talking and called to them to come out and fight. I did not like my situation and wished the matter settled. I soon heard chopping and knocking. I could not imagine what they were doing. Soon after they ran up wheels with a battery on it and fired down without hurting any of us.[123] I called to them again and told them if they were *brave* men to come down and fight us. They gave up the siege and returned to their fort about dusk. There were eighteen in the trap with me. We all got out safe and found one white man dead on the edge of the sinkhole. (They did not remove him for fear of our fire.) We scalped him and placed our dead man upon him. We could not have left him in a better situation than on an enemy.[124] We had now effected our purpose and started back by land, thinking it unsafe to return in our canoes. I found my wife and children and the greater part of our people at the mouth of the Iowa River. I now determined to remain with my family and hunt for them, and humble myself before the Great Spirit and return thanks to him for preserving me through the war. I made my hunting camp on [the] English River (a branch of the Iowa).[125]

4. Campaigning on the Mississippi River, 1814

At this point in his autobiography, Black Hawk reverted back in time from the skirmish at Fort Howard and the Sinkhole in 1815 to his return from the Lake Erie region. He opposed American threats to Sauk independence in his homeland in 1814, bolstered by support from the British, who, despite losing control over Lake Erie, maintained supply lines to the upper Mississippi River from the captured American post at Mackinac, which they supplied along alternative routes that ran northwest from Montreal to Georgian Bay and north from Lake Ontario to the upper lakes. Yet the events on the Detroit front demoralized many native people, and Black Hawk described how some of them ended hostilities with the Americans in light of the Republic's successes on that front.

At one point in 1814 Black Hawk's people entered into a peace agreement with the Americans when their enemy sent an expedition up the Mississippi, threatening Saukenuk and occupying Prairie du Chien to the north of them. Nevertheless, this proved to be short-lived because the Sauks of the Rock River reentered the war against the United States when British and native forces recaptured Prairie du Chien. In the aftermath of that event, Black Hawk led his followers at the Battles of Campbell's and Credit Islands near Saukenuk in the summer of 1814 and otherwise fought the Americans in his homeland.

[1814]

During the winter a party of Potawatomis came from the Illinois to pay me a visit. Among them was Washeown, an old man who had formerly lived in our village.[126] He informed us that in the fall the Americans had built a fort at Peoria and had prevented them from going down to the Sangamon to hunt.[127] He said they were very much distressed, that Gomo had returned from the British army and brought news of their defeat near Malden, and told us that he went to the American chief with a flag, gave up fighting, and told the chief that he wished to make peace for his nation.[128] The American chief gave him a paper for the war chief at the fort at Peoria "and I visited that fort with Gomo. It was then agreed that there should be no more fighting between the Americans and Potawatomis; and that two of their chiefs and eight braves, with five Americans, had gone down to St. Louis to have the peace confirmed."[129] "This," said Washeown, "is good news, for we can now go to our hunting grounds; and, for my part, I never had anything to do with this war. The Americans never killed any of our people before the war, nor interfered with our hunting grounds, and I resolved to do nothing against them." I made no reply to these remarks, as the speaker was old and talked like a child.[130]

We gave the Potawatomis a feast. I presented Washeown with a good horse. My braves gave one to each of his party, and at parting they said they wished us to make peace, which we did not promise but told them that we would not send out war parties against the settlements. A short time after the Potawatomis left, a party of thirty braves belonging to our nation from the *peace camp* on the Missouri paid us a visit. They exhibited five scalps which they had taken on the

Missouri and wished us to dance over them, which we willingly joined in. They related the manner in which they had taken these scalps. Myself and braves then showed the two we had taken near the Cuivre and told them the reason that induced that war party to go out, as well as the manner and difficulty we had in obtaining these scalps. They recounted to us all that had taken place, the number that had been killed by the peace party (as they were called and recognized), which far surpassed what our warriors who had joined the British had done! This party came for the purpose of joining the British. I advised them to return to the peace party and told them the news that the Potawatomis had brought. They returned to the Missouri accompanied by some of my braves whose families were with the peace party.[131]

After sugar making was over in the spring I visited the Fox village at the lead mines. They had nothing to do with the war and were not in mourning. I remained there some days and spent my time pleasantly with them in dancing and feasting. I then paid a visit to the Potawatomi village on the Illinois River and learned that Sanatuwa and Tatapuckey had been to St. Louis.[132] Gomo told me that peace had been made between his people and the Americans, and that seven of his party remained with the war chief to make the peace stronger.[133] He then told me that Washeown was dead, that he had been to the fort to carry some wild fowl to exchange for tobacco, pipes, et cetera, that he had got some tobacco and a little flour, and left the fort before sundown, but had not proceeded far before he was *shot dead* by a war chief who had concealed himself near the path for that purpose and then dragged him to the lake and threw him in, where "I afterward found him. I have since given two horses and my rifle to his relations not to break the peace, which they had agreed to."[134] I remained some time at the village with Gomo and went with him to the fort to pay a visit to the war chief. I spoke the Potawatomi tongue well and was taken for one of their people by the chief. He treated us very friendly and said he was very much displeased about the murder of Washeown and would find out and punish the person who had killed him. He made some inquiries about the Sauks, which I answered.[135]

On my return to Rock River I was informed that a party of [American] soldiers had gone up the Mississippi to build a fort at Prairie du Chien.[136] They had stopped near our village and appeared to be friendly and were kindly treated by our people.[137] We commenced repairing our lodges, putting our village in order, and clearing our cornfields. We divided the fields of the party on the Missouri among those who wanted [them] on condition that they should be relinquished to the owners when they returned from the peace establishment.[138] We were again happy in our village; our women went cheerfully to work and all moved on harmoniously. Some time afterward five or six boats arrived, loaded with soldiers going to Prairie du Chien to reinforce the garrison. They appeared friendly and were well received. We held a council with the war chief. We had no intention of hurting him or any of his party or we could easily have defeated them. They remained with us all day, and used and gave us plenty of whiskey.[139]

During the night a [British] party arrived (who came down Rock River) and brought us six kegs of powder. They told us that the British had gone to Prairie du Chien and taken the fort, and wished us to join them again in the war, which we agreed to [do].[140] I collected my warriors and determined to pursue the [American] boats, which had sailed with a fair wind. If we had known the day before, we could easily have taken them all, as the war chief used no precautions to prevent it. I immediately started with my party by land in pursuit, thinking that some of their boats might get aground or that the Great Spirit would put them in our power if he wished them taken and their people killed. About halfway up the rapids I had a full view of the boats, all sailing with a strong wind. I soon discovered that one boat was badly managed and was suffered to be driven ashore by the wind. They landed by running hard aground and lowered their sail. The others passed on. This boat the Great Spirit gave us! We approached it cautiously and fired upon the men on shore. All that could hurried aboard but they were unable to push off, being fast aground. We advanced to the river's bank under cover and commenced firing at the boat. Our balls passed through the plank and did execution as I could hear them screaming in the boat. I encouraged my braves to continue firing. Several guns were fired from the boat without effect.

I prepared my bow and arrows to throw fire to the sail, which was lying on the boat, and after two or three attempts succeeded in setting the sail on fire. The boat was soon in flames! About this time one of the boats that had passed returned, dropped anchor, and swung in close to the boat on fire and took off all the people except those killed and badly wounded. We could distinctly see them passing from one boat to the other and fired on them with good aim. We wounded the war chief in this way! (Another boat now came down, dropped her anchor, which did not take hold, and was drifted ashore. The other boat cut her cable and rowed down the river, leaving their comrades without attempting to assist them.) We then commenced an attack upon this boat and fired several rounds. They did not return the fire. We thought they were afraid or had but a small number on board. I therefore ordered a rush to the boat. When we got near, they fired and killed two of our people, being all that we lost in the engagement. Some of their men jumped out and pushed off the boat and thus got away without losing a man! I had a good opinion of this war chief. He managed so much better than the others. It would give me pleasure to shake him by the hand.[141]

We now put out the fire on the captured boat to save the cargo when a skiff was discovered coming down the river. Some of our people cried out, "Here comes an express from Prairie du Chien!" We hoisted the British flag but they would not land. They turned their little boat around and rowed up the river. We directed a few shots at them in order to bring them to, but they were so far off that we could not hurt them.[142]

I found several barrels of whiskey on the captured boat and knocked in their heads and emptied out the *bad medicine*. I next found a box full of small bottles and packages, which appeared to be bad medicine also, such as the medicine men kill the white people with when they get sick.[143] This I threw in the river, and continuing my search for plunder found several guns, large barrels full of clothing, and some cloth lodges, all of which I distributed among my warriors.[144] We now disposed of the dead and returned to the Fox village opposite the lower end of Rock Island, where we put up our new lodges and hoisted the British flag.[145] A great many of our braves were dressed in the uniform clothing which we had taken, which gave our encampment the appearance of a regular camp of soldiers! We placed out sentinels and commenced dancing over the scalps we had taken. Soon after, several [American] boats passed down, among them a large boat carrying big guns. Our young men followed them some distance, firing at them, but could not do much damage more than to frighten them.[146] We were now certain that the fort at Prairie du Chien had been taken as this large boat went up with the first party who built the fort. In the course of the day some of the British came down in a small boat. They had followed the large one, thinking she would get fast in the rapids [in the Mississippi at Rock River], in which case they were certain of taking her. They had summoned her on the way down to surrender, but she refused, and now that she had passed over the rapids in safety all hope of taking her had vanished.

The British landed a big gun and gave us three soldiers to manage it.[147] They complimented us for our bravery in taking the boat and told us what they had done at Prairie du Chien, gave us a keg of rum, and joined with us in our dancing and feasting.[148] We gave them some things which we had taken from the boat (particularly books and papers). They started the next morning after promising to return in a few days with a large body of soldiers. We went to work under the direction of the men left with us and dug up the ground in two places to put the big gun in, that the men might remain in with it and be safe. We then sent spies down the river to reconnoiter, who sent word by a runner that several boats were coming up filled with men. I marshaled my forces and was soon ready for their arrival and resolved to fight as we had not yet had a fair fight with the Americans during the war. The boats arrived in the evening and stopped at a small willow island nearly opposite to us. During the night we removed our big gun further down, and at daylight next morning commenced firing. We were pleased to see that almost every fire took effect, striking the boats nearly every shot. They pushed off as quick as possible and I expected would land and give a fight. I was prepared to meet them, but was soon sadly disappointed, the boats having all started down the river. A party of braves followed to watch where they landed, but they did not stop until they got below the Des Moines Rapids, when they landed and commenced building a fort [Johnson].[149]

I collected a few braves and started to the place where it was reported they were making a fort. I did not want a fort in our country, as we wished to go down in the fall to the Two River country to hunt (it being our best hunting ground), and we concluded that if this fort was established we should be prevented from going to our hunting ground.[150] I arrived in the vicinity of the fort in the evening and stopped for the night on the peak of a high bluff. We made no fire for fear of being observed. Our young men kept watch by turns whilst the others slept. I was very tired and soon went to sleep. The Great Spirit, during my slumber, told me to go down the bluff to a creek; that I would there find a hollow tree cut down; to look into the top of it and I would see a large snake; to observe the direction he was looking; and I would see the enemy close by and unarmed. In the morning I communicated to my braves what the Great Spirit had told me, and took one of them and went down a hollow that led to the creek and soon came in sight of the place on an opposite hill where they were building the fort. I saw a great many men. We crawled cautiously on our hands and knees until we got into the bottom, then through the grass and weeds until we reached the bank of the creek. Here I found a tree that had been cut down. I looked in the top of it and saw a large snake with his head raised, looking across the creek. I raised myself cautiously and discovered, nearly opposite to me, two war chiefs walking arm in arm without guns. They turned and walked back toward the place where the men were working at the fort. In a little while they returned, walking immediately toward the spot where we lay concealed but did not come as near as before. If they had they would have been killed, for each of us had a good rifle. We crossed the creek and crawled to a bunch of bushes. I again raised myself a little to see if they were coming but they went into the fort. By this they saved their lives.

We recrossed the creek and I returned alone, going up the hollow we came down. My brave went down the creek; and on rising a hill to the left of the one we came down, I could plainly see the men at work and discovered, in the bottom near the mouth of the creek, a sentinel walking. I watched him attentively to see if he perceived my companion, who had gone toward him. The sentinel walked first one way and then back again. I observed my brave creeping toward him. The sentinel stopped for some time and looked in the direction where my brave was concealed. He laid still and did not move the grass; and as the sentinel turned to walk, my brave fired and he fell. I looked toward the fort and saw that they were all in confusion, running in every direction, some down a steep bank to a boat. My comrade joined me and we returned to the rest of our party and all hurried back to Rock River, where we arrived in safety at our village. I hung up my medicine bag, put away my rifle and spear, and felt as if I should not want them again as I had no wish to raise any more war parties against the whites without they gave new provocation. Nothing particular happened from this time until spring, except news that the fort below the rapids had been abandoned and burnt by the Americans.[151]

5. An End to Fighting, 1815–16

The British garrison holding Prairie du Chien received official word on May 22, 1815, that the War of 1812 had ended (after hearing the same news from American sources in April). They immediately held councils with the natives, distributed presents, and then destroyed the fort on May 25 before retiring north as part of a larger move by the white belligerents to evacuate each other's territory. (Some historians have said that Black Hawk attended these councils, but that was not possible because he was hundreds of miles to the south at the time, having fought the Battle of the Sinkhole the day before.) The Americans and the Mississippi tribes who still were engaged in hostilities that spring brought their conflicts to a close as anticipated in the Treaty of Ghent, although Black Hawk's followers were among the last to do so and became the object of a special British effort later in 1815 to persuade them to negotiate with their old enemy. The tribes signed treaties with the United States between 1815 and 1817, establishing peace and restoring aboriginal rights to their prewar status in accordance with the provisions of the Anglo-American treaty, but the administration of President James Madison used the local treaties to place the First Nations under the government's "protection" in an effort to increase its control over native affairs. The Americans also increased their military presence in the region and worked to cut the ties that bound the tribes to the British in order to assert their sovereignty and destroy the old alliances that had opposed the Republic's interests on its frontier.

The narrative below includes a story of American cruelty to aboriginal people that is out of context chronologically, having occurred in 1814, but which underscores the oppression felt by natives at the end of the war and expresses wrath to mark the larger discussion of the pressures the Americans put on the tribes to sign peace treaties and white accusations that the indigenous population had committed crimes against the settlers without reference to the acts of the Republic's forces that exceeded acceptable limits of wartime behavior.

[1815]

Soon after I returned from my wintering ground we received information that *peace* had been made between the British and Americans, and that we were required to make peace also and were invited to go down to Portage des Sioux for that purpose.[152] Some advised that we should go down, others that we should not.[153] Namoitte, our principal civil chief, said he would go as soon as the Foxes came down from the mines.[154] They came, and we all started from Rock River. We had not gone far before our chief was taken sick. We stopped with him at the village on [the] Henderson River. The Foxes went on, and we were to follow as soon as our chief got better; but he continued to get worse, and died. His brother now became the principal chief. He refused to go down, saying that if he started he would be taken sick and die as his brother had done, which was reasonable. We all concluded that none of us would go at this time.[155]

The Foxes returned. They said they had smoked the pipe of peace with the Americans and expected that a war party would be sent against us because we did not go down. This I did not believe as the Americans had always lost by their war parties that came against us.[156] La Gouthrie and other British traders arrived at our village on Rock River in the fall. La Gouthrie told us that we must go down and make peace—that it was the wish of our English father. He said he wished us to go down to the Two River country, to winter where game was plenty and there had been no hunting there for several years.

Having heard that a principal war chief, with troops, had come up and commenced building a fort [Cantonment Davis] near Rapids des Moines, we consented to go down with the traders to see the American chief and tell him the reason why we had not been down sooner. We arrived at the head of the rapids. Here the traders left their goods and boats, except one, in which they accompanied us to the Americans. We visited the war chief (he was on board a boat) and told him what we had to say, explaining the reason we had not been down sooner. He appeared angry and talked to La Gouthrie for some time. I inquired of him what the war chief said. He told me that he was threatening to hang him up on the yardarm of his boat. "But," said he, "I am not afraid of what he says. He dare not put his threats into execution. I have done no more than I had a right to do as a British subject."[157]

I then addressed the chief, asking permission for ourselves and some Menominees to go down to the Two River country to hunt. He said we might go down but must return before the ice made, as he did not intend that we should winter below the fort. "But," said he, "what do you want the Menominees to go with you for?" I did not know at first what reply to make, but told him that they had a great many pretty squaws with them and we wished them to go with us on that account.[158] He consented. We all started down the river and remained all winter, as we had no intention of returning before spring when we asked leave to go. We made a good hunt. Having loaded our traders' boats with furs and peltries, they started to Mackinac and we returned to our village.

[1814][159]

There is one circumstance, which I omitted to mention in its proper place. It does not relate to myself or people but to my friend Gomo, the Potawatomi chief. He came to Rock River to pay me a visit. During his stay, he related to me the following story.

"The [American] war chief at Peoria is a very good man.[160] He always speaks the truth and treats our people well. He sent for me one day, and told me that he was nearly out of provisions and wished me to send my young men out to hunt to supply his fort. I promised to do so, and immediately returned to my camp and told my young men the wishes and wants of the war chief. They readily agreed to go and hunt for our friend, and soon returned with about twenty deer. They carried them to the fort, laid them down at the gate, and returned to our camp. A few days afterward I went again to the fort to see if they wanted more meat. The chief gave me some powder and lead, and said he wished me to send my hunters out again. When I returned to my camp and told my young men that the chief wanted more meat, Matatah, one of my principal braves, said he would take a party and go across the Illinois, about one day's travel, where game was plenty and make a good hunt for our friend the war chief. He took eight hunters with him. His wife and several other squaws accompanied them. They had traveled about half the day in the prairie when they discovered a party of white men coming toward them with a drove of cattle.[161] Our hunters apprehended no danger, or they would have kept out of the way of the whites who had not yet perceived them. Matatah changed his course as he wished to meet and speak to the whites. As soon as the whites saw our party some of them put off at full speed and came up to our hunters. Matatah gave up his gun to them and endeavored to explain to them that he was friendly and was hunting for the war chief. They were not satisfied with this but fired at, and wounded, him. He got into the branch of a tree that had been blown down to keep the horses from running over him. He was again fired on by several guns and badly wounded. He found that he would be murdered, if not mortally wounded already, and sprung at the nearest man to him, seized his gun, and shot him from his horse. He then fell, covered with blood from his wounds and almost instantly expired."

"The other hunters, being in the rear of Matatah, seeing that the whites had killed him, endeavored to make their escape. They were pursued and nearly all the party murdered! My youngest brother brought me the news in the night, he having been with the hunters and got but slightly wounded. He said the whites had abandoned their cattle and gone back toward the settlement. The remainder of the night was spent in lamenting for the deaths of our friends. At daylight, I blacked my face and started to the fort to see the war chief. I met him at the gate and told him what had happened. His countenance changed. I could see sorrow depicted in it for the death of my people. He tried to persuade me that I was mistaken, as he could not believe that the whites would act so cruelly; but when I convinced him he told me that those cowards who had murdered my people should be punished. I told him that my people would have revenge, that they would not trouble any of his people of the fort, as we did not blame him or any of his soldiers, but that a party of my braves would go toward the Wabash to avenge the death of their friends and relations. The next day I took a party of hunters and killed several deer, and left them at the fort gate as I passed." Here Gomo ended his story. I could relate many similar ones that have come within my knowledge and observation, but I dislike to look back and bring on sorrow afresh. I will resume my narrative.[162]

[1816]

The great chief at St. Louis having sent word for us to go down and confirm the treaty of peace, we did not hesitate but started immediately that we might smoke the peace pipe with him.[163] On our arrival we met the great chiefs in council. They

explained to us the words of our great father in Washington, accusing us of hei-
nous crimes and diverse misdemeanors, particularly in not coming down when
first invited. We knew very well that *our great father had deceived us*, and thereby
forced us to join the British, and could not believe that he had put this speech into
the mouths of these chiefs to deliver to us. I was not a civil chief and consequently
made no reply, but our chiefs told the commissioners that what they had said was
a lie, that our great father had sent no such speech (he knowing the situation in
which we had been placed had been caused by him). The white chiefs appeared
very angry with this reply, and said they would break off the treaty with us and
go to war, as they would not be insulted. Our chiefs had no intention of insulting
them, and told them that they merely wished to explain to them that *they had told
a lie* without making them angry, in the same manner that the whites do when
they do not believe what is told them.[164]

The council then proceeded and the pipe of peace was smoked. Here, for the
first time, I touched the goose quill to the treaty not knowing, however, that by
that act I consented to give away my village. Had that been explained to me I
should have opposed it and never would have signed their treaty, as my recent
conduct will clearly prove.[165] What do we know of the manner of the laws and
customs of the white people? They might buy our bodies for dissection, and we
would touch the goose quill to confirm it without knowing what we are doing.
This was the case with myself and people in touching the goose quill the first
time. We can only judge of what is proper and right by our standard of right and
wrong, which differs widely from the whites. If I have been correctly informed,
the whites may do bad all their lives, and then, if they are sorry for it when about
to die, all is well. But with us it is different: we must continue throughout our
lives to do what we conceive to be good. If we have corn and meat, and know of
a family that has none, we divide with them. If we have more blankets than suf-
ficient, and others have not enough, we must give to them that want (but I will
presently explain our customs and manner we live).

We were friendly treated by the white chiefs, and started back to our village on
Rock River. Here we found that troops had arrived to build a fort [Armstrong] at
Rock Island. This, in our opinion, was a contradiction to what we had done—to
prepare for war in time of peace. We did not, however, object to their building the
fort on the island, but we were very sorry as this was the best island on the Mississippi and had long been the resort of our young people during the summer.[166]
It was our garden (like the white people have near to their big villages), which
supplied us with strawberries, blackberries, gooseberries, plums, apples, and
nuts of different kinds; and its waters supplied us with fine fish, being situated

in the rapids of the river. In my early life I spent many happy days on this island. A good spirit had care of it, who lived in a cave in the rocks immediately under the place where the fort now stands, and has often been seen by our people. He was white, with large wings like a swan's, but ten times larger. We were particular not to make much noise in that part of the island which he inhabited for fear of disturbing him, but the noise of the fort has since driven him away and no doubt a bad spirit has taken his place![167]

Following this section of the autobiography, Black Hawk paused to describe Sauk cultural and subsistence practices (similar to those presented in the introduction to the memoirs in this book), such as describing how his village was surrounded by prairie where his people grazed their horses and cultivated their fields (totaling some eight hundred acres), as he indicated he would do in the second-to-last paragraph above. He also noted how Saukenuk had stood for over a century, and how life had been healthy and prosperous, in contrast to the situation in the 1830s when he dictated his autobiography, noting that "then we were as happy as the buffalo on the plains; but now, we are as miserable as the hungry, howling wolf in the prairie!" Then, he returned to the narrative of his life, emphasizing the events that led to the Black Hawk War in 1832, the hostilities that followed, and his subsequent capture and tour of the eastern United States.

6. Black Hawk's Speeches, 1815–17

Black Hawk's speeches below add more information from his perspective about some of the events he described in his memoirs. As well, they show fundamental consistencies in the way he articulated his views in relation to his memoirs while providing insights into how he expressed himself in diplomatic negotiations. Dating between 1815 and 1817, they also show less familiarity with white society than was the case in the 1830s when he dictated his autobiography, as we might expect given the tremendous changes that occurred in his world after the War of 1812. The major themes that connect these documents, which would have been clear to British officials who heard them, were his disappointment that the king's servants had made peace with the Americans before securing aboriginal independence in the Old Northwest, implied accusations that the Crown consequently had betrayed the First Nations, and a willingness, in spirit if not necessarily in fact, to continue the fight for Sauk freedoms. The first is a speech presented in 1815 before departing on the campaign that would lead to the Battle of the Sinkhole; the second and third were delivered later that year when the British sent a delegation to Prairie du Chien (after withdrawing from the post in May) with the objec-

tive of encouraging the Sauks to negotiate peace with the United States; and the fourth and fifth date to Black Hawk's 1817 visit to the British post on Drummond Island in Lake Huron. The last was controversial, and officials took the unusual and disrespectful step of cutting off Black Hawk during his address, which naturally generated an angry response from him.

A. SPEECH AT PRAIRIE DU CHIEN, APRIL 18, 1815[168]

My father: I am pleased to hear you speak as you have done. I have been sent by our chiefs to ask for a large gun to place in our village. The big knives are so treacherous [that] we are afraid that they may come up to deceive us. By having one of your large guns in our village, we will live in safety. Our women will then be able to plant corn and hoe the ground unmolested, and our young men will be able to hunt for their families without dread of the big knives.

(Taking the war belt in his hand, and advancing a little, he continued.)

My father: you see this belt. When my great father at Quebec gave it to me [it was] to be on terms of friendship with all his red children, to form but one body, to preserve our lands, and to make war against the big knives who want to destroy us all.[169] My great father said: "Take courage, my children, hold tight your war club, and destroy the big knives as much as you can. If the Master of Life favors us, you shall again find your lands as they formerly were. Your lands shall again become green: the trees green, the water green, and the sky blue. When your lands change color, you shall also change." This, my father, is the reason why we Sauks hold the war club tight in our hands and will not let it go.

My father: I now see the time is drawing near when we shall all change color; but, my father, our lands have not yet changed color: they are red, the water is red with our blood and the sky is cloudy. I have fought the big knives and will continue to fight them until they retire from our lands. Till then, my father, your red children cannot be happy.

(Then, laying his tomahawk down before him, he continued.)

My father: I show you this war club to convince you that we Sauks have not forgotten the words of our great father at Quebec. You see, my father, that the club, which you gave me, is still red and that we continue to hold it fast. For what [reason] did you put it in my hands?

My father: when I lately came from [the] war, and killed six of the enemy, I promised my warriors that I would get something for them from my father, the

Red Head; but as he is not here, and you fill his place, I beg of you, my father, to let me have something to take back to them.[170]

My father: I hope you will agree to what I ask, and not allow me to return to my warriors empty-handed, ashamed, and with a heavy heart.[171]

B. SPEECH AT PRAIRIE DU CHIEN, AUGUST 3, 1815[172]

My English father: you have put the war club into the hands of all the Indian warriors, your children. Now is the time we shall know why you did so. You inform us today that you have thrown the Americans on the ground. We are pleased today to learn that we are friends with the Americans. At present we will work to make our women and children live.

My father: what our chief, Namoitte, has said to you is nothing but the truth. He says he has reinforced his village, but the people who come to his assistance are very much in want. He has brought them to his assistance by the authority he has with you.[173]

C. SPEECH AT PRAIRIE DU CHIEN, AUGUST 3, 1815[174]

My father: I thank you for your words today, which instruct us how to live happy. I am also sincerely thankful for the trouble you have taken to save the lives of our women and children for this ensuing winter by the bounty you have bestowed upon us.[175]

My father: you must before have heard that I am one of those very few Indians who speak my sentiments openly and without reserve. Do not therefore be angry at what I am going to say. I shall repeat your own words.

My father: you know that at the commencement of the war we were loath to take up the tomahawk, and did not until you absolutely threatened us seriously with your displeasure. Recollect my father. Your words were these: "My children: those bad spirits the Americans, wishing to rob you of your lands, and having declared war against your great father the king, he has also declared war against them. Your red brethren have all joined him in defense of your lands and of your lives, and I have often pressed you to follow their example, but you are dilatory. I tell you now, for the last time, that if you do not immediately strike upon the Americans, I will turn all the other Indians against you and strike you to the ground." These, my father, you must recollect, were your words conveyed to us by the Red Head (Mr. Dickson).[176] You at the same time told us that if we followed your advice we should want for nothing, and that so soon as we should beat the

Americans, and they would ask to smoke the pipe of peace with our great father the king, then we should see some of your chiefs settled in our lands to make us happy.

My father: you also sent us word to take courage and fear nothing, that when you would smoke the pipe that all your red children would be included in that peace, but this was not to take place until those bad spirits, the Americans, were entirely driven off our lands and those of our ancestors. I believe, my father, you gave us hopes that the Ohio would be the future boundary of the Americans.[177]

My father: you have today recalled to our minds those promises by sending us a supply of goods, which will save our families from perishing in the winter. The Americans, according to their stories, are masters of us and our lands; but this is not your story. We shall therefore listen to your words and remain quiet as my great chief told you just now, and next canoeing season I will go and see my great father at Michilimackinac and perhaps farther.[178]

My father: in the meantime I hope I may not be obliged to dig up my hatchets. I know these big knives have sweet tongues and fear they have cheated us all.

My father: it is a long way to go every year for our supplies, but you say everything is arranged for our good, and next hot season at least one hundred of my warriors will go and see you.

My father: I will take you by the hand. My heart is in it and you may rely on its being the heart and hand of a child who has sense, but when I look down this river some bad blood that remains in my heart jumps up to my throat, and were it not for your counsels I would free myself of it.[179]

D. SPEECH AT THE BRITISH POST ON DRUMMOND ISLAND IN LAKE HURON, AUGUST 7, 1817[180]

Father: I shake our great father by the hand, likewise our fathers at Quebec, Montreal, Fort George, and all you who are now present, and beg you will patiently listen to what I am going to say.

Father: it is not only for my own nation that I speak but I speak for all your red children who are obedient children and always listen to your paroles and counsels.

Father: you have no idea of our miserable situation. A black cloud is overrunning our country, taking our lands from us, and threatening us with destruction.[181] We have not slept, either in peace or tranquility, since we laid down the hatchet and smoked the pipe with the big knives as you desired us.[182] I have a long speech to deliver and hope you will listen with patience to what I have to say. My eyes were dim and I could not see clear until I had passed some bad spirits that are your neighbors, but when I had passed that last hedge or boundary between our country and you I regained the use of my sight.[183] The weather became clear, and as we approached we found the weather quite warm and clear. Our young men began to shout and sing with joy on seeing the redcoats, and when they reached your shores they said, "We now live, and shall once more hear good news from a father whom we love and for whom we would die."

(He then laid the war belt on the floor and said.)

Father: this is the tomahawk you gave me when you desired me to make war on the big knives. You tell me to love it and never abandon it. You told me to fight those bad spirits till the moment that you would cease to fight, which you would not do until they were dispersed and drove off our lands. You told me with the paukumangin that they were not strong; that our great father, when he would be really angry, would blow these bad spirits off the earth if they did not do as he would desire, and that when he made peace we should be considered as Englishmen and brethren.[184] This was not only told us by you, my father [William McKay], but by the Red Head, the agent at Amherstburg, and by our great father's chief warriors at Quebec.[185] This Michnenany[?] was at Quebec and with his own eyes saw the great warrior and with his own ears heard him repeat nearly the same words that you yourself told me.[186] This is what the great war chief said (presenting Sir George Prevost's speech to the Western Indian nations of which the following is a true copy). . . .

> The core points in Sir George's speech, given at Quebec on March 17, 1814, included "Listen to my words. They are the words of truth. You have already heard this from my chiefs and I now repeat them. We have taken each other by the hand and fought together. Our interests are the same. We must still continue to fight together; for the king our great father considers you as his children and will not forget you and your interests at the peace; but to preserve what we hold, and recover from the enemy what belongs to us, we must make great exertions, and I rely on your undaunted courage with the assistance of my chiefs and warriors to drive the big knives from off all our lands the ensuing summer." Overall, Prevost's words affirmed the aboriginal-white alliance, spoke of reinforcements expected from Europe, and encouraged the tribes to remain firm in their commitment despite the American victories in 1813 on Lake Erie and at Moraviantown. Toward the end of the speech, he presented a black wampum belt as a sign of war and as an affirmation of his words.

(The Black Hawk in continuation said.)

This convinces me that you only repeated the words of our great father when you spoke to us, and I believed that a happy day was at hand. On receiving this tomahawk (pointing to the belt, the same that is mentioned in the foregoing speech) I thought myself rising and becoming a great man exceeding all my brethren in magnitude, like a pine tree in the forest higher and stronger than all around me.[187] Proud of the confidence reposed in me, I arose from my seat and flew with your parole to my countrymen and repeated to them what I had heard and showed them what I had got.[188] They jumped and made the hills reecho their shouts of joy. Our wives and children joined in the war song when I told them the good news that ere long they would be happy. You know, McKay, that I do not tell lies, for when you arrived at Prairie du Chien you dispatched this warrior (pointing to one of his brave men) to my village with ammunition.[189] It arrived like lightening; and immediately after you took the fort at Tebisauque from the big knives I afterward sent you the news of our having burnt two large canoes with a great many big guns in them, which you know is true.[190] I was neither idle nor lazy. My young men took the hair off from a great many big knives' heads. We made some slaves and took them to your fire at Tebisauque.[191] You know (pointing to Captain Anderson) that when you were left in charge of our great father's fort at Tebisauque I sent you a pipe to inform you that the river was full of big knives' canoes, full of warriors, and loaded with great guns.[192] The assistance you sent was like thunder. We killed sixty big knives and made the remainder row down the river with all their might.[193]

Father: I have now told you what I heard and what I have done during the war, of which you cannot be ignorant. Our situation and what has happened to us since that time I am now going to relate. Be charitable and listen to the story of your children.

Father: at the moment we were enjoying ourselves in destroying these bad spirits, when they were becoming pale and trembling with fear, and we were driving them away from their cornfields on the River Missouri, and courting their wives, a sudden shock reached my ears. You (pointing to Captain Anderson) washed the great tomahawk, changed its color, and made the bloody hatchet a pipe of peace.[194] You told me that our great father and the big knives had taken each other by the hand and smoked the pipe of peace, and that it was his desire that all his red children should bury the hatchet, smoke with their creditors, live as brethren with all the people of their own color, plant corn, hunt, and they would be happy.[195]

Father: at this news I many times rubbed my eyes and cleared my ears before I could believe what I saw or what I heard, but after thinking and smoking my pipe, I recollected the words of our great father and believed that he had so much frightened the big knives that they consented to give up our lands without losing any more of their hair.[196] I arose from my seat, smoked the pipe, and believed I should soon see our women and children throw off their leather dresses and be clothed in the fine blankets of our great father, in which belief I gave you (pointing to Captain Anderson) a large canoe full of the big knives' hair and slaves that you might be charitable to them.[197]

Father: these promised happy days have not yet made their appearance, and yesterday I got so much frightened by a black cloud that I presented my voyaging pipe to my young men and told them that I would come to hear my great father's voice.[198]

Father: yesterday the big knives below our village sent word that they wanted to talk with me on a matter of consequence. I went to their fort [at St. Louis] with a party of young men.[199] On entering the fort I found a great many American chiefs seated round, as you are today.[200] There were great guns pointed at me, and at each gun, men ready to light them and a great many soldiers surrounding us with lances at the ends of their guns.[201] They looked frightful and were as numerous as the quills on a porcupine.

Father: one of the big knives got up and called us his children [and] talked to us a long time as if he had been drunk. The subject of his discourse was to take away from us our lands, which the Master of Life gave us to live upon. He thought to frighten us with his guns and make us listen to his demands, but I told him he should not have them and that if he thought himself a great man under the shadow of his great father I believed myself at least as great a man as he was under the shadow of my great father.[202] He then said, "Why should you love the English? What have they left you? I have thrown them far away and you will never see them again. Give me some of your lands and be my children." But father, I refused and am come to tell you how we have been treated by this black cloud, and to ask your assistance and support to defend our lands because you told us to fight for them and the Master of Life would be charitable and show us kindness.

Father: your red children [who] with one voice spoke to you yesterday about their grievances are anxious for an answer from our great father, and for fear that any accident should happen to this, our parole, be charitable to me, and you yourself carry it by the same route the other went.[203] You have always been our friend. Do not refuse us this, my request.

Father: the last words I have to speak to you are that your red children never will be slaves to the big knives. They will prefer to die young, like men, and join their forefathers in the scalp song in the great meadow of brave spirits than to live old as slaves and carry water for old women in the miserable land that is the habitation of the spirits of old women.[204]

E. SPEECH AT DRUMMOND ISLAND, AUGUST 9, 1817[205]

Father: when I left my village I made great promises to the warriors, women, and children that remained at home. I told them that when I came back they would see some of their great father's bounty. It is true that those that are come here with me are well clothed and supplied with arms and ammunition, but I expected more than that. I make use of my exertions not only for the support of my own people but also for the numerous other nations that you told me to invite to live on my lands and assist in the war, my village being the key to the road between the big knives and your fort.[206] In consequence of your advice I smoked the pipe with the Mesquakies, Kickapoos, Moovavantics, Osages, Kansas, Iowas, Winnebagos, Menominees, Potawatomis, and Missouris, and the whole of these nations make only one with my people and some of each nation plant corn on my lands.[207] They expect me [to return] with good news from our great father, and that I shall bring them some of his bounty.

Father: there are yet arms, ammunition, and blankets in your store. Empty it for us this day that I may convince my brethren that the word of the English is like thunder.[208]

Father: when you gave the tomahawk you told us a recompense would be granted to the war chiefs, and wounds would be healed, and the blood wiped away from the afflicted. Some of the war chiefs and some of the wounded are now present, and there are many widows and orphans in our village where hearts are still bloody.[209] You were not afraid (pointing to Captain Anderson) to bring our great father's bounty when our hatchet was still red with blood.[210] Why can you not do it now when our women and children are poor and we are threatened with the loss of our lands by the bad spirits? If the great warrior and charitable chief that sent you then was here, he would listen to us and would not fear to heal our wounds.[211]

(This long speech becoming rather insolent and to a point that could not be answered to the Indians' satisfaction, the superintendent thought proper to put a stop to it by saying: "Children: on your arrival here I told you the news from your father at Montreal and Quebec. I gave you good advice, and yesterday I allowed you a greater portion of your great father's bounty than I have done to any of his other children. I have done much more for you than you are aware of; in time you will know it. Your demands are unreasonable and I will not grant them. All that I will do is to give you an additional quantity of powder and tobacco. I have your great father's orders to obey, and all the Indians in the universe will not make me deviate from them. The council is ended, and you must withdraw.")[212]

(The Black Hawk replied and said.)

Father: it is not every day that I trouble you. I have not seen you these three nights; yet you will not listen to our grievances nor comply with my demands.[213] I will not (crying with rage) trouble you any more today but I will come tomorrow with a great many canoes, and if I cannot get assistance on this side, I will cross the great salt lake and beg the assistance of our great father to preserve our lands.[214] (He then shook hands with the officers and retired.)

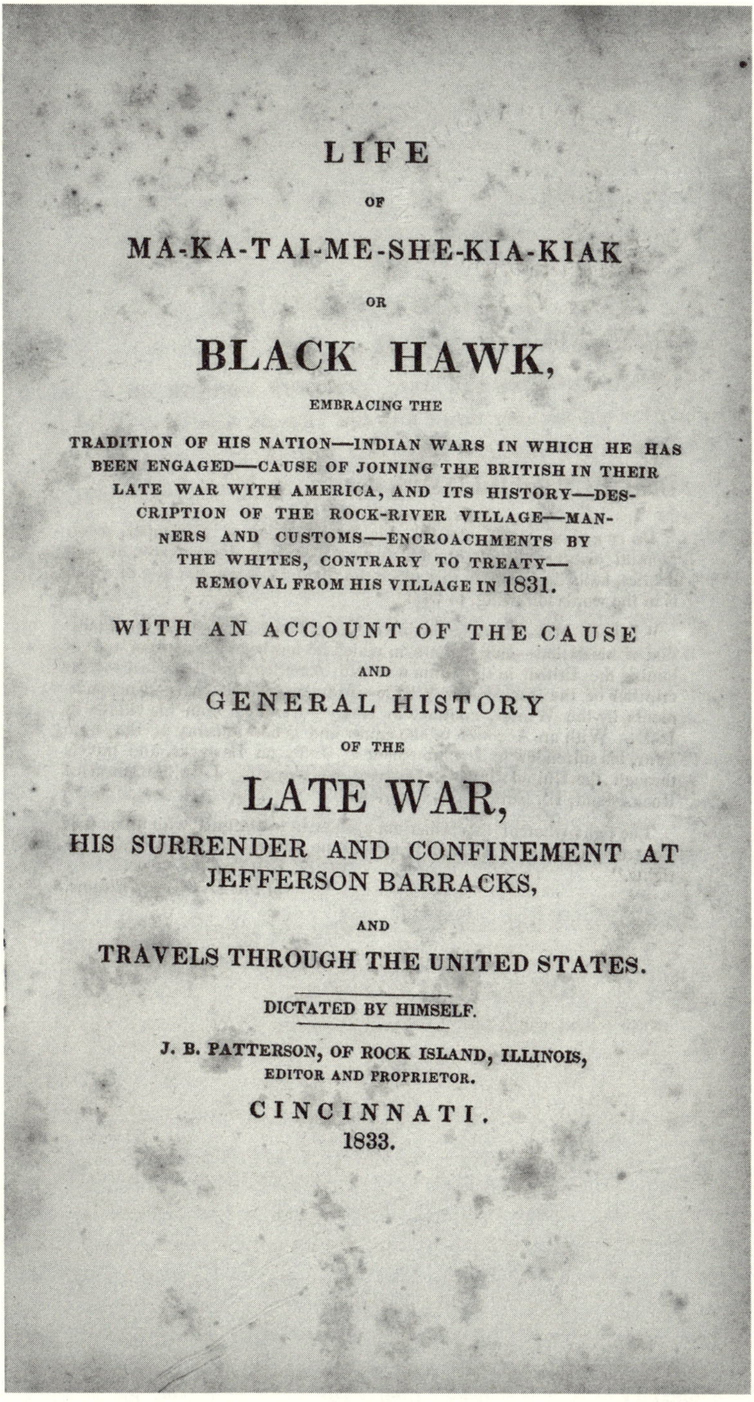

LIFE

OF

MA-KA-TAI-ME-SHE-KIA-KIAK

OR

BLACK HAWK,

EMBRACING THE

TRADITION OF HIS NATION—INDIAN WARS IN WHICH HE HAS
BEEN ENGAGED—CAUSE OF JOINING THE BRITISH IN THEIR
LATE WAR WITH AMERICA, AND ITS HISTORY—DES-
CRIPTION OF THE ROCK-RIVER VILLAGE—MAN-
NERS AND CUSTOMS—ENCROACHMENTS BY
THE WHITES, CONTRARY TO TREATY—
REMOVAL FROM HIS VILLAGE IN 1831.

WITH AN ACCOUNT OF THE CAUSE

AND

GENERAL HISTORY

OF THE

LATE WAR,

HIS SURRENDER AND CONFINEMENT AT
JEFFERSON BARRACKS,

AND

TRAVELS THROUGH THE UNITED STATES.

DICTATED BY HIMSELF.

J. B. PATTERSON, OF ROCK ISLAND, ILLINOIS,
EDITOR AND PROPRIETOR.

CINCINNATI.
1833.

Figure 1. Title page of the first edition of Black Hawk's memoirs, 1833. © American Antiquarian Society.

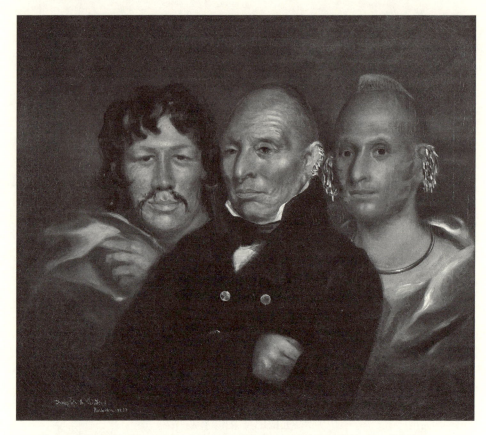

Figure 2. Black Hawk, or Makataimeshekiakiak (center), dictated his memoirs the same year that he sat for this portrait. On the viewer's left is Wabokieshiek, a prophet, and on the right is Black Hawk's son, Whirling Thunder, or Nasheaskuk, all of whom participated in the Black Hawk War of 1832. Oil by James Westhall Ford, 1833. Courtesy of the Special Collections, Library of Virginia.

Figure 3, opposite. Chiefs' medals, given by white powers to aboriginal peoples, were important symbols of alliance relationships and were valued by indigenous wearers, which Black Hawk noted in his memoirs. The Latin legend surrounding the king reads "Georgivs III Dei Gratia Britanniarvm Rex. F[idei]:D[efensor]:" (George III, by the Grace of God, King of the Britains, Defender of the Faith). The American government also issued medals to native peoples. At the time of the War of 1812 and its immediate aftermath, they bore likenesses of either Thomas Jefferson or James Madison on the obverse, and on the reverse, a white hand and a native hand shaking underneath a pipe tomahawk and a peace pipe, accompanied by the words "Peace and Friendship." Silver medal designed by Thomas Wyon Jr., 1814. With permission of the Royal Ontario Museum, © ROM, 929.5.

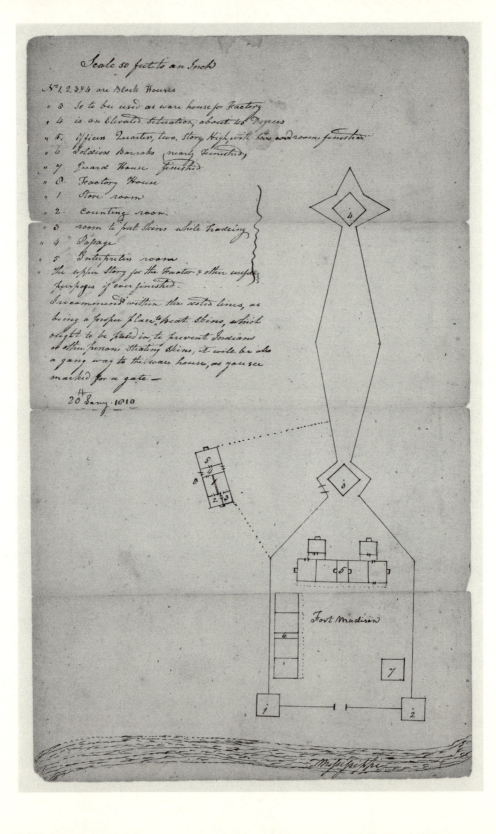

Scale 50 feet to an Inch

Nº 1. 2. 3 & 4. are Block Houses
 „ 3 Is to bee used as ware house for Factory
 „ 4 is an Elevated situation, about 45 Degrees
 „ 5, Officers Quarter, two, Story High with two and rooms finished
 „ 6 Soldiers Barraks (nearly finished,)
 „ 7 Guard House finished
 „ 8 Factory House
 „ 1 Store room
 „ 2 Counting room
 „ 3 room to seat Skins while Trading
 „ 4 Passage
 „ 5 Interpreters room
 „ The upper Story for the Factor & other useful
   purposes if ever finished.
   I recommend within the dotted lines, as
   being a proper place to treat Skins, which
   ought to be staid in, to prevent Indians
   or other persons stealing Skins, it will be also
   a gang way to the ware house, as you see
   marked for a gate —

        20 Jany. 1810

Fort Madison

Figure 5. Crude propaganda played a role in encouraging American hostility toward the British and their native allies, as represented in this cartoon, *A Scene on the Frontiers as Practiced by the "Humane" British and Their "Worthy" Allies,* which affirmed the false claim that the British offered scalp bounties (and which overlooks scalping by Americans and their own scalp bounties). This sort of document, along with lurid tales, racism, ignorance, and greed, combined to foster attitudes and actions by Euro-Americans that haunted the lives of Black Hawk, William Apess, and other indigenous people, while helping to justify the exploitation of the First Nations and the seizure of their lands. Print by William Charles, c. 1812–13. Courtesy of the Library of Congress, LC-DIG-ppmsca-31111.

Figure 4, opposite. Fort Madison beside the Mississippi River in today's Iowa was an unwelcomed American intrusion into the indigenous world. It came under siege during the War of 1812, including a failed attempt to capture the fort during the conflict's first year (with Black Hawk present). The external building on the left is the trading post operated by a factor. The soldiers of the garrison abandoned the site late in 1813 in the face of continuous native harassment. Sketch likely by John Johnson, 1810. Courtesy of the National Archives and Records Administration, RG 75, Entry 56, Box 1, 11E247/20/1.

Figure 6. Whether they allied to the Americans or the British, First Nations warriors regularly fought alongside white soldiers as well as against them. This picture shows typical British infantrymen, who bore the brunt of defending Canada during the War of 1812 and were representative of the men who Black Hawk served with on the Detroit front and who William Apess fought against south of Montreal. As the United States Army followed standard European practices for the most part, American infantry were not dissimilar from their opponents in terms of the tactics they employed, the weapons they carried, or the basic tailoring of their uniforms (albeit in different colors and sporting republican iconography). Print after Charles Hamilton Smith, 1815. Courtesy of the Anne S. K. Brown Military Collection, Brown University Library, 2–Size UC485.G7 S65x 1815.

Figure 7. This naive depiction of the 1813 Battle of Moraviantown represents a scene in the fighting when mounted American troops charged through the thin British and First Nations lines. Tecumseh fell in the battle, and the native confederacy that had formed around him and Tenskwatawa largely collapsed in the weeks and months that followed. Although Black Hawk served on the Detroit front for part of 1813, the historical record is unclear as to whether or not he fought at this battle. Print by Ralph Rawdon, c. 1813–17. Courtesy of Library and Archives Canada, C-007763.

Figure 8. Images of native people from the upper Mississippi River region from the War of 1812 era are very rare, making this representation particularly valuable as a document despite its artistic weakness. The women in this group of individuals who visited the governor in chief of British North America in Quebec City remind us that female members of indigenous society participated in public life, including diplomatic and other exchanges with Euro-Americans, even though they tended to be represented in councils by male speakers and their presence often went unrecorded in period records. One of the men wears a red "chief's coat" of the type given by white authorities to indigenous leaders. The black man symbolizes the "multicultural" diversity that marked much of the First Nations world of North America at the time, where people from outside—native, white, and black—were integrated into aboriginal societies. Watercolor by Rudolph von Steiger, 1814. Courtesy of Library and Archives Canada, 1989-264-1.

Figure 9. In 1816, the American army built Fort Armstrong on Rock Island on the Mississippi close to Black Hawk's village of Saukenuk as part of a larger effort to exercise control over the region and its indigenous populations following the War of 1812. Black Hawk remembered that the post drove away the good spirit who inhabited the island and that "no doubt a bad spirit" took his place. The Battles of Campbell's and Credit Islands in 1814, at which Black Hawk fought, occurred within a short distance of this site. Print after Henry Lewis, c. 1829. Courtesy of the Wisconsin Historical Society, image no. 48766.

Figure 10. This painting shows the site of the massacre at the Bad Axe River during the Black Hawk War of 1832 when American soldiers and their First Nations allies shot many of Black Hawk's followers as they tried to swim across the waterway in their retreat westward. It also portrays the landscape of the upper Mississippi region, which Black Hawk knew so well throughout his life, and captures the grandeur of the region's major rivers, which served as important communications routes for natives and newcomers. Postdating the war by more than two decades, the image speaks to the historical imagination of the settler population of the upper Mississippi River and of Black Hawk's place in the region's past, which contrasts with William Apess, who fell into oblivion in public memory after his passing. Oil from the studio of Samuel Marsden Brookes and Thomas H. Stevenson, 1856. Courtesy of the Wisconsin Historical Society, image no. 2531.

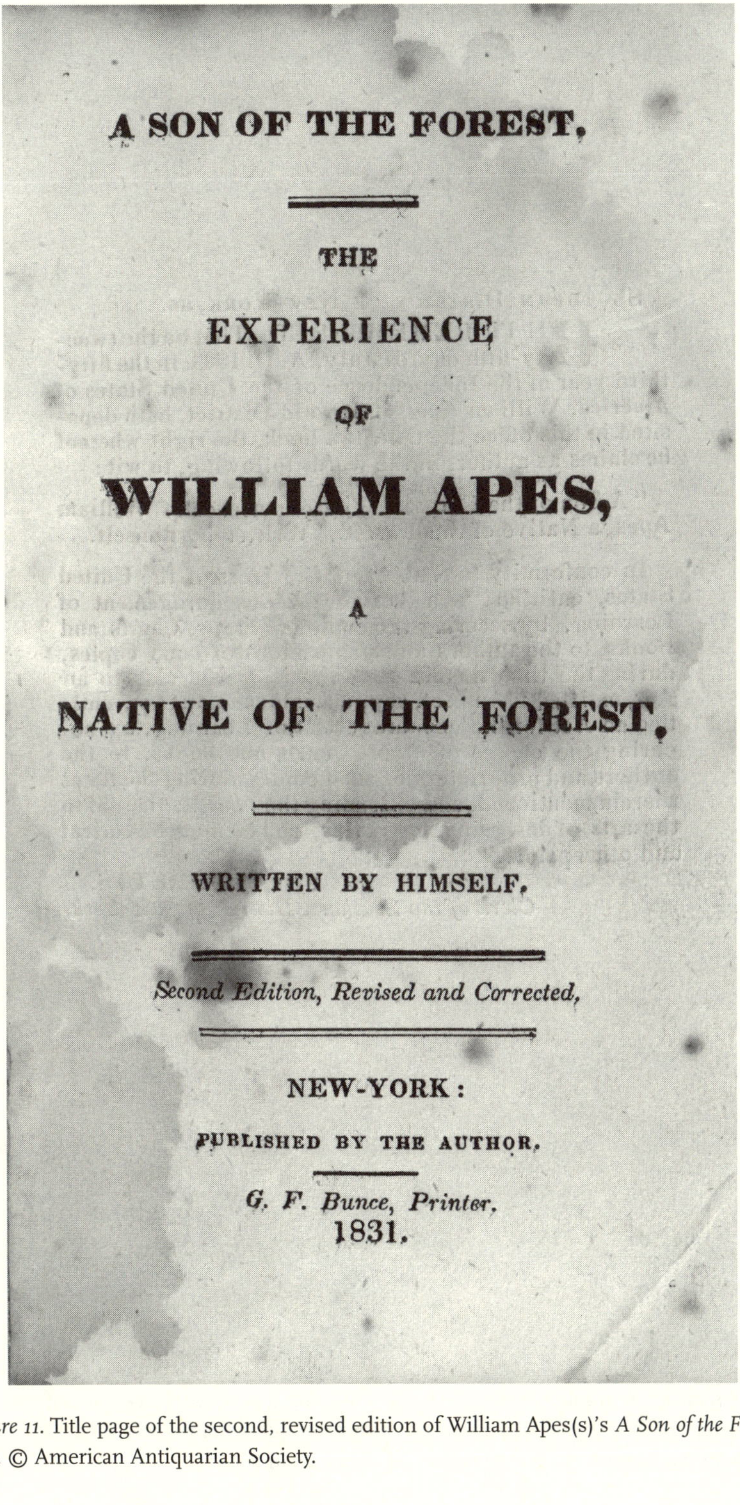

A SON OF THE FOREST,

THE

EXPERIENCE

OF

WILLIAM APES,

A

NATIVE OF THE FOREST,

WRITTEN BY HIMSELF,

Second Edition, Revised and Corrected,

NEW-YORK:

PUBLISHED BY THE AUTHOR,

G. F. Bunce, Printer,
1831.

Figure 11. Title page of the second, revised edition of William Apes(s)'s *A Son of the Forest,* 1831. © American Antiquarian Society.

Mʀ. WILLIAM APES,

A NATIVE MISSIONARY OF THE PEQUOT TRIBE

OF INDIANS.

Figure 12. William Apess included this portrait of himself in the second edition of his auto-biography, *A Son of the Forest*, although it was not present in the first edition of 1829. Print after John W. Paradise, c. 1831. © American Antiquarian Society.

Figure 13. Upon entering the army, William Apess helped garrison Governors Island off Manhattan, where the harbor defenses included the still-extant Castle Williams, visible here. When he arrived in New York in 1813 after running away from indentured servitude in Connecticut, the city was an important port and the nation's largest urban center, with a population of 100,000. Print after W. G. Wall, 1823. Used with permission of the Spencer Collection, the New York Public Library, Astor, Lenox, and Tilden Foundations, image no. 54144.

Figure 14. Unlike most native combatants in the War of 1812, who participated within First Nations war parties, William Apess was a soldier in the American army, first in the 3rd Regiment of Artillery and then in the Corps of Artillery (depicted here). The gun in this image is a "field piece" similar to those Apess served when he participated in the 1813 and 1814 invasions of Canada and the "big guns" that Black Hawk spoke about in his memoirs, such as when he faced one at Fort Bellevue in 1809. Watercolor by Charles Hamilton Smith, 1815. Courtesy of the Houghton Library, Harvard University.

Figure 15. William Apess fought at three major battles in the War of 1812: Châteauguay in 1813, and Odelltown and Plattsburgh in 1814. The latter was both a land and lake battle, with the action between the two naval squadrons on Lake Champlain being the subject of both this depiction and some excited prose in Apess's memoir. The American victory on the water saved the land forces from facing an assault by the British army on the town. Print after Hugh Reinagle, 1816. Courtesy of the Library of Congress, LC-DIG-pga-02823.

Figure 16. The use of alcohol by whites to exploit indigenous peoples was an important theme in William Apess's texts and a problem noted in Black Hawk's autobiography. One of Apess's publications, *Indian Nullification* (1835), included this image to underscore his point. With the ironic title *Manner of Instructing the Indians*, it shows a white man using liquor to distract a native person while someone else steals wood from aboriginal land. The theft of wood was one of the issues in the Mashpee Revolt of 1833, which saw Apess defend indigenous rights energetically and which brought him some notoriety in New England for a time. The portrayal of native housing and dress is inaccurate in relation to Mashpee material culture, but aligned with general conceptualizations of the First Nations world among the period's reading public. Print by an unknown artist, c. 1835. © American Antiquarian Society.

WILLIAM APESS
(PEQUOT)

Introduction to William Apess

In 1813, William Apess (or Apes), a Pequot teenager from New England indentured to a white man, ran away from his master. He then joined the American army and fought at the Battle of Châteauguay, and in 1814 he saw action again at Lacolle Mill and Plattsburgh. After a period of postwar youthful dissipation, he became a Methodist preacher, published his autobiography and other texts, and served as a leading figure in the Mashpee Revolt on Cape Cod in 1833–34.[1] His story represents about as much of a contrast to Black Hawk's memoirs as was possible within the diversity of aboriginal experiences of the early nineteenth century in the territory then claimed by the United States. Among the various reasons for this difference, three in particular stand out. First, Apess lived in a part of North America that had been dominated by Europeans and their descendants for generations; hence, he grew up in entirely different surroundings from Black Hawk's native-white frontier environment along the upper Mississippi River. Apess knew Euro-Americans intimately and communicated his thoughts in a manner that was similar to their ways, even though he expressed a strong aboriginal identity that condemned whites for their treatment of indigenous peoples. Second, the story of his wartime adventures does not possess the complexities of Black Hawk's, being that of a young person caught up in the conflict because of personal desperation, and so he presents a worm's-eye view of events in contrast to Black Hawk, whose autobiography articulates the perspectives of a mature military leader engaged in the intricacies of tribal politics and external relations. Third, Apess prepared his life story in English and clearly knew white-authored texts, which served as models when he composed his story within preexisting conventions of Euro-American literature. This, of course, contrasts to Black Hawk's translated memoirs that flowed from deep within the thought patterns of Sauk culture.

Despite its structural debts to the white world, William Apess's autobiography is a fascinating aboriginal document by someone who lived within a part of North America where First Nations people formed a tiny minority, as would become increasingly common elsewhere across the continent in the decades following the War of 1812. The power of the dominant society was so great in his New England homeland that Apess did not take up arms as a member of a tribal war party, but instead enlisted in a white artillery regiment. His recruitment and life in the army captured many of the experiences of the common soldiers in the American military who fought against aboriginal warriors, such as the debilitating conditions of life in the ranks in contrast to the freer experience of the still-independent natives. While his story is unusual for indigenous participants in the conflict of 1812–15, it fits a pattern of military service for them that had emerged in his region during the Seven Years' War of the 1750s and 1760s and that continued through the American Revolution of the 1770s and 1780s, and which presaged the future for aboriginal communities as they fell behind the westward-moving procession of newcomer colonization. There is evidence, for example, to suggest that his father or another relative may have joined a "white" regiment in one or both of the earlier conflicts.[2] We see this tradition of natives serving within Euro-American military environments continuing in 1861–65, when aboriginal men on the south side of the Great Lakes put on blue uniforms to fight for the Union during the American Civil War, and in 1884–85, when Canadian-resident Mohawks and Ojibwas served as river pilots in a British expedition that sailed up the Nile River during the Sudan War. Later, of course, aboriginal history filled with the service of men and women who joined the Canadian and American armed forces, especially after 1914 (although, like William Apess during the War of 1812, they often endured the prejudices of other soldiers). While Apess's story is unusual in comparison to those of most native participants in the War of 1812, its distinctiveness underscores how diverse indigenous experiences were in the past, as they remain today.

William Apess was born in January 1798 in a tent pitched by his father in the woods in the sparsely settled neighborhood of Colrain, Massachusetts.[3] His parents were William Apes Sr., a shoemaker, and, possibly, a woman called Candace, whose maiden name has been lost to history. Both came from the Colchester, Connecticut, area. One record stated that Candace was a black slave until freed in 1805 by her master in Colchester (although she had married before her putative manumission, had children, and had experienced some degree of liberty in her movements). Candace may have been an indentured servant rather than a slave and more likely was of mixed aboriginal and black parentage (and possibly partly white too), even though William Apess Jr. affirmed that his mother was of pure native ancestry (which, combined with other uncertainties, raises the possibility that Candace was not his mother). William Sr. was the son of a Pequot woman and a white man. Mixed-racial origins among the aboriginal population in New England (and elsewhere) were normal, and while people today generally realize that white-native marriages were not uncommon, Candace's supposed African heritage, whatever her relationship with William Jr., represents a generally over-looked feature of indigenous life. A significant number of blacks lived in the native world, where they tended to be accepted with less prejudice than among whites and where children of mixed unions normally grew up primarily as First Nations people in terms of their cultural formation and self-identity. It also re-minds us that individuals chose their social affiliations to some degree because William Jr. tended to celebrate his indigenous heritage rather than his nonnative connections in his life and writing.[4]

Long before William Apess's birth, at the beginning of European settlement in the early years of the seventeenth century, the Pequot nation was one of the southern New England Algonquian tribes. Its territory extended from the Connecticut River in modern Connecticut to the border with today's Rhode Island, and from the Atlantic coast to a point three-quarters of the way toward the present Connecticut-Massachusetts border, and also included offshore lands, including part of Long Island. The Pequots shared their land with a people who lived in a subordinate position to them, the Mohegans. Like other aboriginal people in the region, the Pequots supported themselves primarily through growing corn, beans, squash, and other crops. They also traded, hunted (especially deer), fished in both salt- and freshwater, and gathered materials, medicines, and foods across a range of ecological zones to meet their needs.

In 1636, war broke out with the English at a time of serious native population loss due to smallpox and food shortages. In 1637, the newcomers, aided by their aboriginal allies, won a decisive victory over the Pequots when they assaulted the tribe's main village on the Mystic River. The attackers torched it, burned a great many people to death, and slaughtered others who tried to flee. Hostilities continued until 1638, when the victors forced the surviving two thousand Pequots who had not disappeared as refugees into the forests to agree to a treaty that dissolved their nation and banished them from their homeland. The whites enslaved some and sent hundreds of others into captivity with their native allies. Despite this attempt to eradicate their nation, the Pequots survived. After the tragedy of the war, they maintained many aspects of their traditional ways of life while participating in the growing Euro-American economy that changed the landscape of New England. In the 1650s, some of them reestablished their independence from their native captors and received their first reservation in Connecticut within their old territory. By the end of the 1600s, there were two Pequot settlements serving as homelands for what had emerged as two separate Pequot political entities. Their residents became the objects of Christian missionizing, which led to some conversions of varying levels of intensity and longevity, along with the grafting of the new faith onto older forms of spirituality, such as during the "Great Awakening" that swept through New England and much of the rest of the Protestant world in the early eighteenth century (which called on believers to embrace their faith with new levels of emotional self-awareness in their personal relationship with God through Jesus Christ). Through the 1700s, however, periodic epidemics, casualties suffered in colonial wars, ongoing persecutions, the miseries of poverty, and newcomer encroachments onto reservation land continued to afflict the Pequot population, which gradually declined. Around the time of the American Revolution (in which the Pequots fought against the Crown), some members of the tribe moved to the Oneida lands in today's Upstate New York to join other New England Christian Algonquians at the Brothertown community (which subsequently resettled in Wisconsin in the 1830s).

When William Apess Jr. entered the world of postrevolutionary America at the end of the eighteenth century, one hundred or so Pequots lived at Ledyard and North Stonington in Connecticut. Others, such as William's parents, lived away from these reservations, regularly if not permanently, among the general population of the northeastern United States; but most Pequots thought of the reservations as "home." In that period, Pequots usually were small-scale farmers, laborers, and servants, although various seafaring occupations employed some, and many produced craft items, such as baskets and shoes, or collected medicines across the landscape to sell. In general, gathering and hunting were more important for them than for their white neighbors in New England but were less significant in their economy than among natives who lived to the west or north. They also generated income by leasing land or selling reservation resources, such as timber. Their possessions and homes were similar to those of poor Euro-Americans for the most part. A portion of their cultural heritage had been lost by the turn of the nineteenth century, although the language survived and William Apess was familiar with it, although we do not know how fluent he was.[5] Much of the subsequent story of the Pequots in the decades that followed was one of declining fortunes despite attempts to preserve their distinct identity, but in the 1970s some interrelated people asserted their Pequot heritage with renewed vigor, invited others with Pequot ancestry to join the nation, and achieved federal government recognition for the Mashantucket Pequot tribe in 1983. Today, there are two Pequot reservations in Connecticut: Mashantucket (Ledyard) and Lantern Hill (North Stonington).

After William Jr.'s birth in 1798, his parents returned to Colchester near the Pequot reservations. About three years later, his father and mother separated and moved away, leaving William and his siblings with his mother's impoverished parents. William continued to see his father at least periodically but did not meet his mother again for sixteen or seventeen years (although the parents may have been together at least occasionally during that period, given the birth dates of their children).[6] His grandparents abused alcohol and often neglected or beat the children. Once, while intoxicated in 1802, William's grandmother attacked him with a club, breaking his arm in three places. She might have killed him had an uncle not intervened to save the little boy. In looking back on the incident as an adult, William believed white society was partly to blame for such "unnatural conduct" because Europeans had introduced liquor to indigenous people to befuddle them, steal their lands and possessions, exploit native women with "violence of the most revolting kind," and drive the tribespeople into a state of impoverished desperation.[7]

In the wake of the assault, the uncle obtained medical care for William and had him removed to a safer home. Consequently, William Apess became a ward of the Euro-American town in which he lived, whose selectmen bound him out to a white cooper and farmer by the name of Furman and his wife, who previously had given food to William and his hungry siblings when they had lived with their grandparents. The indenture was to last until William turned twenty-one, and his labor was to benefit the Furmans in return for the care they gave him. The Furmans were Baptists who sent William to school for six winters and attended to his religious instruction. Like many indentured native children in New England, he likely maintained contact with aboriginal people through his relatives and perhaps other individuals in the neighborhood, which preserved his sense of cultural distinctiveness.[8] The Furmans, however, told William frightening stories about First Nations history, which filled his young imagination with dread. On one occasion, influenced by these tales, he came across some dark-skinned Euro-American women picking berries, which led him to run away in terror out of fear that they were "natives in the woods" who intended to commit bloodthirsty horrors upon him! Years later, he reflected on how whites had failed to tell him "that they were in the great majority of instances the aggressors, that they had imbrued their hands in the lifeblood of my brethren, driven them from their once peaceful and happy homes," and "introduced among them the fatal and extermi-nating diseases of civilized life."[9] These opinions on white culpability for both his grandmother's alcohol-induced violence and his mistaken fear of his own people were representative of thoughts that William Apess expressed throughout his writing and which captured the resentment and injury he felt as an indigenous victim of the European settlement of North America. They also probably spoke to the perspectives of New England aboriginal people in general, especially among those who had experienced indenture or other servitude within white households where they regularly were mistreated and overworked, and where their native heritage was devalued but where ongoing interactions with their family and other connections created opportunities to hear alternative histories and appreciate the qualities of aboriginal society.[10]

In spite of the fantastic tales told to him and the occasional beatings inflicted by his guardians (as was common in the white world at the time), Apess gener-ally lived contentedly with the Furmans and spoke warmly of the care they gave him.[11] Yet he made a grim decision in his eleventh year when he concocted a plan to run away from home under the influence of an older boy. The Furmans found out and responded by selling his indenture to Judge William Hillhouse, a senior member of one of Connecticut's leading families. The Furmans falsely told Apess that his move would be temporary. The new circumstances proved to be miserable for both Hillhouse and Apess, as young William turned out to be too unruly for the elderly man. Within a year the judge resold the indenture to William Williams, another elite gentleman. Unlike the humble Furmans, neither of these wealthy people sent Apess to school.

During his residence with the Williams family, Apess's interest in Christian-ity deepened, especially in its Methodist version, which commonly appealed to humbler and less educated people at the time, and he experienced a powerful conversion to the faith. The Williamses, who were Congregationalists, objected to Apess's sort of religion, ordered him not to attend Methodist meetings, and oc-casionally beat him when he slipped away to hear the Gospel in his preferred church. This clash, combined with other abuses, led him to join another boy in the household and run away to New York City. There, he enlisted in the American army and served first at the port's fortifications and then along the Canadian bor-der between 1813 and 1815. As was typical of many recruits, he lost his way spiritu-ally, drank heavily, and participated in the other dissipations of a soldier's life.

Despite having fought against the British and Canadians, William Apess briefly lived in Canada after the return of peace, spending part of his time among its native population. He subsequently crossed back into the United States and led a life at the margins of society, doing odd jobs, begging, and falling in with bad characters with whom he drank too much and otherwise engaged in conduct that troubled his soul. By 1816, he had returned to Connecticut, and he passed the winter of 1817–18 in or near the Ledyard Reservation or at nearby Groton with one of his father's relatives, Sally George, a devout Christian and respected individual within both the native and white communities, who was, according to Apess, "almost a preacher" and whose example may have provided inspiration for his later work as an indigenous Christian missionary.[12] William became temperate, and in 1818, at the age of twenty, while attending a camp meeting of the Methodist Episcopal Church, he came to believe he had a religious vocation. A minister or speaker invited him to address the congregation, and Apess recorded that in rising, "I found all impediment of speech removed; my heart was enlarged, my soul glowed with holy fervor, and the blessing of the Almighty sanctified this, my first public attempt to warn sinners of their danger and invite them to the marriage supper of the Lamb." Even though he suffered from doubts and fears afterward, he concluded then that "I was now in my proper element, just harnessed for the work, with the fire of divine love burning on my heart."[13] In December 1818, William Apess was baptized by immersion at Bozrah north of New London.[14] In 1819, he visited his father, now reunited with his mother in Colrain. He learned how to be a shoemaker and worked in the trade and at various menial jobs, earning enough money to pursue his religious calling, but noted that some of his success in the church occurred because people merely were curious "to hear the Indian preach."[15]

His faith was an unsophisticated and emotional one dominated by the dangers people faced when they did not repent their depravities and allow God to save them. The expressive and unrefined nature of Apess's beliefs was typical among many Methodists in the decades before a large part of that denomination moved away from its early evangelicalism (and, to some degree, its status as a religion of outsiders) into the realm of ecclesiastical regularity and social respectability by the mid-nineteenth century. Apess's Methodism was a version of Christianity that non-evangelical Protestants condemned as fraught with perils because people fell under the sway of uneducated clergy who lacked the qualifications needed to address questions of deep importance with theological precision. In contrast, individuals like Apess, while not opposed to learning (as we shall see below), declared that preachers in his church spoke with the authority of the indwelling Holy Spirit rather than through the limitations of formal study. Of course, it was only through a church that accepted such ministries that the comparatively uneducated William Apess could pursue his vocation. Nevertheless, some in his own denomination had doubts about him, which he found devastating, and which led to his alienation from his church. Feeling like an "outcast from society," he "gave way for a little while" to his despair; however, he recovered among the company of fellow Pequot Christians and continued to work for the promotion of the faith.[16]

In 1821, William Apess married Mary Wood of Salem, Connecticut. She too was a devout Methodist and likely a person of mixed ancestry (most likely white along with black, native, and/or Hispanic heritage), who William Apess described as "nearly of the same color as myself."[17] She was a decade older than her husband and had lived her early life as an indentured servant, having been bound out by her impoverished and widowed mother, who could not afford to keep her.[18] Mary and William were to have at least two girls and a boy together. Like many people without property, William frequently had to live away from his family to find enough work to support his wife and children. In the mid-1820s, while living in Providence, Rhode Island, with or near his sister, he became a class leader in the Methodist Episcopal Church. Subsequently, church authorities gave him an exhorter's license to work as a missionary in New England and New York between 1827 and 1829, but they would not grant him the more prestigious role of lay preacher. These developments transpired as the church's members were growing in material comfort and self-conscious "respectability" and increasingly embraced hierarchical structures along with gender and racial biases. The denial seems to have been based partly on Apess's indiscipline to ecclesiastical authority, but possibly because of his nonwhite origins as well. In 1829, he left the denomination and moved to one of the Methodist societies then in existence that would form the Methodist Protestant Church in 1830, receiving a license to preach as a layperson, although it seems he did not enter the ranks of the clergy despite assertions that he was an ordained minister.[19] In 1831 William Apess went to proclaim the Gospel to the Pequots in Connecticut but also traveled among other people as part of his missionizing, such as occurred in Boston in 1832 when he delivered lectures and sermons on such topics as the "purity of the Gospel," the "judgment of the great day," and an "address on the subject of slavery," where he came to the favorable notice of various reformers in the city.[20]

In 1833, William Apess moved to Mashpee (or Marshpee) on Cape Cod in Massachusetts to preach to the New England Algonquian people of the Wampanoag nation who resided there, among whom lived individuals of black, white, and mixed origins (the latter being the most numerous), including people of various native identities. He helped the Mashpees in their struggle to free themselves both from the arbitrary regime imposed on them by three white overseers appointed by the state and from the indifference and bigotry of their resident Congregationalist missionary, the Reverend Phineas Fish. The overseers leased land to outsiders, granted woodlot rights, bound out people in employment contracts, controlled residency, and otherwise imposed their will to benefit whites at the expense of the aboriginal population of three hundred or more souls. Appointed by Harvard College, Phineas Fish was not popular with the natives, largely because of his lack of interest in serving their spiritual needs, his views that the Mashpees were inferior to whites, and his appropriation of tribal resources for his personal use. Few Mashpees, whose faith was more conservative and evangelical than Fish's, attended his services, so most people who came to the community's "Indian meetinghouse" were Euro-American. Meanwhile, Fish forbade an aboriginal Baptist preacher, Blind Joe Amos, from using the building for his services.

The Mashpees adopted Apess and agreed to give his family a home, presumably hoping that the Methodist missionary could strengthen their community and help them in their struggles. Apess opposed Fish, joined Amos in forming a temperance society, founded a congregation called the "Free and United Church," and took up the cause of Mashpee rights. He saw the fight as paralleling the American drive for independence from Britain in the late eighteenth century and as affirming Mashpee equality in the eyes of God in distinction from the prejudice of their white neighbors. Presumably theological tensions between William Apess and Phineas Fish magnified their mutual hostility. (Fish, in surveying his opponents, stated that it gave him "pain" to see Baptist and Methodist "busybodies" working at "demolishing the remnant of Congregationalism" at Mashpee.)[21] Apess likely was the author of petitions to Harvard University and the government of Massachusetts designed to promote Mashpee rights and interests. The one to Harvard announced that the Mashpees had discharged Fish and declared that they wanted Apess to take his place, with, they hoped, financial support from the college. The second petition was a proclamation from the tribe's "national assembly" announcing that the Mashpees wanted independence from state interference after having been "distressed, and degraded, and robbed daily."[22] In July 1833, William Apess led a small group of natives in preventing some white men from removing wood from the settlement in an act to assert indigenous rights. The outsiders, one of whom was a justice of the peace and a member of Fish's congregation, seem to have tried to take the wood specifically to challenge the Mashpees. Three days later, Apess found himself arrested for riot with "force of arms" and other offenses. His incarceration seems to have led the Mashpees to back down and attempt to find less confrontational solutions to their problems. Apess was released on bail until his trial, when the court found him guilty and sentenced him to thirty days in jail, fined him one hundred dollars, and ordered him to post bond in the same amount to keep the peace. Two of the Mashpees who were with him at the incident were imprisoned for ten days.[23]

Despite the conviction, Apess continued to work for the Mashpees and represent the community at public meetings in Boston and appeared before a committee of the Massachusetts legislature. In 1834 he and his supporters won a partial victory when the state gave the natives fundamentally the same rights to municipal self-government that people in white townships enjoyed, which represented an improvement over their previous condition. Phineas Fish hung on in his living until 1846 in spite of ongoing hostility, although he was ejected from the meetinghouse in 1840. During the Mashpee Revolt, Fish, the anti-Mashpee press, and others labeled Apess an outside agitator and blamed him for the troubles, choosing to overlook the issues that had led up to the events of 1833–34. In contrast, some newspapers, such as the *Liberator,* published by the famous abolitionist and social reformer William Lloyd Garrison, supported Apess, who had gained some prominence in the public realm during the crisis. The Mashpees and William Apess, however, fell out toward the end of 1834.[24] As well, non-Mashpee supporters of the tribe seemed to have turned their back on Apess; and later, after his death, various newspapers, without providing evidence, hinted that he may not have lived with the integrity expected of him, possibly having misappropriated some Mashpee funds, which he had been accused of doing earlier in his life as well when suggestions were made that he had raised money to support church projects but had used it to meet personal needs, although on the earlier occasion he successfully won a court case for slander in protecting his reputation.[25]

In 1835, William Apess published the history of the Mashpee Revolt in *Indian Nullification of the Unconstitutional Laws of Massachusetts Relative to the Marshpee Tribe: or, The Pretended Riot Explained.* His use of the word "nullification" was provocative because of its association with a constitutional crisis in the public mind over affirmations by South Carolinians that their state had the right to nullify federal laws within their borders when they believed Washington acted unconstitutionally. Then, in 1836, in Boston, he continued to challenge the dominant society when he delivered and published his *Eulogy on King Philip* on the famous Wampanoag leader (also known as Metacomet) in the white-native war in New England in 1675–76. In his address, Apess (who made the mistake of thinking that Metacomet was a Pequot) proclaimed two important points as part of his demands for racial equality. First, he affirmed that much of the exploitation of people of color could be traced to white America's Puritan founders and their sense of being a chosen people with racial and moral superiority over others; and second, he declared that the native leader King Philip ought to be seen as a patriotic figure of the same standing as George Washington. In the 1830s, these thoughts represented aggressive challenges to the worldview of Americans at the time of the Black Hawk War, Indian Removal and its racist agenda, tightening antiblack laws directed against the Republic's other great oppressed minority, a growing affirmation of the formative importance of New England Puritanism in shaping America's distinctiveness as a nation, and the saintly status Washington enjoyed among the population at large.[26] Apess pursued his ministry at least until the end of 1837, as he appeared in the national capital of Washington that year, again speaking in public on native rights.[27]

While working as a preacher, public figure, and writer in the 1830s (supported partly by craft work and manual labor), Apess's financial affairs were precarious. He was the subject of several debt actions and lost his property, including his Mashpee home. His wife Mary may have died in the mid-1830s (although it also is possible that the marriage failed and he left her and their children).[28] He then seems to have married or formed a bond with another person in 1836, of whom we know little aside from her Christian name, Elizabeth, and a sentence in a newspaper that stated that Apess had married a "good looking white woman." (The comment on her appearance seems impertinent by the standards of the day, and we might wonder if it was meant to be pejorative.)[29]

Hardship marked William Apess's existence, from his early impoverishment, to being left with abusive grandparents when he was very small, to his indentured servitude with white families, to a demeaning and dissipated life as a common soldier and a wanderer during and after the War of 1812. Yet his Christian faith and his Pequot identity offered him visions of a better and more just world for himself and his people, and so he struggled against drink and the other demons that plagued him and tried to rise to a position of respectability and utility within Methodism. In the church, he engaged in a ministry directed partly toward native people and enjoyed some success. Nevertheless, even after his baptism in 1818 and his church work, he faced ongoing challenges, poverty, prejudice, and hostility; and like other talented people, he found the struggle against so many difficulties to be too much in the end. Early in 1839, Elizabeth and William moved into a New York City boardinghouse in fallen circumstances. Elizabeth noted that she and William "always lived on good terms," although she described him as being "formerly a preacher"—which surely was a sad confession—who "lately" had "been somewhat intemperate." Then, after several days of consuming large quantities of liquor (at a time when binge drinking, or "frolicking," was common), William

Apess complained of feeling ill. Two doctors treated him at the boardinghouse, mainly with purgatives, which critically weakened his body. Within three days of their treatment, on April 10, 1839, he was dead. Apess was forty-one. The physician who performed the autopsy diagnosed the cause of death as "apoplexy," or what we would call a cerebral hemorrhage, although possibly some other bodily catastrophe had carried him away. Perhaps the medical care he had received had brought on or hastened his demise, as some newspapers suggested, but part of the blame almost certainly falls to his abuse of alcohol, a curse that he had identified so plainly as a threat to native peoples and which he had condemned so strongly during his life.[30]

William Apess printed his autobiography, *A Son of the Forest*, in New York in 1829, using sales of the self-published book to supplement his family's income, and then brought out a revised edition in the same city in 1831. He also published *The Increase of the Kingdom of Christ* (New York, 1831); two editions of *The Experiences of Five Christian Indians of the Pequod Tribe* (Boston, 1833 and 1837), which included the autobiography of his wife, Mary Wood; an essay appended to the first edition of *Experiences of Five Christian Indians* titled "An Indian's Looking-Glass for the White Man"; *Indian Nullification* (Boston, 1835); and two editions of *Eulogy on King Philip* (Boston, 1836 and 1837). Collectively, these fascinating texts embrace three important unifying themes. One is the assertion that Euro-Americans had denied indigenous peoples their rights, and even their humanity, since the beginning of the colonial era, but justice demanded that the relationship between natives and newcomers be revived on an equal and honorable basis. Another is that true Christianity is color-blind and thus stands as a condemnation of white treatment of indigenous and black peoples, and as a censure of those churches that fail to live up to the imperatives in the Gospel proclamations of equality and liberation. The third is an affirmation of the goodness of First Nations society within an aboriginal self-identification that integrated Christianity into it, as was common in William Apess's world. His very being as a Christian missionary and writer (and advocate of republican virtues) who was proud of his indigenous identity represented an act of defiance against whites who wanted to use faith, education, and their perceptions of American values as vehicles to assimilate native peoples and eradicate their separate cultures.[31]

Apess's writing put him in the company of a number of First Nations Christians who wrote lengthy texts that integrated faith with indigenous personal experiences, along with native perspectives on history and culture. The best known of his era were fellow Methodists Peter Jones, or Kahkewaquonaby, of the Mississaugas (1802–56), and George Copway, or Kahgegagahbowh, of the Ojibwas (1818–69), along with the Mohawk Congregationalist-turned-Episcopalian Eleazer Williams, or Onwarenhiiake (1788–1858), the first two of whom lived in Canada, while the last spent most of his life in the United States.[32] The autobiographical nature of *A Son of the Forest* sets it apart from William Apess's other publications, except for a comparable section of *Experiences of Five Christian Indians*. Perhaps he found inspiration for his work in two books from the 1820s which told the stories of native women, the adopted Seneca, Mary Jemison, and the Cherokee, Catharine Brown, although their memoirs were taken down from oral testimony and organized by white men who added their own glosses to the texts.[33] Essentially a conversion narrative (a literary genre Apess must have known as a Methodist), *A Son of the Forest* also follows the format of other biographical and autobiographical texts of the period. One is the slave narrative, in which a vulnerable person, alienated from the surrounding world, escapes his or her bonds, embarks on an adventurous journey, and explores issues of racial oppression. A second and similar form is the soldier's tale, typically of a young man, who, feeling persecuted, runs away from his troubles, finds himself down on his luck, joins the army, and then experiences the trials of military life, but transcends them to emerge as a better and wiser person. A third literary construct possessing similarities to Apess's autobiography is the "Indian captivity narrative," in which a white person recounts the tribulations experienced after being seized by aboriginal people (and in the process justifies white hostility toward them), but of course Apess inverted that form by speaking as a native captured—through his indenture—by whites.[34]

While there is no reason to doubt the authenticity of William Apess's voice in his publications, we do not know the details of how his works came to be published, and the quality of his texts might seem more advanced than we might expect from someone with a limited education. (The appendix to *A Son of the Forest* on the origins of the First Nations was a reworking of other people's writing, particularly those of Elias Boudinot, a prominent public figure from New Jersey —not the famous Cherokee of the same name—but the appendix falls outside of Apess's autobiography of concern to us and differs from his more obviously self-authored efforts.) Yet William Apess's aboriginal Methodist contemporaries, Peter Jones and George Copway, wrote complex and skilled works after receiving similarly modest educations, and the famous Mohawk leader of an earlier generation, Joseph Brant, could communicate on paper with competence with only two years of Euro-American education. (He even had the literary proficiency to translate parts of the Bible and the Book of Common Prayer from English into written Mohawk and to draft a history of the Six Nations Iroquois.) We also probably should assume that Apess developed his literary skills beyond his primary education while attending classes and through reading as part of his theological development and maturation as an adult. As well, other people may have read, commented upon, and copyedited his various works before they went to press, or even helped him draft some of his texts, possibly through writing down his dictated words in some instances. His printers may have made corrections also. Yet none of these normal aspects of the writing process, if they occurred, seem to have blunted the strength of Apess's voice as an aboriginal person from New England.[35]

The excerpt from *A Son of the Forest* presented below consists of part of chapter 3 and all of chapters 4, 5, and 6 of the Toronto Public Library's copy of the "revised and corrected" edition, published in New York in 1831, between pages 30 and 71 of the original 214-page book. That publication contains 110 pages of autobiography, with most of the rest comprising Boudinot's appendix mentioned above.

1. An Indentured Servant's Struggles, 1809–13

We enter William Apess's autobiography in the rural mill town of Colchester, Connecticut, in 1809, partway in chapter 3 of his A Son of the Forest. *It was the eleventh year of his life and toward the end of his time living with the Euro-American Furman family, who had looked after him following his removal from the home of his native grandmother after she had beaten him severely. Much of this section consists of descriptions of his subjugation as an indentured servant and discussions of a religious crisis generated by his sense of sinfulness, which had been made plain to him by the lessons learned among the Methodists. Despite that crisis, he felt at home spiritually and emotionally within that church and among its adherents who, like him, had been mistreated by the wider world. While this section differs from the more adventuresome segments that follow, it sets Apess's subsequent enlistment in the army in context and captures much of the essence of the autobiography as a whole, which we would miss in focusing entirely on Apess's life as a soldier during the War of 1812. Central to autobiographical conversion narratives such as* A Son of the Forest *is the story of becoming painfully aware of the author's sinfulness, followed by embracing Christianity, tales of backsliding, and a recovery into a harmonious and promising relationship with God.*

[1809–12]

Nothing very extraordinary occurred until I had attained my eleventh year. At this time it was fashionable for boys to run away, and the wicked one put it into the head of the oldest boy on the farm to persuade me to follow the fashion.[36] He told me that I could take care of myself and get my own living. I thought it was a very pretty notion to be a man—*to do business for myself and become rich*. Like a fool I concluded to make the experiment, and accordingly began to pack up my clothes as deliberately as could be, and in which my adviser assisted. I had been once or twice at New London where I saw, as I thought, everything wonderful. Thither I determined to bend my course as I expected that on reaching the town I should be metamorphosed into a person of consequence. I had the world and everything my little heart could desire on a string when behold, my companion, who had persuaded me to act thus, informed my master that I was going to run off. At first he would not believe the boy, but my clothing already packed up was ample evidence of my intention. On being questioned I acknowledged the fact. I did not wish to leave them—told Mr. Furman so. He believed me but thought best that for a while I should have another master. He accordingly agreed to transfer my indentures to Judge Hillhouse for the sum of twenty dollars.[37] Of course, after the bargain was made, my consent was to be obtained, but I was as unwilling to go now as I had been anxious to run away before. After some persuasion I agreed to try it for a fortnight on condition that I should take my dog with me, and my request being granted, I was soon under the old man's roof as he only lived about six miles off. Here everything was done to make me contented because they thought to promote their own interests by securing my services. They fed me with knickknacks, and soon after I went among them I had a jackknife presented to me, which was the first one I had ever seen. Like other boys, I spent my time either in whittling or playing with my dog, and was withal very happy; but I was homesick at heart, and as soon as my fortnight had expired I went home without ceremony. Mr. Furman's family was surprised to see me but that surprise was mutual satisfaction in which my faithful dog appeared to participate.

The joy I felt on returning home as I hoped was turned to sorrow on being informed that I had been *sold* to the judge and must instantly return.[38] This I was compelled to do; and reader, all this sorrow was in consequence of being led away by a bad boy. If I had not listened to him I should not have lost my home. Such treatment I conceive to be the best means to accomplish the ruin of a child, as the reader will see in the sequel. I was sold to the judge at a time when age had rendered him totally unfit to manage an unruly lad. If he undertook to correct me, which he did at times, I did not regard it as I knew that I could run off from him if he was too severe, and besides I could do what I pleased in defiance of his authority.[39]

Now the old gentleman was a member of the Presbyterian Church and withal a very strict one. He never neglected family prayer and he always insisted on my being present. I did not believe, or rather, had no faith in his prayer because it was the same thing from day to day, and I had heard it repeated so often that I knew it as well as he. Although I was so young, I did not think that Christians ought to learn their prayers, and knowing that he repeated the same thing from day to day is, I have no doubt, the very reason why his petitions did me no good. I could fix no value on his prayers.[40]

After a little while the conduct of my new guardian was changed toward me. Once secured, I was no longer the favorite. The few clothes I had were not taken care of, by which I mean no pains were taken to keep them clean and whole, and the consequence was that in a little time they were all tattered and torn, and I was not fit to be seen in decent company. I had not the opportunity of attending meeting as before.[41] Yet as the divine and reclaiming impression had not been entirely defaced, I would frequently retire behind the barn and attempt to pray in my weak manner. I now became quite anxious to attend evening meetings a few miles off.[42] I asked the judge if I should go and take one of the horses, to which he consented. This promise greatly delighted me; but when it was time for me to go, all my hopes were dashed at once as the judge had changed his mind. I was not to be foiled so easily: I watched for the first opportunity and slipped off with one of the horses, reached the meeting, and returned in safety. Here I was to blame. If he acted wrong, it did not justify me in doing so; but being successful in one grand act of disobedience, I was encouraged to make another similar attempt whenever my unsanctified dispositions prompted. For the very next time I wished to go to meeting I thought I would take the horse again, and in the same manner too, without the knowledge of my master. As he was by some means apprised of my intention, he prevented my doing so and had the horses locked up in the stable. He then commanded me to give him the bridle. I was obstinate for a time, then threw it at the old gentleman and ran off. I did not return until the next day, when I received a flogging for my bad conduct, which determined me to run away. Now the judge was partly to blame for all this. He had in the first place treated me with the utmost kindness until he had made sure of me. Then the whole course of his conduct changed, and I believed he fulfilled only one item of the transferred indentures, and that was *work*. Of this there was no lack. To be sure I had enough to eat, such as it was, but he did not send me to school as he had promised.

A few days found me on my way to New London where I stayed awhile. I then pushed on to Waterford, and as my father lived about twenty miles off, I concluded to go and see him. I got there safely, and told him I had come on a visit and that I should stay one week. At the expiration of the week he bid me go home and I obeyed him. On my return I was treated rather coolly, and this not suiting my disposition, I ran off again but returned in a few days. Now, as the judge found he could not control me, he got heartily tired of me and wished to hand me over to someone else, so he obtained a place for me in New London. I knew nothing of it and I was greatly mortified to think that I was sold in this way. If my consent had been solicited as a matter of form, I should not have felt so bad; but to be sold to, and treated unkindly by, those who had got our fathers' lands for nothing was too much to bear.[43] When all things were ready, the judge told me that he wanted me to go to New London with a neighbor to purchase salt. I was delighted and went with the man, expecting to return that night. When I reached the place I found my mistake. The name of the person to whom I was transferred this time was General William Williams, and as my treatment at the judge's was none the best, I went home with him contentedly.[44] Indeed, I felt glad that I had changed masters, and more especially that I was to reside in the city. The finery and show caught my eye and captivated my heart. I can truly say that my situation was better now than it had been previous to my residence in New London. In a little time I was furnished with good new clothes. I had enough to eat, both as it respects quality and quantity, and my work was light. The whole family treated me kindly, and the only difficulty of [the] moment was that they all wished to be masters but I would not obey all of them.

There was a French boy in the family who one day told Mr. Williams a willful lie about me, which he believed and gave me a horsewhipping without asking me a single question about it. Now, I do not suppose that he whipped so much on account of what the boy told him as he did from the influence of the judge's directions.[45] He used the falsehood as a pretext for flogging me, as from what he said he was determined to make a good boy of me at once, as if stripes were calculated to effect that which love, kindness, and instruction can only successfully accomplish. He told me that if I ever ran away from him he would follow me to the uttermost parts of the earth. I knew from this observation that the judge had told him that I was a runaway. However cruel this treatment appeared, for the accusation was false, yet it did me much good as I was ready to obey the general and his lady at all times, but I could not and would not obey any but my superiors. In short, I got on very smoothly for a season.

The general attended the Presbyterian Church, and was exact in having all his family with him in the house of God. I of course formed one of the number. Though I did not profess religion, I observed and felt that their ways were not like the ways of the Christians.[46] It appeared inconsistent to me for a minister to read his sermon. To turn over leaf after leaf and at the conclusion say "amen" seemed to me like an "empty sound and a tinkling cymbal."[47] I was not benefited by his reading. It did not arouse me to a sense of my danger, and I am of the opinion that it had no better effect on the people of his charge. I liked to attend church as I had been taught in my younger years to venerate the Sabbath day; and although young, I could plainly perceive the difference between the preachers I had formerly heard and the minister at whose church I attended. I thought (as near as I can remember) that the Christian depended on the Holy Spirit's influence entirely, while this minister depended as much upon his learning. I would not be understood as saying anything against knowledge; in its place it is good and highly necessary to a faithful preacher of righteousness. What I object to is placing too much reliance in it, making a god of it, et cetera.

[1812–13]

Everything went on smoothly for two or three years. About this time the Methodists began to hold meetings in the neighborhood and consequently a storm of persecution gathered; the Pharisee and the worldling united heartily in abusing them.[48] The gall and wormwood of sectarian malice were emitted, and every evil report prejudicial to this pious people was freely circulated; and it was openly said that the character of a respectable man would receive a stain—and a deep one too—by attending one of their meetings. Indeed, the stories circulated about them were bad enough to deter people of "character" from attending the Methodist ministry, but it had no effect on me. I thought I had no character to lose in the estimation of those who were accounted great. For what cared they for me? They had possession of the red man's inheritance and had deprived me of liberty. With this they were satisfied and could do as they pleased; therefore, I thought I could do as I pleased, measurably. I therefore went to hear the *noisy Methodists*.[49] When I reached the house I found a clever company. They did not appear to differ much from "respectable" people. They were neatly and decently clothed, and I could not see that they differed from other people except in their behavior, which was more kind and gentlemanly. Their countenance was heavenly; their songs were like sweetest music; in their manners they were plain; their language was not fashioned after the wisdom of men. When the minister preached he spoke as one having authority. The exercises were accompanied by the power of God. His people shouted for joy while sinners wept. This being the first time I had ever attended a meeting of this kind, all things of course appeared new to me.[50] I was very far from forming the opinion that most of the neighborhood entertained about them. From this time I became more serious and soon went to hear the Methodists again, and I was constrained to believe that they were the true people of God. One person asked me how I knew it. I replied that I was convinced in my own mind that they possessed something more than the power of the devil.

I now attended these meetings constantly, and although I was a sinner before God, yet I felt no disposition to laugh or scoff. I make this observation because so many people went to these meetings to make fun. This was a common thing, and I often wondered how persons who professed to be considered great (i.e., "ladies and gentlemen") would so far disgrace themselves as to scoff in the house of God and at his holy services. Such persons let themselves down below the heathen in point of moral conduct—below the heathen, yes, and below the level of the brute creation who answers the end for which they were made.

But notwithstanding the people were so wicked, the Lord had respect unto the labors of his servants; his ear was open to their daily supplications, and in answer to prayer he was pleased to revive his work. The power of the Holy Ghost moved forth among the people: the Spirit's influence was felt at every meeting; the people of God were built up in their faith; their confidence in the Lord of hosts gathered strength while many sinners were alarmed and began to cry aloud for mercy. In a little time the work rolled onward like an overwhelming flood. Now the Methodists and all who attended their meetings were greatly persecuted. All denominations were up in arms against them because the Lord was blessing their labors and making them (a poor, despised people) his instruments in the conversion of sinners; but all opposition had no other effect than of cementing the brethren more closely together.[51] The work went on, as the Lord was with them of a truth and signally owned and blessed their labors. At one of these meetings I was induced to laugh. I believe it must have been to smother my conviction as it did not come from my heart. My heart was troubled on account of sin, and when conviction pressed upon me I endeavored not only to be cheerful, but to laugh, and thus drive away all appearance of being wrought upon. Shortly after this I was affected even unto tears. This the people of the world observed and immediately inquired if I was one of the Lamb's children. Brother Hill was then speaking from this passage of scripture: "Behold the Lamb of God that taketh away the sins of the world."[52] He spoke feelingly of his sufferings upon the cross, of the precious blood that flowed like a purifying river from his side, of his sustaining the accumulated weight of the sins of the whole world, and dying to satisfy the demands of that justice, which could only be appeased by an infinite atonement. I felt convinced that Christ died for all mankind—that age, sect, color, country, or situation made no difference. I felt an assurance that I was included in the plan of redemption with all my brethren. No one can conceive with what joy I hailed this *new* doctrine, as it was called. It removed every excuse, and I freely believed that all I had to do was to look in faith upon the Lamb of God that made himself a freewill offering for my unregenerate and wicked soul upon the cross. My spirits were depressed, my crimes were arrayed before me, and no tongue can tell the anguish I felt.

After meeting I returned home with a heavy heart, determined to seek the salvation of my soul. This night I slept but little. At times I would be melted down to tenderness and tears, and then again my heart would seem as hard as adamant. I was greatly tempted. The evil one would try to persuade me that I was not in the pale of mercy. I fancied that evil spirits stood around my bed—my condition was deplorably awful—and I longed for the day to break as much as the tempest-tossed mariner who expects every moment to be washed from the wreck to which he fondly clings. So it was with me upon the wreck of the world: buffeted by temptations, assailed by the devil, sometimes in despair, then believing against hope. My heart seemed at times almost ready to break, while the tears of contrition coursed rapidly down my cheeks; but sin was the cause of this, and no wonder I groaned and wept. I had often sinned, and my accumulated transgressions had piled themselves as a rocky mountain on my heart; and how could I endure it? The weight thereof seemed to crush me down. In the night season I had frightful visions and would often start from my sleep and gaze round the room as I was ever in dread of seeing the evil one ready to carry me off. I continued in this frame of mind for more than seven weeks.

My distress finally became so acute that the family took notice of it. Some of them persecuted me because I was serious and fond of attending meeting. Now, persecution raged on every hand, within and without, and I had none to take me by the hand and say, "Go with us and we will do thee good," but in the midst of difficulties so great to one only fifteen years of age I ceased not to pray for the salvation of my soul.[53] Very often my exercises were so great that sleep departed from me—I was fearful that I should wake up in hell. And one night when I was in bed, mourning like the dove for her absent mate, I fell into a doze. I thought I saw the world of fire: it resembled a large solid bed of coals, red and glowing with heat. I shall never forget the impression it made upon my mind. No tongue can possibly describe the agony of my soul, for now I was greatly in fear of dropping into that awful place, the smoke of the torment of which ascendeth up forever and ever. I cried earnestly for mercy. Then I was carried to another place, where perfect happiness appeared to pervade every part of the inhabitants thereof. Oh, how I longed to be among that happy company.[54] I sighed to be free from misery and pain. I knew that nothing but the attenuated thread of life kept me from falling into the awful lake I beheld. I cannot think that it is in the power of human language to describe the feelings that rushed upon my mind or thrilled through my veins. Everything appeared to bear the signet of reality. When I awoke, I heartily rejoiced to find it nothing but a dream.

I went on from day to day with my head and heart bowed down, seeking the Savior of sinners, but without success. The heavens appeared to be brass.[55] My prayers wanted the wings of faith to waft them to the skies. The disease of my heart increased, the heavenly physician had not stretched forth his hand and poured upon my soul the panacea of the Gospel, the scales had not fallen from my eyes, and no ray of celestial light had dispelled the darkness that gathered around my soul. The cheering sound of sincere friendship fell not upon my ear. It seemed as if I were friendless, unpitied, and unknown; and at times I wished to become a dweller in the wilderness. No wonder then that I was almost desponding. Surrounded by difficulties and apparent dangers, I was resolved to seek the salvation of my soul with all my heart, to trust entirely to the Lord, and if I failed, to perish pleading for mercy at the foot of the throne. I now hung all my hope on the Redeemer, and clung with indescribable tenacity to the Cross on which he purchased salvation for the "vilest of the vile."[56] The result was such as is always to be expected when a lost and ruined sinner throws himself entirely on the Lord—"perfect freedom."[57] On the fifteenth day of March in the year of our Lord 1813, I heard a voice in soft and soothing accents saying unto me, "Arise, thy sins, which were many, are all forgiven thee, go in peace and sin no more!"[58]

There was nothing very singular (save the fact that the Lord stooped to lift me up) in my conversion. I had been sent into the garden to work, and while there I lifted up my heart to God when all at once my burden and fears left me, my heart melted into tenderness, my soul was filled with love—love to God, and love to all mankind. Oh, how my poor heart swelled with joy, and I could cry from my very soul, "Glory to God in the highest!"[59] There was not only a change in my heart but in everything around me. The scene was entirely altered. The works of God praised him, and I saw him in everything that he had made. My love now embraced the whole human family. The children of God I loved most affectionately.

Oh, how I longed to be with them, and when any of them passed by me, I would gaze at them until they were lost in the distance. I could have pressed them to my bosom as they were more precious to me than gold, and I was always loath to part with them whenever we met together. The change, too, was visible in my very countenance.[60]

I enjoyed great peace of mind, and that peace was like a river: full, deep, and wide, and flowing continually. My mind was employed in contemplating the wonderful works of God and in praising his holy name; [I] dwelt so continually upon his mercy and goodness that I could praise him aloud even in my sleep. I continued in this happy frame of mind for some months. It was very pleasant to live in the enjoyment of pure and undefiled religion.

2. A Runaway Joins the Army, 1812–13

This segment reproduces chapter 4 of A Son of the Forest. *It describes how the oppression William Apess experienced because of his faith and the abuse he endured from a maid in the Williams household led him, at the age of fifteen, to run away with another boy. It then presents the adventures of the naive teenagers as they made their way from New London to New York, where the other boy left Apess. As recounted below, William, like so many other vulnerable young men through the ages, became an easy mark for a recruiting party, who enlisted him into an artillery regiment in the United States Army. Once in the military he turned from his quest for a life within the faith to spend the next few years as a debauched soldier and drifter who found it difficult to resist temptation.*

[1812–13][61]

The calm and sunshine did not, however, continue uninterrupted for any length of time. My peace of mind, which flowed as a river, was disturbed. While the adversary tempted me, the fire of persecution was rekindled. It was considered by some members of the family that I was too young to be religiously inclined, and consequently that I was under a strong delusion. After a time, Mr. Williams came to the conclusion that it was advisable for me to absent myself entirely from the Methodist meetings. This restriction was the more galling as I had joined the class and was extremely fond of this means of grace.[62] I generally attended once in each week; so when the time came round, I went off to the meeting without permission. When I returned, Mrs. Williams prepared to correct me for acting contrary to my orders. In the first place, however, she asked me where I had been. I frankly told her that I had been to meeting to worship God. This reply completely disarmed her and saved me a flogging for the time, but this was not the end of my persecution or my troubles.

The chambermaid was in truth a treacherous woman. Her heart appeared to me to be filled with deceit and guile, and she persecuted me with as much bitterness as Paul did the disciples of old.[63] She had a great dislike toward me and would not hesitate to tell a falsehood in order to have me whipped; but my mind was stayed upon God and I had much comfort in reading the Holy Scriptures. One day after she had procured me a flogging (and no very mild one either), she pushed me down a long flight of stairs. In the fall I was greatly injured, especially my head. In consequence of this I was disabled and laid up for a long time. When I told Mr. Williams that the maid had pushed me downstairs, she denied it, but I succeeded in making them believe it. In all this trouble the Lord was with me of a truth. I was happy in the enjoyment of his love. The abuse heaped on me was in consequence of my being a Methodist.

Sometimes I would get permission to attend meetings in the evening, and once or twice on the Sabbath, and oh, how thankful I felt for these opportunities for hearing the word of God; but the waves of persecution and affliction and sorrow rolled on and gathered strength in their progress, and for a season overwhelmed my dispirited soul. I was flogged several times very unjustly for what the maid said respecting me. My treatment in this respect was so bad that I could not brook it, and in an evil hour I listened to the suggestions of the devil, who was not slow in prompting me to pursue a course directly at variance with the Gospel. He put it into my head to abscond from my master, and I made arrangements with a boy of my acquaintance to accompany me.[64]

[1813]

So, one day, Mr. Williams had gone to Stonington. I left his house, notwithstanding he had previously threatened, if I did so, to follow me to the ends of the earth. While my companion was getting ready I hid my clothes in a barn and went to buy some bread and cheese, and while at the store, although I had about four dollars in my pocket, I so far forgot myself as to buy a pair of shoes on my master's account. Then it was that I began to lose sight of religion and of God.[65]

We now set out.[66] It being a rainy night, we bought a bottle of rum, of which poisonous stuff I drank heartily. Now the shadows of spiritual death began to gather around my soul. It was half-past nine o'clock at night when we started, and to keep up our courage we took another drink of the liquor. As soon as we left the city, that is, as we descended the hill, it became very dark, and my companion, who was always fierce enough by daylight, began to hang back. I saw that his courage was failing and endeavored to cheer him up. Sometimes I would take a drink of rum to drown my sorrows, but in vain. It appears to me now as if my sorrows neutralized the effects of the liquor.

This night we traveled about seven miles, and being weary and wet with the rain, we crept into a barn by the wayside, and for fear of being detected in the morning if we should happen to sleep too long, we burrowed into the hay a considerable depth. We were aroused in the morning by the people feeding their cattle. We laid still and they did not discover us. After they had left the barn we crawled out, made our breakfast on rum, bread, and cheese, and set off for Colchester, about fourteen miles distant, which we reached that night. Here we ventured to put up at a tavern. The next morning we started for my father's, about four miles off. I told him that we had come to stay only one week, and when that week had expired he wished me to redeem my promise and return home. So I had seemingly to comply, and when we had packed up our clothes, he said he would accompany us part of the way; and when we parted I thought he had some suspicions of my intention to take another direction as he begged me to go straight home. He then sat down on the wayside and looked after us as long as we were to be seen. At last we descended a hill, and as soon as we lost sight of him, we struck into the woods. I did not see my father again for eight years. At this time, I felt very much disturbed. I was just going to step out on the broad theater of the world as it were, without father, mother, or friends.

After traveling some distance in the woods, we shaped our course toward Hartford. We were fearful of being taken up, and my companion coined a story, which he thought would answer very well. It was to represent ourselves whenever questioned as having belonged to a privateer, which was captured by the British who kindly sent us on shore near New London, that our parents lived in the city of New York, and that we were traveling thither to see them.[67] Now, John was a great liar. He was brought up by dissipated parents and accustomed in the way of the world to all kinds of company. He had a good memory, and having been where he heard war songs and tales of blood and carnage, he treasured them up. He therefore agreed to be spokesman, and I assure my dear reader that I was perfectly willing, for abandoned as I was, I could not lie without feeling my conscience smite me. This part of the business being arranged, it was agreed that I should sell part of my clothing to defray our expenses.

Our heads were full of schemes, and we journeyed on until night overtook us. We then went into a farmhouse to test our plan. The people soon began to ask us questions, and John as readily answered them. He gave them a great account of our having been captured by the enemy, and so straight that they believed the whole of it. After supper we went to bed, and in the morning they gave us a good breakfast, and some bread and cheese, and we went on our way satisfied with our exploits. John now studied to make his story appear as correct as possible. The people pitied us, and sometimes we had a few shillings put in our hands.[68] We did not suffer for the want of food.

At Hartford we stayed some time, and we here agreed to work our passage down to New York on board of a brig, but learning that the British fleet was on the coast, the captain declined going.[69] We then set out to reach New York by land. We thought it a good way to walk. We went by way of New Haven, expecting to reach the city from that place by water. Again we were disappointed. We fell in company with some sailors who had been exchanged, and we listened to their story.[70] It was an affecting one, and John concluded to incorporate a part of it with his own. So shortly afterward he told some people that while we were prisoners we had to eat bread mixed with pounded glass. The people were foolish enough to believe us. At Kingsbridge an old lady gave us several articles of clothing.[71] Here we agreed with the captain of a vessel to work our way to New York. When we got under way, John undertook to relate our sufferings to the crew. They appeared to believe it all until he came to the incredible story of the "glass bread." This convinced the captain that all he said was false. He told us that he knew that we were runaways, and pressed us to tell him but we declined. At length he told us that we were very near to Hell Gate (Hurl Gate); that when we reached it the devil would come on board in a stone canoe with an iron paddle, and make a terrible noise, and that he intended to give us to him.[72] I thought all he said was so. I therefore confessed that we were runaways [and] where and with whom we had lived. He said he would take me back to New London, as my master was rich and would pay him a good price. Here the devil prompted me to tell a lie, and I replied that the general had advertised me [for a] one-cent reward.[73] He then said that he would do nothing with me further than to keep my clothes until we paid him.[74] When the vessel reached the dock, John slipped off, and I was not slow to follow.

In a few days we got money to redeem our clothing. We took board in Cherry Street at two dollars per week. We soon obtained work and received sixty-two-and-a-half cents per day. While this continued, we had no difficulty in paying our board. My mind now became tolerably calm, but in the midst of this I was greatly alarmed as I was informed that my master had offered fifteen dollars reward for me and that the captain of one of the packets was looking for me.[75] I dared not go back and therefore determined to go to Philadelphia. To this John objected and advised me to go to sea but I could find no vessel. He entered on board a privateer and I was thus left entirely alone in a strange city.[76]

Wandering about, I fell in company with a sergeant and a file of men who were enlisting soldiers for the United States Army. They thought I would answer their purpose; but how to get me was the thing. Now they began to talk to me, then treated me to some spirits, and when that began to operate, they told me all about the war and what a fine thing it was to be a soldier. I was pleased with the idea of being a soldier, took some more liquor and some money, had a cockade fastened to my hat, and was off in high spirits for my uniform. Now my enlistment was against the law but I did not know it. I could not think why I should risk my life and limbs in fighting for the white man who had cheated my forefathers out of their land. By this time I had acquired many bad practices.[77]

I was sent over to Governors Island opposite the city and here I remained some time.[78] Too much liquor was dealt out to the soldiers, who got drunk very often. Indeed, the island was like a hell upon earth in consequence of the wickedness of the soldiers. I have known sober men to enlist who afterward became confirmed drunkards and appeared like fools upon the earth. So it was among the soldiers, and what should a child do who was entangled in their net? Now, although I made no profession of religion, yet I could not bear to hear sacred things spoken of lightly or the sacred name of God blasphemed, and I often spoke to the soldiers about it, and in general they listened attentively to what I had to say. I did not tell them that I had ever made a profession of religion. In a little time I became almost as bad as any of them [and] could drink rum, play cards, and act as wickedly as any. I was at times tormented with the thoughts of death, but God had mercy on me and spared my life, and for this I feel thankful to the present day. Some people are of [the] opinion that if a person is once born of the Spirit of God he can never fall away entirely, and because I acted thus, they may pretend to say that I had not been converted to the faith. I believe firmly that, if ever Paul was born again, I was; if not, from whence did I derive all the light and happiness I had heretofore experienced? To be sure it was not to be compared to Paul's but the change I felt in my very soul.[79] I felt anxious to obtain forgiveness from every person I had injured in any manner whatever. Sometimes I thought I would write to my old friends and request forgiveness—then I thought I had done right. I could not bear to hear any order of Christians ridiculed, especially the Methodists; it grieved me to the heart.

3. Campaigning on the Canadian Border, 1813–15

The material below, comprising chapter 5 of the autobiography, continues the story of William Apess's military service, from his training on Governors Island off New York through to the return of peace in 1815, and includes descriptions of the grim experiences of common soldiers on campaign and in action on the border between New York and Lower Canada.

In 1813, the Americans launched their largest offensive of the war, a two-pronged campaign against Montreal, although they did so with incompetent generals and limited optimism. If they captured that important port and commercial center at the confluence of the Ottawa and St. Lawrence Rivers, however, they could sever Upper Canada's lifeline to the rest of the British Empire and cripple the defensive efforts of the military authorities in that province. Apess participated in one of the thrusts, which ended in a humiliating defeat for the United States on the Châteauguay River south of Montreal near the international border. (The other half of the campaign also saw the British achieve victory when, outnumbered three thousand to twelve hundred, they beat the Americans on the banks of the St. Lawrence at Crysler's Farm.) In 1814 Apess took part in another move north against Canadian territory, but it too came to a failed end at Lacolle Mill. Later that year, after Britain won the war against Napoleon and dispatched reinforcements from Europe to North America, a British army marched south against Plattsburgh to secure Lower Canada's vulnerable underbelly. William Apess again saw action, but this time as a defender rather than an invader, in a land battle that the British withdrew from early in its course after the Americans emerged triumphant in a naval encounter on the waters of Lake Champlain beside Plattsburgh. Apess left the army after the return of peace, although it is unclear whether he deserted or was discharged.

[1813]

It appeared that I had been enlisted for a musician, as I was instructed while on the island in beating a drum.[80] In this I took much delight.

While on the island I witnessed the execution of a soldier who was shot according to the decision of a court-martial. Two men had been condemned for mutiny or desertion. It is impossible for me to describe the feelings of my heart when I saw the soldiers parade, and the condemned, clothed in white with Bibles in their hands, come forward. The band then struck up the *Dead March*, and the procession moved with a mournful and measured tread to the place of execution, where the poor creatures were compelled to kneel on the coffins, which were alongside two newly dug graves. While in this position the chaplain went forward and conversed with them. After he had retired, a soldier went up and drew the caps over their faces. Thus blindfolded, he led one of them some distance from the other. An officer then advanced and raised his handkerchief as a signal to the platoon to prepare to fire. He then made another for them to aim at the wretch, who had been left kneeling on his coffin, and at a third signal, the platoon fired, and the immortal essence of the offender in an instant was up in the spirit land. To me this was an awful day. My heart seemed to leap into my throat. Death never appeared so awful; but what must have been the feelings of the unhappy man who had so narrowly escaped the grave? He was completely overcome and wept like a child, and it was found necessary to help him back to his quarters. This spectacle made me serious, but it wore off in a few days.

Soon after this we were ordered to Staten Island, where we remained about two months.[81] Then we were ordered to join the army destined to conquer Canada. As the soldiers were tired of the island, this news animated them very much. They thought it a great thing to march through the country and assist in taking the enemy's land. As soon as our things were ready we embarked on board a sloop for Albany and then went on to Greenbush, where we were quartered.[82] In the meantime I had been transferred to the ranks. This I did not like: to carry a musket was too fatiguing and I had a positive objection to being placed on the guard, especially at night.[83] As I had only enlisted for a drummer, I thought this change by the officer was contrary to law, and as the bond was broken, liberty was granted me. Therefore, being heartily tired of a soldier's life, and having a desire to see my father once more, I went off very deliberately. I had no idea that they had a lawful claim on me and was greatly surprised as well as alarmed when arrested as a deserter from the army.[84] Well, I was taken up and carried back to the camp where the officers put me under guard. We shortly after marched for Canada, and during this dreary march the officers tormented me by telling me that it was their intention to make a fire in the woods, stick my skin full of pine splinters, and after having an Indian powwow over me, burn me to death. Thus they tormented me day after day.[85]

We halted for some time at Burlington but resumed our march and went into winter quarters at Plattsburgh. All this time God was very good to me as I had not a sick day. I had by this time become very bad. I had previously learned to drink rum, play cards, and commit other acts of wickedness, but it was here that I first took the name of the Lord in vain, and oh, what a sting it left behind. We continued here until the ensuing fall, when we received orders to join the main army under General Hampton.[86] Another change now took place. We had several pieces of heavy artillery with us, and of course horses were necessary to drag them, and I was taken from the ranks and ordered to take charge of one team. This made my situation rather better. I now had the privilege of riding. The soldiers were badly off as the officers were very cruel to them, and for every little offense they would have them flogged. One day the officer of our company got angry at me and pricked my ear with the point of his sword.

We soon joined the main army and pitched our tents with them. It was now very cold, and we had nothing but straw to lie on. There was also a scarcity of provisions and we were not allowed to draw our full rations.[87] Money would not procure food, and when anything was to be obtained the officers had always the preference, and they, poor souls, always wanted the whole for themselves. The people generally have no idea of the extreme sufferings of the soldiers on the frontiers during the last war. They were indescribable: the soldiers ate, with the utmost greediness, raw corn and everything edible that fell in their way. In the midst of our afflictions, our valiant general ordered us to march forward to subdue the country in a trice.[88] The pioneers had great difficulty in clearing the way.[89] The enemy retreated, burning everything as they fled. They destroyed everything, so that we could not find forage for the horses. We were now cutting our way through a wilderness, and were very often benumbed with the cold. Our sufferings now for the want of food were extreme. The officers too began to feel it and one of them offered me two dollars for a little flour, but I did not take this money and he did not get my flour. I would not have given it to *him* for fifty dollars.[90] The soldiers united their flour and baked unleavened bread; of this we made a *delicious* repast.

After we had proceeded about thirty miles, we fell in with a body of Canadians and Indians—the woods fairly resounded with their yells. Our "brave and chival- rous" general ordered a picked troop to disperse them. We fired but one cannon, and a retreat was sounded to the great mortification of the soldiers who were ready and willing to fight; but as our general did not fancy the smell of gunpow- der, he thought it best to close the campaign by retreating with seven thousand men before a "host" of several hundred. Thus were many a poor fellow's hopes of conquest and glory blasted by the timidity of one man. This little brush with an enemy that we could have crushed in a single moment cost us several men in killed and wounded. The army now fell back on Plattsburgh, where we remained during the winter.[91]

[1813–14]

We suffered greatly for the want of barracks, having to encamp in the open fields a good part of the time. My health, through the goodness of God, was preserved notwithstanding many of the poor soldiers sickened and died. So fast did they go off that it appeared to me as if the plague was raging among them.[92]

[1814]

When the spring opened, we were employed in building forts. We erected three in a very short time.[93] We soon received orders to march and joined the army under General Wilkinson to reduce Montreal. We marched to Odelltown in great splendor, "heads up and eyes right," with a noble commander at our head and the splendid city of Montreal in our view.[94] The city, no doubt, presented a scene of the wildest uproar and confusion; the people were greatly alarmed as we moved on with all the pomp and glory of an army flushed with many victories; but when we reached Odelltown, John Bull met us with a picked troop.[95] They soon retreated, and some took refuge in an old fortified mill, which we pelted with a goodly number of cannonballs. It appeared as if we were determined to sweep everything before us. It was really amusing to see our feminine general, with his nightcap on his head and a dishcloth tied round his precious body, crying out to his men, "Come on, my brave boys, we will give John Bull a bloody nose."[96] We did not succeed in taking the mill, and the British kept up an incessant cannon-ade from the fort. Some of the balls cut down the trees so that we had frequently to spring out of their way when falling.[97] I thought it was a hard time, and I had reason too, as I was in the front of the battle assisting in working a twelve-pounder, and the British aimed directly at us.[98] Their balls whistled around us and hurried a good many of the soldiers into the eternal world, while others were most horribly mangled. Indeed, they were so hot upon us that we had not time to remove the dead as they fell. The horribly disfigured bodies of the dead, the pierc-ing groans of the wounded and the dying, [and] the cries for help and succor from those who could not help themselves were most appalling. I can never forget it.[99] We continued fighting till near sundown when a retreat was sounded along our line; and instead of marching forward to Montreal, we wheeled about, and having once set our faces toward Plattsburgh and turned our backs ingloriously on the enemy, we hurried off with all possible speed. We carried our dead and wounded with us. Oh, it was a dreadful sight to behold so many brave men sacrificed in this manner. In this way our campaign closed. During the whole of this time the Lord was merciful to me, as I was not suffered to be hurt.[100]

We once more reached Plattsburgh and pitched our tents in the neighborhood. While here, intelligence of the capture of Washington was received. Now, says the orderly sergeant, the British have burnt up all the papers at Washington (and our enlistment of the war among them) we had better give in our names as having enlisted for five years.[101]

We were again under marching orders as the enemy, it was thought, contemplated an attack on Plattsburgh. Thither we moved without delay and were posted in one of the forts. By the time we were ready for them, the enemy made his appearance on Lake Champlain with his vessels of war. It was a fine thing to see their noble vessels moving like things of life upon this mimic sea, with their streamers floating in the wind. This armament was intended to cooperate with the army, which numbered fourteen thousand men, under the command of the captain-general of Canada, and at that very time in view of our troops.[102] They presented a very imposing aspect. Their red uniforms and the instruments of death, which they bore in their hands, glittered in the sunbeams of heaven like so many sparkling diamonds. Very fortunately for us and for the country, a brave and noble commander was placed at the head of the [American] army. It was not an easy task to frighten him. For notwithstanding his men were inferior in point of number to those of the enemy, say as one to seven, yet relying on the bravery of his men, he determined to fight to the last extremity.[103]

The enemy, in all the pomp and pride of war, had sat down before the town and its slender fortifications and commenced a cannonade, which we returned without much ceremony. Congreve rockets, bombshells, and cannonballs poured upon us like a hailstorm.[104] There was scarcely any intermission, and for six days and nights we did not leave our guns, and during that time the work of death paused not, as every day some shot took effect. During the engagement, I had charge of a small magazine.[105] All this time our fleet, under the command of the gallant Macdonough, was lying on the peaceful waters of Champlain.[106] But this little fleet was to be taken or destroyed: it was necessary in the accomplishment of their plans. Accordingly the British commander bore down on our vessels in gallant style. As soon as the enemy showed fight, our men flew to their guns. Then the work of death and carnage commenced. The adjacent shores resounded with the alternate shouts of the sons of liberty and the groans of their parting spirits. A cloud of smoke mantled the heavens, shutting out the light of day, while the continual roar of artillery added to the sublime horrors of the scene. At length, the boasted valor of the haughty Britons failed them. They quailed before the incessant and well-directed fire of our brave and hardy tars and, after a hard-fought battle, surrendered to that foe they had been sent to crush. On land the battle raged pretty fiercely. On our side the Green Mountain Boys behaved with the greatest bravery.[107] As soon as the British commander had seen the fleet fall into the hands of the Americans, his boasted courage forsook him, and he ordered his army of heroes, fourteen thousand strong, to retreat before a handful of militia.[108] This was indeed a proud day for our country. We had met a superior force on the lake, and "they were ours."[109] On land, we had compelled the enemy to seek safety in flight. Our army did not lose many men, but on the lake many a brave man fell—fell in the defense of his country's rights.[110] The British moved off about sundown.

[1815]

We remained in Plattsburgh until the peace.[111] As soon as it was known that the war had terminated and the army disbanded, the soldiers were clamorous for their discharge, but it was concluded to retain our company in the service. I, however, obtained my release. Now, according to the act of enlistment, I was entitled to forty dollars bounty money and 160 acres of land. The government also owed me for fifteen months' pay. I have not seen anything of the bounty money, land, or arrearages from that day to this.[112] I am not, however, alone in this: hundreds were served in the same manner; but I could never think that the government acted right toward the *natives*, not merely in refusing to pay us but in claiming our services in case of perilous emergency, and still deny us the right of citizenship. And as long as our nation is debarred the privilege of voting for civil officers, I shall believe that the government has no claim on our services.[113]

4. A Wandering Life, 1815–16

The contents from chapter 6 of A Son of the Forest *cover a period of drifting and dissipation, when the teenaged William Apess left the United States for Montreal, possibly to avoid being punished for deserting the American army, as his military records claim he did. Like many veterans, Apess carried the bad habits learned in uniform into civilian life and found it impossible to settle down. He roamed from one job to another in Upper and Lower Canada through 1815 and 1816 where he met native peoples in the two British colonies, whose presence contributed to his ongoing reflections on the subjugation*

*experienced by indigenous populations and the imperatives of Christian equality and
justice to oppose that oppression.*

[1815–16]

No doubt there are many good people in the United States who would not tram-
ple upon the rights of the poor; but there are many others who are willing to roll
in their coaches upon the tears and blood of the poor and unoffending natives
[and] those who are ready at all times to speculate on the Indians and defraud
them out of their rightful possessions. Let the poor Indian attempt to resist the
encroachments of his white neighbors, what a hue and cry is instantly raised
against him. It has been considered as a trifling thing for the whites to make war
on the Indians for the purpose of driving them from their country and taking possession thereof. This was, in their estimation, all right, as it helped to extend the
territory and enriched some individuals. But let the thing be changed. Suppose
an overwhelming army should march into the United States for the purpose of
subduing it and enslaving the citizens: how quick would they fly to arms, gather
in multitudes around the tree of liberty, and contend for their rights with the last
drop of their blood. And should the enemy succeed, would they not eventually
rise and endeavor to regain [their] liberty? And who would blame them for it?

When I left the army, I had not a shilling in my pocket. I depended upon the
precarious bounty of the inhabitants until I reached the place where some of my
brethren dwelt.[114] I tarried with them but a short time and then set off for Montreal. I was anxious in some degree to become steady and went to learn the business of a baker. My bad habits now overcame my good intentions. I was addicted
to drinking rum and would sometimes get quite intoxicated. As it was my place
to carry out the bread, I frequently fell in company, and one day, being in liquor, I
met one of the king's soldiers, and after abusing him with my tongue, I gave him
a sound flogging. In the course of the affair I broke a pitcher which the soldier
had; and as I had to pay for it, I was wicked enough to take my master's money
without his knowledge for that purpose. My master liked me, but he thought if I
acted so once I would a second time, and he very properly discharged me. I was
now placed in a bad situation; by my misconduct I had lost a good home!

I went and hired myself to a farmer for four dollars per month. After serving him two months, he paid me, and with the money I bought some decent
clothes.[115] By spells, I was hired as a servant, but this kind of life did not suit me
and I wished to return to my brethren. My mind changed, and I went up the
St. Lawrence to Kingston, where I obtained a situation on board of a sloop in the

capacity of a cook at twelve dollars per month. I was on board the vessel some time, and when we settled the captain cheated me out of twelve dollars. My next move was in the country. I agreed to serve a merchant faithfully, and he promised to give me twelve dollars a month. Everything went on smooth for a season. At last I became negligent and careless, in consequence of his giving me a pint of rum every day, which was the allowance he made for each person in his employment.[116] While at this place, I attended a Methodist meeting. At the time I felt very much affected, as it brought up before my mind the great and indescribable enjoyments I had found in the house of prayer when I was endeavoring to serve the Lord. It soon wore off, and I soon relapsed into my former bad habits.

I now went again into the country and stayed with a farmer for one month. He paid me five dollars. Then I shifted my quarters to another place and agreed with a Dutch farmer to stay with him all winter at five dollars a month. With this situation I was much pleased. My work was light—I had very little to do except procuring firewood. I often went with them on hunting excursions; besides, my brethren were all around me, and it therefore seemed like home. I was now in the Bay of Quinte.[117] The scenery was diversified. There were also some natural curiosities. On the very top of a high mountain in the neighborhood there was a large pond of water, to which there was no visible outlet. This pond was unfathomable. It was very surprising to me that so great a body of water should be found so far above the common level of the earth.[118] There was also in the neighborhood a rock that had the appearance of being hollowed out by the hand of a skillful artificer. Through this rock wound a narrow stream of water. It had a most beautiful and romantic appearance, and I could not but admire the wisdom of God in the order, regularity, and beauty of creation.[119] I then turned my eyes to the forest, and it seemed alive with its sons and daughters. There appeared to be the utmost order and regularity in their encampment.

Oh, what a pity that this state of things should change. How much better would it be if the whites would act like a civilized people, and instead of giving my brethren of the woods *rum* in exchange for their furs, give them food and clothing for themselves and [their] children. If this course were pursued, I believe that God would bless both the whites and natives threefold. I am bold to aver that the minds of the natives were turned against the Gospel and soured toward the whites because *some* of the missionaries have joined the unholy brethren in speculations to the advantage of themselves, regardless of the rights, feelings, and interests of the untutored sons of the forest. If a good missionary goes among them, and preaches the pure doctrines of the Gospel, he must necessarily tell them that they must "love God and their neighbor as themselves" [and] "to love men, deal justly, and walk humbly."[120] They would naturally reply, "Your doctrine is very good, but the whole course of your conduct is decidedly at variance with your profession; we think the whites need fully as much religious instruction as we do." In this way many a good man's path is hedged up and he is prevented from being useful among the natives in consequence of the bad conduct of those who are, properly speaking, only "wolves in sheep's clothing."[121] However, the natives are on the whole willing to receive the Gospel, and of late, through the instrumentality of *pious missionaries*, much good has been done. Many of them have been reclaimed from the most abandoned and degrading practices, and brought to a knowledge of the truth as it is in Jesus!

After the end of this chapter, William Apess continued his autobiography with both a defense of native interests against white prejudices and the story of his return to the United States, where he gradually reformed his behavior and went on to pursue his career as a Methodist missionary.

5. Another Version of William Apess's Autobiography, c. 1813–c. 1820

William Apess and his wife, Mary Wood, wrote The Experiences of Five Christian Indians of the Pequod Tribe *(Boston, 1833; second edition, 1837). An autobiographical section of that pamphlet tells the story of William's life in a shorter version than the one above from* A Son of the Forest. *The excerpt below begins with the religious persecution he experienced in the household of William Williams, includes an affirmation of the solidarity of people of color in the face of white intolerance, and then covers the period of his life from the point he ran away until his return to Methodism after his wartime service and sojourn in Canada. Thus, it extends somewhat further chronologically than the excerpt from the memoirs presented above but possesses the virtue of covering the important story of his postwar return to the church and the beginnings of his own work in it more concisely than the other book does.*

The text below is from the first edition of Experiences of Five Christian Indians *in the collection of the Library of Congress (and available online) between pages 17 and 20 of the sixty-page pamphlet.*

I can say I had none to make me the object of their care [or] to encourage me to press forward in the ways of well doing; but, on the other hand, persecution raged most bitterly, and soon I was deprived of that privilege that was near and dear to me, such as the privilege of class meetings and other means of grace that are usually among the Methodists; and being young, I was again led astray. How hard it is to be robbed of all our earthly rights and deprived of the means of grace merely because the skin is of a different color. Such has been the case with me. I would ask the white man if he thinks that he can be justified in making just such a being as I am or any other person in the world unhappy; and although the white man finds so much fault because God has made us thus, yet if I have any vanity about it, I choose to remain as I am, and praise my Maker while I live, that an Indian he has made.

But again, the burden that was heaped upon me at this time was more than I could bear, being only about fifteen years old, and I now began to relapse back again into my former state.[122] I now became acquainted with wicked and silly youths, and one of them, whose name was Miner, and myself, agreed to try some other parts of the world. Children as we were, we made the best arrangements for our journey that we could; and so off we started, and steered our course for New York. With difficulties and fears, we arrived there. Many of the people thought that we were sailor boys as we informed them that we had been privateering, and had been taken [prisoner] and set on shore near New London, and were going home to New York to our parents; and it being wartime, we informed the people all we knew about it. When we had arrived at New York City, and almost alone in the world, and but little economy to take care of ourselves, we thought best to engage in the war.[123] So I became a musician in the army, while my comrade went on board a privateer.

We now parted, and I went with the soldiers to Canada, where I experienced all the horrors of war, fought in the great Battle of Lake Champlain with General Macomb, with Hampton, and [with] Wilkinson at the Mills.[124] After the war was over, I went to Montreal and from thence to Upper Canada [and] Fort Niagara, from thence to Kingston and through the wilderness, and saw many of my brethren who ornamented the wood with their camps and [en]chanted the wild beasts of prey with their songs.[125] Being now satisfied with these regions and their curiosities, I now began to think of home, and those kindred friends who had long before buried me beneath the sods of the forest, to behold my face no more forever here, being gone so long, nearly five years.[126]

This journey was not instructing to the paths of virtue but of vice. Though I did not forget the past and often recollected those happy moments and sighed on account of my condition, but [I] had no heart to pray, no pious parents to instruct me, no minister of God's holy word to notice me and pour into my ear the blessed truths of God, but [was] a poor, destitute, helpless child of the forest, all alone in the world, as it were. I now made the best of my way home to my kindred in the flesh, and when I arrived there, I found them surprised and rejoiced to see me on this side of the grave. After a while I became more steady and began once more to attend the worship of God, and had a desire to return from my backsliding state to the worship of God that I might enjoy his smiles again. For it was now that I had become wretched and miserable through the deceitfulness of sin and bad examples of the white soldiers, and nothing but thick darkness gathered around me; and, apparently, my situation was worse than before. It was now harder to seek the Lord than it was when I was young, for now my sins were redoubled, and it appeared indeed that there was no mercy for me. And when I went to pray and call upon God for mercy, I was met by the enemy of souls who very readily thrusted a dart at me filled with a message of despair: that there was nothing but eternal death for me, that I had committed the unpardonable sin by having sinned against the Holy Ghost, and it was all in vain for me to try again for help in God—that he was sure that I should make up his host in hell.

My distress became more acute than ever, but I attended the meetings where God's children meet and at last I made known my distress to them; and they, the dear children of God, comforted me by saying that Christ would have mercy upon the worst of sinners, and encouraged me to pray, and then prayed with and for me. I sought the Lord for weeks and months, and at last began to see that I had received some of his divine approbation. To say that I immediately had as clear an evidence as I had before, I cannot; but when I acknowledged myself a sinner before the people and confessed what a sinner I had been, then the light of God's countenance broke into my soul, and I felt as if I were on the wings of angels and ready to leave this world. I united with the Methodists, and was baptized by immersion, and strove to walk with them in the way of heaven; and can say that I spent many happy hours with them in the worship of God, and to this day, I most heartily rejoice that I was brought again from the dead to praise God.

After a while I began to exercise my gift in the way of prayer and exhortation, and was blessed in so doing. I began to be exercised more abundantly about the salvation of precious souls, and began to have a desire to call sinners to repentance in a public way, and it appeared I could not rest in any other way; but I knew that I was weak and ignorant as to the letter; and not only so, I was already a hissing-stock and a byword in the world, merely because I was a child of the forest; and to add any more occasion to the weak and scornful family of the whites was more than I wished to do, but there was no peace for me, either by day or night.[127] Go I must, and expose my ignorance to the world, and strive to preach, or exhort sinners to repentance.

Epilogue

In the preface, I mentioned two native combatants from Canada who wrote extended autobiographical texts about their participation in the War of 1812 but who are not explored in this book because of its focus on American-resident indigenous veterans. One is an unusually trustworthy witness, Mohawk chief John Norton, who I study in another work. The other is Mohawk warrior Eleazer Williams, but I will not examine his wartime service in detail because his memoir is so unreliable that I would not be able to deploy my particular historian's skills effectively in making sense of the document (although another scholar with different talents could uncover its meanings for us). Perceptive readers of the annotations that accompany the autobiographies of Black Hawk and William Apess will note that both men sometimes shifted the telling of their stories from how the events they describe unfolded and even misled their audiences on occasion. While I believe they are less candid than John Norton, they are far more reliable than Eleazer Williams and without doubt deserve careful study as overwhelmingly dependable and significant witnesses to the aboriginal world during the period of the War of 1812 (and beyond when reading their texts in their entirety).

On one level, the problems in their autobiographies are typical of the limitations of personal memory and the frailty of the human condition. While it might be tempting to devalue the memoirs produced by Black Hawk and William Apess because we have identified these challenges, such a response logically would condemn us to reject most extensive personal documents from the past because of the imperfections that pervade them, especially those that have arguments to make, as do the autobiographies presented in this book. In contrast, a mature reading of their words allows us to identify weaknesses, contextualize them, and use them to deepen our understanding of the authors' concerns with more discernment than if we either did not recognize the dissembling or let it cause us to discard their texts more or less entirely. Acknowledging the ambiguities in their documents ought not blind us to the tremendous value these memoirs possess, especially as there are so few direct and detailed First Nations voices from the early nineteenth century in existence. In fact, the challenges in their autobiographies actually can improve our appreciation of these men's lives, such as by allowing us to identify contexts where the authors thought they had made mistakes or felt uncomfortable with their behavior and thus tried to obscure their stories. On another level, each autobiography, to a large extent, is a production similar to a diplomatic document, in which a representative of one society speaks to an audience in another in order to advance a cause. The authors of such communications typically structure them to make the best arguments possible, even when their case is as strong as the cry for fundamental justice for native populations which forms the central concern of both narratives. This is a significant point because it reminds us that, despite the articulation of their voices through the comforts of the familiar Euro-American medium of printed text, Black Hawk and William Apess were non-Western authors who saw the white realm as alien and hostile, wanted the dominant society to recognize the wrongs inflicted on aboriginal peoples, and hoped it would respond through positive actions rather than treat their autobiographies merely as interesting diversions into the life of foreign cultures.

The preface also noted that the memoirs of Black Hawk and William Apess as a whole are very different from each other, even within the sections of their autobiographies presented in these pages, which study the narrow time frame of the War of 1812 and the years immediately surrounding the conflict. The dissimilarities underscore the diversities of native North America in contrast to the tendency of Euro-Americans to homogenize First Nations experiences. At a personal level, for instance, they held divergent religious views: Black Hawk followed the quietly expressed traditional beliefs of the Sauks in contemplating his place within creation while articulating criticism of the defects of Christians he met; William Apess embraced a demonstrative evangelical version of the newcomer's faith, but one in which the Gospel demand for liberation for all peoples gave him strength and inspired visions of a better future. Beyond religious differences, their personal characteristics, their standing within their communities, the social contexts in which they came to maturity, and the pressures placed on them by white society were profoundly dissimilar. Owing mainly to these men's geographical origins, those pressures defined two fundamental realities for First Nations in the nineteenth century as they came to bear the growing burdens placed on them by Euro-Americans, either in the years preceding the loss of much of their independence or in the bleakness of indigenous life that typically followed. Like the majority of natives on the continent in the late eighteenth century, Black Hawk lived beyond the western reaches of white settlement, but gradually, as began to occur in the 1804 treaty that haunts his memoir, newcomers increasingly threatened the Sauks and their way of life. Like some aboriginal people, he fought back through long-established methods of warfare and, as we saw, successfully defended Sauk lands along the upper Mississippi River during the War of 1812 against American forces. Yet, in the end, these victories only slowed the expansion in the United States and the imposition of the Republic's domination over the tribe. The sheer weight of numbers generated by a rapidly growing settler population as it spread uncontrollably westward, combined with new technologies, shifting cultural values, and bureaucratic expansion, generated a sort of inevitability that would see the Sauks—like many First Nations—displaced and forced onto reservations with far fewer options and opportunities than they had enjoyed during their earlier years. At the same time, the benefits of modernization in the 1800s offset only a fraction of the traumas caused by this process for most native peoples. At a personal level, Black Hawk witnessed those immense transformations between his birth in the 1760s and his passing in the 1830s, and then his earthly body suffered indignities associated with the common white belief that aboriginal people were a disappearing race when someone stole his corpse and reduced it to that of a curiosity in a small museum. In contrast to Black Hawk, William Apess grew up in a native community that had lost most of its tribal freedoms long before his birth in 1798 due to the geographical location of the Pequots on the Atlantic Seaboard. There, permanent Euro-American settlement had begun early in the seventeenth century, and his ancestors had been forced onto reservations beyond living memory at the time he came into the world owing to the conflicts associated with white expansion. Like many indigenous peoples who lived on reservations and in surrounding white communities once their independence and economy had been shattered, poverty and its associated miseries marked his life as a Pequot. We see this, for instance, in the alcohol abuse that turned his earliest years into a desperate horror and in the control over his life exercised by outsiders, some of whom, in the Furman family, seem to have been kindly despite their racist views, but most of whom oppressed him. Yet Apess struggled against these challenges, sought fulfillment through marriage and a career proclaiming his faith and promoting native rights, and enjoyed some success at Mashpee and in the public realm in the 1830s. In the end, however, like many talented individuals afflicted by impoverishment, its accompanying curses, and the constant hostility of prejudiced people, the strains upon him proved to be too much, and his life came to an early and miserable end.

Despite the agendas of Euro-Americans and their governments to make First Nations disappear through assimilation, or the common nineteenth-century view that the native world was doomed to extinction, aboriginal people—including the Pequots and Sauks—survived through the decades and still form a vibrant part of the North American mosaic. In fact, the indigenous population has gone through a tremendous resurgence in recent decades. Furthermore, aboriginal people retained their cultural identities in opposition to external pressures as their communities continually adjusted to evolving challenges and opportunities despite the disadvantages they faced, and still face, as a result of the baleful legacies of the contact experience over the past five hundred years. Much of their survival today and their success in the future as distinct societies rests upon efforts by aboriginal people to demand their rights and otherwise work to protect their communities, and a portion of those endeavors occur when natives speak out in defense of their world. Within the continuum of that broad venture through the centuries, Black Hawk and William Apess present eloquent and persuasive voices that demand respect for First Nations' societies, aspirations, dignity, and justice.

Notes

PREFACE

1. Apess, *On Our Own Ground*, ed. O'Connell; Black Hawk, *Black Hawk: An Autobiography*, ed. Jackson.

2. E.g., Ashwill, "Savagism and Its Discontents," 217.

CHRONOLOGICAL OVERVIEW

1. These guides to the level of native participation are based on the figures I believe are the most reliable after examining the battles from a range of sources. This summary of the war derives from my understanding of the conflict after studying it for several decades, with a particular focus on native history, but important books consulted for this particular survey were Stagg, *Mr. Madison's War* (perhaps the best single-volume study of the conflict); Hickey, *War of 1812*; Hickey, *Don't Give up the Ship!*; Hitsman, *Incredible War of 1812* (revised by Graves); Lambert, *Challenge*; and Arthur, *How Britain Won the War of 1812*. Two short histories of the war are Benn, *War of 1812*, and Stagg, *War of 1812*, while Hickey's *Don't Give up the Ship!*, 323–46, presents a more extensive chronology than outlined here. There is a large body of literature on native participation in the war and related themes and periods, but recommended studies include Allen, *His Majesty's Indian Allies*; Benn, *Iroquois in the War of 1812*; Calloway, *Crown and Calumet*; Dowd, *Spirited Resistance*; Horsman, *Expansion and American Indian Policy*; Sugden, *Tecumseh*; White, *Middle Ground*; and Willig, *Restoring the Chain of Friendship*. Excellent maps may be found in Tanner, *Atlas of Great Lakes Indian History*.

2. The Old Northwest conventionally included American territory north of the Ohio River between Pennsylvania and the Mississippi River which had been formed into the Northwest Territory in 1787. In 1800 the United States established a separate Indiana Territory out of most of the region, with the remnant Northwest Territory consisting only of land that would form most of the state of Ohio in 1803 (and which tends to be excluded from the concept of the Old Northwest by many historians of the War of 1812). A small portion of Indiana also became part of Ohio. Then in 1805 and 1809 the American government created the Michigan and Illinois territories and separated them from the remaining portions of Indiana. These political entities continued in existence until further changes occurred after the War of 1812. Farther west, much of the area of the Louisiana Purchase became the Louisiana Territory in 1805, but it was renamed the Missouri Territory in early

June 1812 to avoid confusion with the State of Louisiana, formed in April of that year. The Missouri Territory also continued in existence until the return of peace.

3. The Ohio Country conventionally comprised the upper Ohio River region, south of Lake Erie and west of the Appalachian Mountains.

4. Hagan, *Sac and Fox Indians*, 42.

5. Stagg, *Mr. Madison's War*, 3–47.

6. Thomas Jefferson to William Duane, August 4, 1812, Jefferson Papers, Library of Congress, http://memory.loc.gov/cgi-bin/query/r?ammem/mtj:@field(DOCID+@lit(tj110109)).

7. Benn, "Native Military Forces," 302–3.

8. As explored in the Black Hawk section of this book, his presence at the Battle of Moraviantown cannot be confirmed.

9. The commonly held date of September 3 for the evacuation is incorrect (Bennett, "New Perspective," part 3, 19–20; Ferguson, *Illinois in the War of 1812*, 281).

BLACK HAWK (SAUK)

1. The best annotated complete version of the memoirs is *Black Hawk: An Autobiography*, trans. Leclair; original ed. Patterson; modern ed. Jackson (henceforth *BHA*), but it does not explore the 1812–period memoirs in the detail that this book does and does not capture more recent scholarship, having been published in 1955. J. B. Patterson released a nearly identical version of the 1833 autobiography the next year and then issued a revised edition in 1882. The last is not used much because Patterson altered the text from the original. Some of his revisions were inconsequential and even helpful, such as adjusting punctuation and capitalization, as well as reducing the quantity of italicized text to make the book read better and conform to modern publishing conventions. Some, however, were problematic, such as changing words to improve the narrative. In a few cases, Patterson added information in 1882 that cannot be linked to Black Hawk (henceforth BH) with confidence; yet he also included appendices about BH's life after 1833 along with other information.

2. Ford, *History of Illinois*, 110n. J. B. Patterson refuted the accusation that the autobiography was a fraud, affirming its integrity, repeating the claims of authenticity printed in the original edition, and discussing his views of BH from his acquaintance with him. He also pointed out that Thomas Ford's putative hoaxer, fur trader and entrepreneur George Davenport, was an enemy of BH and a friend of his main Sauk rival, Keokuk, which proved the falsity of the governor's statement because Davenport would not have produced something as sympathetic as the *Life*. Most damning, Patterson said that Ford's comments demonstrated that he had not read the text (Patterson, "Black Hawk's Autobiography Vindicated," 1855, 300–304). A review of Davenport's papers in the Iowa State Historical Society for this book did not produce any documents to suggest a connection between Davenport and BH's memoirs.

3. Jackson, "Introduction," *BHA*, 25; Horr, *Sac, Fox, and Iowa Indians*, 3:132–33 et passim.

4. People noticed these problems with the text from an early time while affirming its overall authenticity, such as literary notices in the 1830s (e.g., Review of *Life of Black Hawk*, 69–70).

5. Examples of authors who use the autobiography as a primary text include A. Wallace,

"Prelude to Disaster"; Hagan, *Sac and Fox Indians*; Hallwas, "Black Hawk." Examples of scholars who came to believe it to be authentic after exploring the question are Jackson, "Introduction," *BHA*, 24–31; Nichols, *Black Hawk*, 160–61.

6. Generally, "Mesquakie" (or "Meskwaki") is preferred today instead of "Fox," but this book employs the latter to reduce confusion because BH's autobiography uses "Fox."

7. Thomas Forsyth to William Clark, December 23, 1812, Forsyth Papers; List of Indian Warriors, 1814, Strachan Papers (likely based on information from Robert Dickson). These figures seem correct because warriors tended to compose between one-fifth and one-quarter of the population of the First Nations of the Great Lakes and upper Mississippi River regions.

8. *BHA*, 47.

9. Nichols, *Black Hawk*, 13–14.

10. A. Wallace, "Prelude to Disaster," 264.

11. White, *Middle Ground*, 511–13.

12. Newquist, "Reading of Black Hawk's *Autobiography*," 183–84 et passim.

13. *BHA*, 101.

14. Ibid., 97.

15. Memorandum, June 4–7, 1831, M. Wallace, "Black Hawk's *An Autobiography*," 42; see also *BHA*, 111. A. Wallace, "Prelude to Disaster," 274–88, provides a summary of the Black Hawk War and the events leading up to it, while the body of literature on the period as a whole is reasonably extensive.

16. Scheckel, *Insistence of the Indian*, 110.

17. *BHA*, 147.

18. J. Snyder, "Burial of Black Hawk," 494–99; Trask, *Black Hawk*, 303–4.

19. *BHA*, 152.

20. Walker, *Indian Nation*, 67 et passim.

21. *BHA*, 152.

22. Ibid., 37.

23. LeClair, untitled certification, ibid., 35.

24. Ibid. For linguistic skills, see C. Snyder, "Antoine LeClaire," 85, 89.

25. Patterson, "Advertisement," *BHA*, 39.

26. LeClair, untitled certification, ibid., 35.

27. Jackson, "Introduction," ibid., 28.

28. Krupat, *For Those Who Came After*, 31.

29. See BH's speeches related to the War of 1812 in section 6 of BH's texts in this book.

30. J. B. Patterson to Lyman Draper, February 23, 1883; Schmitz, "Captive Utterance," 7–8.

31. Schmitz, "Captive Utterance," 2–5; T. Sweet, "Masculinity and Self-Performance," 462–65; Newquist, "Reading of Black Hawk's *Autobiography*," 171.

32. Walker, *Indian Nation*, 65–66.

33. This copy is available on microfiche via the Canadian Institute for Historic Microreproduction microfiche 27473 and electronically from Early Canadiana Online: www.canadiana.ca/en/eco through subscribing libraries, and freely through the Wisconsin Historical Society at www.wisconsinhistory.org/turningpoints/search.asp?id=248.

34. Aboriginal diplomats generally did not use the term "father" in a patriarchal Euro-American sense but understood the concept within the norms for a biological father in

native society, as someone who exercised little control over his children and who acted with generosity and kindness toward them and who protected their interests.

35. The visit took the form of a formal council, with the Sauks painting their bodies and dressing appropriately for the occasion, and with white officials distributing gifts as symbols of friendship and alliance.

36. American soldiers entered St. Louis in late February 1804; the formal transfer of the upper part of the Louisiana Purchase to the control of the United States occurred in March. Some Sauks at the time apparently showed their contempt for the new order by dragging an American flag, which had been presented to them, through the dirt from a horse's tail (Mackay Wherry to Amos Stoddard, September 15, 1804; Jung, "Toward the Black Hawk War," 29).

37. The "friends" probably were non-American whites, blacks, and people of mixed ancestry in St. Louis.

38. The insertion in square brackets is an intervention in the 1833 edition of the *Life*. Zebulon Pike met the Sauks while on a mission to find the headwaters of the Mississippi, search for locations for military and trading posts, and establish or improve diplomatic relations with the region's tribes. He became a brigadier general during the War of 1812.

39. Natives often preferred to engage in diplomatic relations with two white powers to play them off each other and thereby compel Euro-Americans to be sensitive toward aboriginal concerns lest they be driven into the other power's orbit. This behavior also forced whites to respond in other ways, such as through offering more presents when engaged in diplomatic initiatives and lowering prices in trade. The medals BH mentioned were accepted by aboriginal leaders from white authorities and worn around their necks as tokens of alliance and symbols of white obligations toward the tribes. Aside from their wariness about the Americans, the Sauks needed to be careful because British subjects on the upper Mississippi (often francophones from Canada) were both their primary trading partners and potential allies should Sauk-American relations collapse. In many cases, these people were integrated into native communities through marriage and other relationships, which further complicated diplomacy while creating important cross-cultural links.

40. When Zebulon Pike returned south in 1806, the Sauks expressed anger because his arrival looked like a reinforcement to another party of soldiers looking for Osage prisoners that the Sauks had taken, and thus represented a threatening intrusion into Sauk affairs. At the time, the natives interpreted the plumes in the soldiers' hats as signs that the Americans intended to engage in hostilities (Hagan, *Sac and Fox Indians*, 32–34).

41. The American government ordered medals in 1815 to replace the British medals, with the intention of giving them out at the peace negotiations that year, although it is unclear if all of those who gave up their medals to Zebulon Pike received replacements after the war (Prucha, *American Indian Treaties*, 133).

42. Zebulon Pike fell at the 1813 Battle of York (in modern Toronto).

43. Several Sauks killed three or more squatters north of St. Louis near the Cuivre River in 1804, before Zebulon Pike's journey to Saukenuk. The Sauks were worried about increasing white settlement and the evident friendliness Americans showed toward the tribe's Osage enemies at that moment. The Sauks apparently acted in opposition to the chiefs and perhaps in self-defense, although details are vague and unverifiable stories surround the event. After the incident, settlers prepared to retaliate, causing tribespeople living close to St. Louis to move away for their safety. The Sauks tried to ease tensions

by handing over one of the people involved (whose name is now lost to us but who volunteered to serve as a hostage), while attempting to negotiate a resolution of the crisis in response to demands that they turn in the men or face retribution, possibly from a combined white and Osage force. (See Jackson, note 25, *BHA*, 54; A. Wallace, "Prelude to Disaster," 261–63.)

44. Quashquame (or Jumping Fish) came from a village on the Mississippi River north of the Des Moines River at that time and was the leading chief on this mission. He usually tried to be accommodating to the Americans in order to protect native interests, which partly accounts for BH's generally negative assessments of him (Communication from William E. Whittaker of the University of Iowa, June 22, 2012). Pashepaho was a civil chief, also known as the Spear Fisher or the Stabber; Ouchequaka was referred to as the Sun Fish; and Hashequarhiqua as the Bear. Another, now-obscure person, Layauvois or Laiyuwa, accompanied them. At least one of these men came from the Fox nation. In native societies a killing normally had to be avenged by the victim's family or community unless the perpetrator's relations made restitution by giving presents and performing a condolence ceremony to "cover" the grave of the deceased.

45. The American father was William Henry Harrison, the prominent military officer, government official, and politician who had fought the native peoples in the 1790s, led efforts to alienate aboriginal territory, served as a major general during the War of 1812, and won the 1840 presidential election (but died within a month of taking office). At the time of the treaty, he was governor of both the Indiana and Louisiana Territories (the latter of which became the Missouri Territory in 1812). His attitude toward the acquisition of First Nations land was captured in his annual message to the Legislative Council and House of Representatives of Indiana Territory on November 12, 1810, in which he stated, "Is one of the fairest portions of the globe to remain in a state of nature, the haunt of a few wretched savages, when it seems destined by the Creator to give support to a large population, and to be the seat of civilization, of science, and true religion?" (Eustace, *1812*, 165–66).

46. The identity of the Jeffreon is uncertain, although it likely was the North River in modern Missouri.

47. Treaty negotiations occurred during the autumn of 1804, but the Americans kept the hostage in custody. He broke out of jail before May 5, 1805, and sentries shot at him as he ran away. At first, people assumed he had escaped; however, he had been hit in the neck and died of his wound. The Americans later discovered his body seven miles from St. Louis (Pierre Chouteau to William Henry Harrison, May 5, 8, and 10, 1805, Harrison Papers, 167, 168, 173). Earlier, President Thomas Jefferson had pardoned the prisoner on William Henry Harrison's recommendation as part of an attempt to demonstrate American benevolence toward the tribespeople, but word of that decision did not reach St. Louis in time to save the man. Some observers believed it would have been impossible to convict him in court because there were certain legal constraints on the government's ability to prosecute, as well as some doubts that native witnesses could give testimony because they were not Christians (James Bruff to James Wilkinson, November 5, 1804, Carter, *Territorial Papers*, 13:77).

48. Keeping native delegates intoxicated was a common tactic when negotiating land cessions. Research by Robert Owens of Wichita State University, however, indicates that Harrison tended not to rely on alcohol at that time, but may have achieved his objectives through intimidation, slanted translation, and other disreputable means. For his part, Quashquame may have blamed alcohol to excuse or mitigate his culpability for the treaty

disaster (Communication from Robert Owens, July 15, 2004). Nevertheless, while the aboriginal delegates intended to offer presents to restore harmony, they do not seem to have
been authorized by their people to sell territory and certainly had no power to sign away
large quantities of land, while Harrison had been ordered to seek a cession as part of an
aggressive plan of the administration of President Thomas Jefferson to acquire indigenous
territories. The Sauk delegates may have panicked into giving up land as payment to "cover
the graves" of the dead whites in order to avoid war, although the price was astoundingly
high. It seems more likely that the chiefs believed they only were acknowledging Washington's sovereignty rather than giving up ownership of their country, which they may
have thought would relieve tensions and perhaps give the tribe the same standing that
their Osage enemies had achieved with the newcomers and, in the process, improve Sauk
security and trade opportunities. A fundamental problem with the Treaty of 1804 was that
it did not comply with acceptable aboriginal protocols for land cessions. These included
the failure of the Americans to invite the natives to attend a treaty for the express purpose
of alienating territory, and hence the tribespeople's inability to obtain the views of the bulk
of the men and women of their communities on whether they wanted to sell and on what
terms they would do so. The lack of a large representation of people at the negotiations
also meant that the Americans could not legitimize the sale in native eyes by distributing
payments and presents to the Sauk and Fox populations at large. The territory lost comprised modern Illinois between the Illinois and Mississippi Rivers and lands in today's
Wisconsin, Iowa, and Missouri (including areas the Sauks and Foxes did not claim as their
own). For this huge tract, the aboriginal delegates received gifts and clothing purportedly
worth a little more than twenty-two hundred dollars while in St. Louis (although the dollar
amount seems grossly inflated in comparison to clothing and other gifts that this small
delegation could have obtained by any reasonable measure), and the Sauk and Fox nations
respectively were given annuities of six hundred and four hundred dollars. These modest
amounts contrasted with the estimated worth of the Sauk and Fox fur trade in St. Louis of
between forty and sixty thousand dollars per annum, a figure that did not include the trade
the tribes enjoyed to the north, the proceeds from their lead mines, or the value of their
territories in supporting their populations through farming, hunting, and other means,
all of which combine to underscore the profound unfairness of the treaty. (The treaty is
printed in *BHA*, 157–60, and in Kappler, *Indian Affairs*, 2:74–77; see also Jackson, note 28,
BHA, 54–56; Owens, *Mr. Jefferson's Hammer*, 86–92; and the important article A. Wallace,
"Prelude to Disaster," 247–88, which also reprints the treaty.)

49. "Council after council" suggests that the natives regarded the white presence with
anxiety. The Des Moines Rapids on the Mississippi were located just above the mouth of
the Des Moines River.

50. The army established Fort Bellevue on the Mississippi (today's Fort Madison, Iowa)
one hundred miles south of Saukenuk in the autumn of 1808 as a temporary post while
they constructed a permanent establishment, Fort Madison, beside it. Soldiers completed
the latter in 1809. The initiative was part of an effort to undermine British influence by
erecting rival and subsidized trading posts, asserting American authority among the aboriginal peoples, and suppressing the low-level hostilities then occurring both among the
tribes and between natives and whites.

51. The commanding officer was Lieutenant Alpha Kingsley of the 1st Regiment of
Infantry.

52. One observer noted that the pickets at Fort Bellevue were "so low that the Indians could with great ease *jump* over them," which was a problem because the natives had "become very insolent at that place" (William Clark to William Eustis, April 5, 1809, Carter, *Territorial Papers*, 14:260). The incident occurred at the temporary Fort Bellevue, on April 10, 1809, which did not have strong defenses, unlike the permanent Fort Madison, built of thick oak logs that stood twelve or thirteen feet tall, into which the Americans moved on April 14 (John Johnson to Clark, April 12, 1809, Private Collection; Alpha Kingsley to Henry Dearborn, April 19, 1809, Office of the Adjutant General Papers). The artillery piece possibly was a six-pounder ([Hunt?], "Personal Narrative," n.d. [post-1833], 665). This type of gun fired a six-pound iron round shot (or cannonball) that did not explode but smashed through its target, as well as other projectiles, such as grape and case shot, which were cloth and metal containers full of musket or other small balls that, when fired, sprayed out like enormous shotgun blasts and that were effective against enemy personnel. From a six-pounder, round shot could travel over a thousand yards, whereas grape and case were effective at less than three hundred.

53. These incidents from the spring of 1809 reflected aboriginal hostility toward American threats to their independence, expressed through both humor and an event that BH recorded as an almost spontaneous attempt to overwhelm the post but which the warriors aborted because of the precautions taken by the garrison. At the time, there were sixty soldiers in the fort, while the surrounding native force numbered in the hundreds. (At Michilimackinac at the head of Lake Michigan in 1763, Ojibwas and Sauks surprised the forty-man British garrison at the outbreak of Pontiac War's by using a lacrosse game as cover, causing the soldiers to let down their guard and permit the warriors inside the defenses, who then killed or captured the men of the garrison.) John Johnson recorded the events at Fort Bellevue and challenged BH's affirmation of spontaneity: "we have now in sight of the garrison across the river the whole nation of Sauks, who have been counseling and trading here for ten days. They declare themselves our friends, which we believe not to be the case altogether, and the only breach of that promise was two days past when the chiefs were in counsel . . . in the garrison. A dancing party came up and asked leave to dance around the garrison. One of the gates being opened near the guardhouse, they attempted to force in by a crowd. The guard put themselves in the position to charge bayonet, and was obliged to step a few paces back or run them through. The cannon was drawn up and charged, which put a stop to the dancing. They returned out of the garrison with a yell, raising the arm which held the weapon of defense." Johnson also noted that the Americans had heard news beforehand that the Sauks planned to take the post: "Mr. Garrod [Nicholas Jarrott?], who arrived here two days before this took place, informed us [that] the traders told him the plan of the Indians was to take the garrison and factory [trading post]; to come under the pretense of trading and counseling, et cetera, get possession by the use of the knife and tomahawk, which corroborated with their movements of that day" (Johnson to William Clark, April 12, 1809, Private Collection). Another, now-unidentified person (who may have been George Hunt) stated in a document composed some time after the Black Hawk War of 1832 that the plan to seize Fort Bellevue in 1809 had been premeditated and recorded that the dance stratagem was BH's idea, whereas other leaders had suggested alternative schemes ([Hunt?], "Personal Narrative," 664–66).

54. The "friends" presumably were people of Spanish, French, Métis, and possibly African origins with whom the Sauks had enjoyed positive relations earlier. Their presence

with the reinforcements perhaps sent the unsettling message that these people had accepted the authority of the United States and were willing to march in potential opposition to the Sauks, which contrasted with the sadness that BH had noted that they had expressed when American soldiers first arrived in the region in 1804.

55. The prophet was Tenskwatawa, Tecumseh's half brother, who began to preach his message of revitalizing spirituality and who advocated the formation of a pan-tribal confederacy to oppose American expansion onto First Nations lands in 1805. The Sauks had communicated with Tenskwatawa since at least 1807, and Tecumseh visited the Mississippi tribes in 1810 and 1812.

56. The council took place in the spring of 1810 and stemmed from the enormous upset caused by the 1809 Treaty of Fort Wayne (in the Indiana Territory) when a large tract of land to the east of the Sauks' territory had been lost. About 250 Sauks and Foxes attended the council and then traveled to Canada to confer with British officials, who gave them weapons and ammunition but cautioned them against going to war. Some returned home, while others stayed with Tecumseh.

57. The identity of this prophet is uncertain but may have been Main Poc, a Potawatomi leader and shaman who hated Americans and who visited the Sauks in the spring of 1811. Although some Sauks embraced Tenskwatawa's message and joined him, the nation as a whole remained on the periphery of the confederacy that formed around him and Tecumseh.

58. The Battle of Tippecanoe between the Americans under William Henry Harrison and the people allied with Tenskwatawa and Tecumseh occurred on November 7, 1811, outside Prophetstown in Indiana, where Tenskwatawa had established a village in 1808. Tecumseh was not present at the time. Harrison moved against Prophetstown to break up the developing confederacy in response to raids against settlers by natives wanting to avenge the deaths of their people and protect their lands, although at that moment responsibility for encouraging hostilities did not fall at the feet of the Shawnee half brothers, who believed they needed more time to build native unity in order to negotiate or fight for aboriginal rights from a position of strength. Instead, militancy centered on Main Poc and his associates. Harrison camped close to Prophetstown, then occupied by people from various nations (Shawnees, Piankashaws, Winnebagos, Potawatomis, and others), in expectation of attacking. During the night, American sentries fired on and killed two Winnebago men engaged in a patrol near the American camp (although we do not know who fired the first shot), after which natives launched an early morning assault to avenge the deaths they had suffered but which the Americans repulsed. Five hundred warriors fought twice as many American regulars and militia; casualties seem to have been about fifty for the natives and almost two hundred for the Americans. Harrison's soldiers then burned Prophetstown, but Tenskwatawa's followers rebuilt it shortly afterward. The effect of the battle was the opposite of what Harrison had wanted because it encouraged rather than undermined First Nations militancy in the Old Northwest.

59. Against the wishes of the indigenous population, sixty white men had moved to the lead mines around modern Dubuque, Iowa, in the summer of 1811, but most withdrew in the face of Winnebago resistance. The Foxes and Sauks subsequently burned the miners' abandoned buildings. On New Year's Day, 1812, natives killed two whites, looted stores, and torched buildings at one mine to avenge the loss of the Winnebagos at Tippecanoe. Normally, the tribespeople only allowed Euro-Americans who had married aboriginal women to extract lead, such as Julien Dubuque, who worked there from the 1780s until his death

in 1810, and who BH called "our relation" (*BHA*, 150). The lead deposits were important to aboriginal people, who had intensified mining efforts over previous years to replace trading opportunities lost through the decline of the fur-bearing animal population. Prairie du Chien, also mentioned by BH, was a largely Canadian and Métis trading community of thirty or forty homes near the mouth of the Wisconsin River, 170 miles north of Saukenuk along the Mississippi. American Indian subagent Nicolas Boilvin resided there at the time, as did pro-British traders. The Winnebagos presumably went to consult with people from both sides to gain information to help them decide the course of action they should take and to acquire presents and supplies. The warriors in the incident described in this paragraph did not attack Fort Madison itself, but killed settlers in the vicinity of the post and a soldier caught away from the safety of the garrison.

60. BH and a few of his followers joined two hundred Winnebagos in late August 1812 to besiege the fifty-man garrison at Fort Madison, with the first shots being fired on September 5 (although harassment of the post had occurred over previous months). The natives had been inspired in part by news of American reverses at Mackinac and elsewhere to the north and east once the Anglo-American War of 1812 had broken out in June, and the move against the post was part of a widespread outbreak of violence in the upper Mississippi region, which included both indigenous raids against settlers and white actions to destroy aboriginal villages, although most Sauks did not participate in the fighting at that time.

61. The beating probably consisted of the playing of reveille and morning duty calls.

62. The garrison's losses were one killed and one wounded (Communication from Daniel Colbert, July 20, 2004). We need to remember that BH recalled his story over twenty years after the event and thus did not remember some details accurately.

63. The besiegers burned some of the fort's outbuildings and boats and killed the garrison livestock; however, the defenders made "squirts" from old gun barrels to soak their blockhouses and thus save them (Thomas Hamilton to D. Bissell, September 10, 1812, Brannan, *Official Letters*, 63–66).

64. While being able to fire so accurately as to shoot through the ropes of the flagpole sounds like an old soldier's tale, the flag did fall after a large quantity of small-arms fire had been directed at it (ibid., 64). Most combatants in the War of 1812 used muskets, which could fire two or three times per minute, but which possessed only limited range and accuracy because the barrel interiors were smooth and the balls were loose fitting. (For instance, the barrel of a British military musket was .75 caliber [i.e., 75/100 of an inch], while the bullet was .69, whereas the American equivalent had a .69 caliber barrel and a .64 ball.) In contrast, BH used a rifle, a form of firearm that saw much less service in the war than muskets. A rifle had a tight-fitting ball and a grooved barrel interior, which meant that it could shoot farther and with more accuracy in comparison to a musket, but it took about a minute to load and could not fire as many shots between cleanings as a musket could because gunpowder debris clogged the barrel quickly, making it impossible to push a tight bullet with a ramrod down the barrel from the muzzle. (For a description of native and white warfare and weaponry in 1812–15, see Benn, *Iroquois in the War of 1812*, 67–85.)

65. John Johnson was the trader (or factor); the Winnebago's identity has been lost to history. The warriors lifted the siege on September 8.

66. BH in fact knew that war already had broken out before his attack on Fort Madison, given that the general move against the post had been inspired by news from other fronts.

67. Robert Dickson (or Dixon) was a trader married to a prominent Sioux woman,

Totowin, sister of a chief named Red Thunder. He played an important role in building alliances between Great Britain and the First Nations of the western Great Lakes and upper Mississippi and was rewarded with the rank of lieutenant colonel for his services at the end of hostilities. BH's comments on Dickson at this point most likely referred to his engagement of natives to support the British in the summer of 1812 at the capture of both Mackinac and Detroit before the attack on Fort Madison. Although hostile to the Americans, BH did not join him at that time, unlike some Sauks who did.

68. The affirmation that the British could be relied upon to do as they said seems positive; however, in factoring in the next paragraph of his autobiography, which expressed ambivalence toward them, it seems that BH suggested something more sinister but chose to do so with restraint.

69. While the meaning of this story is not completely clear, it contains a strong affirmation of the value of a native person's word. BH's decision to call the executed person "one of our people" is notable because the man was a Sioux, not a Sauk. In this instance, BH affirmed a wider aboriginal identity that distinguished natives from whites. The murder occurred in December 1814 when a Dakota Sioux man, Chunksah, who belonged to a band that had been suspected of pro-American sympathies, killed a Canadian (Antoine Dubois) and mortally wounded a Métis (Louis Champagney), apparently during a robbery. The British sent soldiers from Prairie du Chien to the man's village and seized a chief of the Gens de la Feuille Tiré band, Le Corbeau François (or Wabasha), to hold hostage until his people turned over the culprit. Shortly afterward, Wabasha's people produced the accused and the British released the chief. A court martial convicted Chunksah of the crime, and he died in front of a firing squad in January 1815. There is no independent record to confirm that Chunksah visited his family before his execution, and it is possible that BH may have conflated Wabasha and Chunksah as one person.

There is more of significance to this story. First, it would have been acceptable in native society to offer presents to the families of the victims to prevent retaliation; however, Chunksah had committed other crimes and seems to have lost the goodwill of his community. Second, the British used the incident to force Wabasha's Sioux into a treaty with them, thereby reducing the danger to Crown interests and sending an uncompromising message to the larger aboriginal population of the upper Mississippi, which BH probably found to be a hard one that underscored the difficult lesson he had learned when Robert Dickson threatened the Sauks if they did not join the British military effort, as we shall see subsequently in relation to an incident that occurred earlier in the war but which BH placed later in his narrative. Third, it was members of Chunksah's band of Sioux who massacred and captured BH's followers who had escaped the slaughter by American and native forces at the Bad Axe River in 1832 (described in the introduction to BH's memoirs). His narrative, however, did not address that connection, either here or later when he described the horror, only recording that "a large body of Sioux had pursued and killed a number of our women and children who had got safely across the Mississippi. The whites ought not to have permitted such conduct, and none but *cowards* would ever have been guilty of such cruelty, which has always been practiced on our nation by the Sioux" (*BHA*, 140). BH's comment on the role of whites in the affair stemmed from pressure the American government had put on the Sioux to attack his followers, although there had been incidents of violence between the Sauks and Sioux before the Black Hawk War broke out. A further complication arises out of BH's statement that he hunted for the executed person's family because it was that family's community that later killed BH's people, and thus we have an example of a betrayal that offended his sense of honor and decency, which he chose to articulate, but which must have eluded virtually all readers of his autobiography because it was so vague, as were some of his other allusions.

For details on the Chunksah incident, see Andrew Bulger to Robert McDouall, December 13, 1814, Bulger to Robert Dickson, January 6, 1815, Proceedings of a Court Martial, January 7, 1815, and Bulger to McDouall, January 7, 1815, Thwaites, "Bulger Papers," 36–37, 47–52; Memorandum, January 7, 1815, "Captain T. G. Anderson's Journal, 1814," 274–75; "Personal Narrative of Captain Thomas G. Anderson," c. 1870, 200–201; Dickson to Noah Freer and Dickson to Gordon Drummond, both January 17, 1815, British Military Records, 258:4–11.

70. This statement appears to acknowledge that BH's story is out of sequence chronologically in terms of the relationship between his attack on Fort Madison, the execution, and the decision by most Sauks to remain neutral in the late summer of 1812. His "late visit," of course, referred to his tour of the American East Coast a few months before dictating his memoirs in 1833.

71. This presumably refers to a delegation that went to Washington in May 1812 to see President James Madison. It returned to the west in the fall at an uncertain date, but as of late September the delegates only had reached Pittsburgh, Pennsylvania (Viola, *Diplomats in Buckskins*, 22–23, 202).

72. BH's friend at Peoria (a fur trade community on the lake of the same name) was Thomas Forsyth, an important trader who provided intelligence to the Americans and who secretly had been appointed American subagent for Indian Affairs in the Illinois District in April 1812. BH's chronology is unclear, but Forsyth went to Fort Dearborn (Chicago) early in July 1812 and again immediately after the destruction of the fort's garrison by natives on August 15 (Forsyth to Ninian Edwards, July 13, 1812, Carter, *Territorial Papers*, 16:250; Franke, *French Peoria*, 95; Ferguson, *Illinois in the War of 1812*, 104). While BH thought of Forsyth as a friend, Forsyth described the Sauks and Foxes as "a dastardly, cowardly set of Indians" (Forsyth to William Clark, December 23, 1812, Forsyth Papers).

73. In the early stages of the war, the American government generally wanted the First Nations to remain neutral, mainly because it believed neutrality was the best it could obtain from the tribes as there was little reason for indigenous people to ally with the United States. As the war progressed, officials increasingly sought native assistance where they thought they could obtain it, such as among the Iroquois who resided in New York.

74. Traders commonly provided goods to aboriginal people on credit because natives could not pay for them until they had completed their hunting and other subsistence endeavors. Giving them the materials needed to earn their living and feed their families in advance of payment thus was an important feature in the indigenous economy.

75. This period of hopefulness related to American trade promises probably occurred in September 1812.

76. We do not know what the quantities of presents were, but the story can be read to suggest that they were modest, which would have made BH's party anxious about American intentions, given that generosity in gift giving was a fundamental virtue in maintaining and building alliances between natives and newcomers. The war chief presumably was Lieutenant Thomas Hamilton of the 1st Regiment of Infantry.

77. BH's visit to Fort Madison happened after his September attack on the post. The trader was John Johnson.

78. As the Sauk delegation that went to Washington did not return until later in the autumn, BH may have erred on the sequence of events or may have chosen to present them in a chronologically imprecise way to facilitate his narrative of American betrayal through simplifying the story. Alternatively, the words of the "great father" in this part of the text may have been expressed earlier by local officials, possibly speaking on behalf of the president, and therefore existed independently of the message from Washington, in which case BH may have represented them as coming directly from the American capital to make his story more compelling while lessening its complexity. Simplifying stories and structuring them to enhance narrative drive were common features of First Nations diplomatic speeches, and BH may have conformed to that practice here. We know that government traders did extend credit to aboriginal people occasionally, contrary to authorized practice, but it seems likely that the trader in 1812 held back from doing so. What is more certain is that the quality of goods was thought to be inferior to the materials that came via British-based suppliers while also generally being more expensive. (See "Personal Narrative," 662–64; "Operations of the Factory System," March 8, 1822, 326–64; Morrell Marston, "Memoirs of the Sauks and Foxes," 1820, Blair, *Indian Tribes*, 2:176–78; Hagan, *Sac and Fox Indians*, 49–50.)

79. Edward La Gouthrie (or La Gutrie) was a trader who enjoyed a close relationship with the Sauks and who worked with Robert Dickson to win native support for the British. He camped on Rock Island on the Mississippi close to Saukenuk in the autumn of 1812, most likely in October, because Dickson sent supplies to the region in late September and early October to encourage the tribespeople to ally with the British (Dickson to Jacob Franks, October 2, 1812, "Dickson and Grignon Papers," 287–88). The majority of Sauks chose not to go to war against the United States. For those who did, there were reasons to do so beyond BH's simple statement, with the poor state of Sauk-American relations and the expectation that a successful war might lead to the creation of a native homeland outside of white control being primary motivations. Why BH emphasized trade and credit is unclear, although the focus on the broken promise fits with the theme of betrayal that is central to his memoirs, but he gave additional reasons on other occasions, such as "to preserve our lands, and to make war against the big knives who want to destroy us" (BH Speech, April 18, 1815, "Prairie du Chien Documents," 278), or to drive the Americans off aboriginal lands, or to respond to British threats of attack if they did not take up arms against the United States (BH Speech, August 3, 1815, British Military Records, 258:285–87). See more of these speeches in section 6 of BH's texts in this book.

80. This short section conflates two separate incidents, consisting of Edward La Gouthrie's supply of goods on Robert Dickson's orders in the autumn of 1812, followed by Dickson's subsequent recruiting of war parties in March 1813. Between the two, Dickson left Mackinac for Montreal in October 1812 but returned to the West early in 1813. While in Montreal, he was appointed agent and superintendent in the Indian Department for the nations west of Lake Huron and received resources to carry out his responsibilities.

81. It was customary in native diplomacy to give arriving parties a day to rest before engaging in business. Smoking a pipe with delegates was an important collective act where minds could be calmed and high-minded thoughts could be generated, in part because tobacco possessed sacred qualities and its rising smoke symbolized the establishment of rapport with the good spirits above the earth.

82. The willingness of Edward La Gouthrie to provide goods without receiving pay-

ment at that moment contrasted with BH's description of how the Americans would not extend credit, although it may be possible that the expression "do as we pleased with them" indicates that La Gouthrie did not expect compensation at all, offering these supplies as diplomatic gifts.

83. There was one francophone and a number of native communities in the Green Bay area on the west side of Lake Michigan, closely linked to the fur trade based at Mackinac. One Menominee-centered tradition placed Robert Dickson somewhat farther south at the time, in the Lake Winnebago area (Powell, "Recollections," 151).

84. Edward La Gouthrie and BH did not know about their "friend" Thomas Forsyth's links to the American cause at that point. In fact, Forsyth worked to keep as many Potawatomis as possible out of a British alliance.

85. The identity of these people is uncertain, but the son had been described as a brother to Quashquame, although the term may have been used loosely or inaccurately (Maurice Blondeau to Benjamin Howard, January 23, 1813, Carter, *Territorial Papers*, 14:644–65).

86. It was common practice for white powers to equip native allies for military campaigns.

87. This meeting took place in mid-March 1813. Detroit had fallen to the British the previous August. BH lost the paper in 1832.

88. Contrary to BH's text, Robert Dickson had not received orders to wage war against white settlements, but had been directed to prevent acts of inhumanity while recruiting indigenous forces to support operations in defense of Canada (Ferguson, *Illinois in the War of 1812*, 73). Nevertheless, there was logic behind BH's desire to attack American settlers because it was these people who posed the greatest immediate threat to Sauk independence and the retention of tribal lands. Furthermore, such a strategy would have conformed to his earlier experiences in conducting hostilities against native enemies for control of particular territories. Perhaps he also hoped that campaigning on the upper Mississippi would represent an adequate show of support for the British to prevent possible retribution from them should they take offense at the limited amount of Sauk participation in their war effort elsewhere. At some point (but certainly by early 1813) the British had said they would organize attacks on the Sauks if they did not provide more help; thus, the discussion recorded here may represent a fragment of the difficult negotiations that took place, which BH may have softened for his American readers because acknowledging the issue could undermine his affirmations that it was American behavior that drove him to take up arms against the United States. The British threat weighed on his mind because BH reminded Crown officials about it at Prairie du Chien in 1815 (BH Speech, August 3, 1815, British Military Records, 258:285–87, reproduced in section 6 of BH's texts in this book). Robert Dickson acknowledged that he had intimidated BH's people, stating, "I have told the Sauks and Renards [Foxes] that they sleep too long. If they do not get up, that I should rouse them with the hatchet, and that Britain suffers no neutrals" (Dickson to John Lawe, March 20, 1814, "Lawe and Grignon Papers," 116). The Americans knew about these warnings, as they mentioned them in several documents, noting that Sioux and other indigenous forces were to be used to carry through the threat if necessary (e.g., Maurice Blondeau to Benjamin Howard, April 3, 1813, and Report of August La Roche and Louis Chevalier, April 4, 1813, Carter, *Territorial Papers*, 14:659, 654). In trying to convince BH to assist the British, Dickson at some point apparently indicated that an objective of their alliance was to create a boundary between the Americans and the First Nations far to the east of the upper

Mississippi (BH Speech, August 3, 1815, British Military Records, 258:285–87, reproduced in section 6 of BH's texts in this book).

89. Gomo (or Masseno or Nasimo) was an important Potawatomi chief from a village twenty miles upriver of Peoria. He had been friendly toward the Americans but cautiously allied with the British in 1812; however, he then negotiated peace and supplied intelligence to the Americans after their forces burned his vacant village early in the autumn of 1813 and defeated the British and western tribes at Moraviantown in Upper Canada in October. The person that Robert Dickson wanted to capture was Thomas Forsyth, whose American connections finally had been uncovered, but Gomo did not seize him and in fact did not seem to want to do so. In 1814 Dickson again sent warriors to take Forsyth; however, he escaped a second time. (See Edmunds, *Illinois River Potawatomi*, 341–62; Ferguson, *Illinois in the War of 1812*, 108, 110–11.)

90. BH and Robert Dickson did not travel together, so the British chief mentioned was someone else. Dickson at first remained in the West to recruit more men and then took a native contingent north to Mackinac before heading south to the Detroit front. In contrast, BH marched eastward to the Detroit River with his warriors (and a number of women and children), arriving ahead of Dickson. This has confused some historians who thought they accompanied each other, leading them to assume, incorrectly, that BH missed the first siege of Fort Meigs, which he described in the next paragraph (Dickson to George Prevost, March 16 and May 31, 1813, Department of State, War of 1812 Papers; Dickson to Roger Sheaffe, March 22, 1813, and Dickson to Noah Freer, June 23, 1813, British Military Records, 257:67, 86; Cruikshank, "Robert Dickson," 140–49).

91. Several hundred natives, mainly Potawatomis, killed or captured most of the American garrison of fifty-four men from Fort Dearborn at today's Chicago on August 15, 1812, when the soldiers and forty civilians and military dependents fled the post in the face of widespread aboriginal hostility. The commanding officer had negotiated a surrender in which he was allowed to evacuate the fort in return for handing over government supplies, but when the natives discovered that he had destroyed the arms, ammunition, and whiskey they had expected to seize, they felt betrayed and attacked a mile or two from the post. Indigenous losses are not known yet likely were modest. After the battle the Potawatomis burned the fort.

92. BH arrived among the British on the Detroit front about April 21, 1813 (Antal, *Wampum Denied*, 221–22).

93. The text refers to the first siege of Fort Meigs (in modern Perrysburg, Ohio) between April 27 and May 9, 1813, but is somewhat confused, which has led some historians to assume mistakenly that BH was present at the fighting at Frenchtown (today's Monroe, Michigan) in January 1813, but that was not possible because he did not leave for the Detroit front until March. At Fort Meigs, Tecumseh and Brevet Colonel Henry Procter of the 41st Regiment of Foot led a native and white force of over two thousand against the post and its garrison of eleven hundred men. The fort had been under construction from February 1813 as part of the American effort to regain control of the Michigan Territory, lost with the surrender of Detroit in August 1812. The attackers set up batteries outside the post and bombarded it but could not coerce its commandant, William Henry Harrison, to surrender. BH's reference to the boats and subsequent fighting described events on May 5 when part of an American relief contingent, numbering twelve hundred men, attacked the British and natives, drove them some distance, but then suffered defeat with heavy losses

in a counterattack at about the same time that a sortie from the post assaulted the British batteries. Much of the aboriginal force left shortly afterward, and the Canadian militia either departed or clamored to go home, so Procter, with a comparatively small number of regular soldiers, lifted the siege on May 9. British and native casualties were seventy or eighty; the Americans lost 350 killed and wounded along with six hundred captured. After the fighting related to the relief force ended, some warriors wanted to kill American prisoners, while others argued that their lives should be spared. During the debate, some men started shooting and tomahawking the captured soldiers. According to most witnesses (which overlook BH's statement), warriors continued to do so until Tecumseh and some British Indian Department officers intervened. About two dozen Americans and a British sentry who tried to protect them lost their lives in this incident.

94. Although this sentence appears to relate to the first siege of Fort Meigs, it refers to the second investment, of July 21–28. After failing to capture the post in May, Henry Procter (now a major general) and Tecumseh returned to try again. The two thousand Americans then inside its walls, however, were entrenched securely, and the white and aboriginal attackers, numbering between two thousand and three thousand men, lacked the heavy artillery needed to breach the defenses. The natives staged a mock battle in the forest outside the fort in imitation of the destruction of the American relief column in the spring, hoping that its garrison would sally to rescue their nonexistent comrades and thus be caught in a trap; but the men in the fort did not come out, having learned earlier that there were no supporting troops near the post. When the ruse did not work, Procter and Tecumseh withdrew. The defenders lost six men killed or captured; the attackers had no casualties. The British and natives then attacked Fort Stephenson on the Sandusky River (at modern Fremont, Ohio), thirty miles east of Fort Meigs, on August 1–2, 1813. Their objective was to destroy the post to clear the way for an assault against the American naval squadron being built at Presque Isle on the south side of the lake that threatened the Royal Navy's control of Lake Erie.

95. Robert Dickson was present, but the flag was carried by Captain Peter Chambers of the 41st Regiment of Foot. Lieutenant Colonel Matthew Elliott of the Canadian militia and the Indian Department also accompanied them to demand the American surrender, which the fort's commandant refused.

96. Major George Crogham of the 17th Regiment of Infantry was twenty-one years old. He commanded 167 men. The British had five hundred soldiers along with an unknown number of native allies.

97. The light caliber British artillery could not breach the walls, so Henry Procter ordered a frontal assault on August 2, which the natives would not join, and which the Americans repulsed because the soldiers could not cut through the walls of the fort. As in the attacks on Fort Meigs, the Americans defended their post successfully and thus secured their staging areas for a subsequent thrust to reclaim Michigan and invade southwestern Upper Canada. Losses at Fort Stephenson were just over one hundred on the British and First Nations side, eight on the American.

98. There are three interpretations for what BH meant by "retreat." First, it could refer to the British withdrawal to Canada after the attack on Fort Stephenson in August 1813, as seems logical from the way he presented his memoirs and because we know that a portion of the Sauk force returned to the upper Mississippi at that time. Second, it might refer to a point six weeks later, after the British lost the naval Battle of Lake Erie on September 10.

When the British evacuated the Detroit River area and withdrew eastward through Upper Canada toward Niagara after the defeat, some Sauks and other tribespeople decided not to stay with their allies but moved to Michigan, where they raided settlements and awaited the outcome of the clash that was expected to follow on land because the Americans followed up their victory on the lake by pursuing the British. If the king's forces were to win, these warriors could fall upon the retreating American army, but if they were to lose, the natives could go home in comparative safety. The third possibility is that BH remained with the British following the loss of Lake Erie when they marched toward the Niagara Peninsula and was present at the Battle of Moraviantown on October 5, in which the Americans under William Henry Harrison triumphed, Tecumseh fell, and, in the aftermath, the Western Tribal Confederacy largely collapsed. The first possibility, that he went home right after the attack on Fort Stephenson, seems to be least likely because he was still away from Saukenuk late in September and October 1813 at the time when it was threatened by an American raid and when his rival, Keokuk, rose to power, described later in his autobiography. Of the second and third possibilities, perhaps BH's presence at Moraviantown is the more probable because he apparently told several people in the years after dictating his memoirs that he had been there (e.g., Drake, *Life and Adventures of Black Hawk*, 237–41, 245). We also know, for example, that sixty Sauk and Fox men, with a hundred women and children, retreated to the Niagara Peninsula after the battle, indicating a continued Sauk presence with the British army at the time (Return by William Claus, October 26, 1813, British Military Records, 681:10). Some Sauks even remained in the lower Great Lakes theater until the return of peace in 1815, although BH clearly did not because he fought on the upper Mississippi in 1814 (Claus Speech at Burlington Heights, April 24, 1815, ibid., 258:60). If BH did see action at Moraviantown, he then slipped through American-controlled areas in order to travel back to Saukenuk.

It is difficult to understand why BH did not discuss the famous events of the 1813 campaign in more detail, although he seems to have been reluctant to talk about things related to Tecumseh at the time he dictated his life story (as discussed in the introduction to his section of this book), and the Battle of Moraviantown was a critical element in the saga of the famous Shawnee leader. As well, BH's presence in support of British operations on the lower Great Lakes that year was not essential to the main thematic concerns of his autobiography, focused on the history of the defense of Sauk interests on the upper Mississippi, and he may not have realized how much his white audience might have wanted to hear about the campaigning around Lake Erie. Another problem in tracing BH's service in 1813 is the existence of some obviously incorrect traditions related to him. For example, one report quotes him saying that he was on the Niagara Peninsula "when the Americans walked into Fort Erie" (Drake, *Life and Adventures of Black Hawk*, 235). While he may have been at that fort at some point in 1813, it is not possible for him to have been there when the British lost the post, either briefly that year or again in 1814. There are other sources that cannot be dismissed quite so easily, although they probably are spurious, such as a supposed BH account of the Battle of Moraviantown (published in various American newspapers in 1838, and reprinted in ibid., 244). Nevertheless, the questionable value of such a text does not preclude his presence at the event, especially given that his return to Saukenuk almost certainly occurred after the October 1813 battle.

99. His wife was Asshewequa (Singing Bird). They had several children, of whom two sons and a daughter survived BH.

100. Leaving a military campaign was a warrior's prerogative according to aboriginal custom and was not considered to be desertion the way it was in white armies.

101. In November 1812, during a larger campaign against native villages in the Illinois Territory, Americans burned much of Peoria, believing that its francophone residents were aiding Kickapoos, Potawatomis, and Piankashaws against the United States. The militiamen on the expedition, apparently not knowing Thomas Forsyth's pro-American allegiance, took him prisoner when relations between the villagers and their occupiers deteriorated badly.

102. The old man and his son are the same people who BH had visited before leaving for the Detroit front.

103. This was Fort Mason, built in 1812, south of modern Hannibal, Missouri.

104. The officer was Lieutenant John Campbell of the 1st Regiment of Infantry.

105. One source noted that on January 16, 1813, American soldiers from Fort Mason "took a young Sauk prisoner, a young man who was out on the deer hunt at the Bay of Charles [north of today's Hannibal, Missouri] on the other side of the Mississippi. They took him across, killed him with a rifle, and took his scalp." This suggests that the Americans (from Captain Nathan Boone's company of mounted Missouri Rangers) brought him over to the side of the river on which he was not supposed to be found in order to justify the murder. This same source recorded that the victim's family had asked for presents "to put out the blood that had been spilt" in order to avoid the need to avenge the death but had been refused, which in native society demanded that a war party take action against the perpetrators' community. In the end, however, the Americans complied with the request (Maurice Blondeau to Benjamin Howard, January 23, 1813, Carter, *Territorial Papers*, 14:644–45; see also Frederick Bates to Howard, January 28, 1813, and Blondeau to Howard, April 3, 1813, ibid., 14:642, 658–59; Ferguson, *Illinois in the War of 1812*, 117). Boone's rangers were volunteers raised in Missouri under the authority of the federal government and who received a per diem for their services. Of fundamental significance in the story of the killing was the older man's reason quoted earlier in the text for refusing to let his son join BH, as the latter remembered that "he said he did not like the war. He had been down the river and had been well treated by the Americans and could not fight against them."

106. The story of how BH visited his friend in the last hours of his life might have been a construct to enhance BH's narrative, although the fundamentals of how his friend's son had been murdered are accurate.

107. Perhaps the last sentence of this paragraph is J. B. Patterson's editorial addition because BH's experience on the Detroit front ought to have conflicted with such a view, although it did reflect a pervasive but inaccurate American mythology about their military prowess in comparison to the British, and it may have been Patterson's way of redeeming BH's condemnation of both armies, which undermined American readers' self-perceptions of their country's military competence. As well, the British army in the Detroit region, operating at the end of an uncertain supply line, suffered from serious shortages of clothing and footwear. The other material in the paragraph largely seems to accord with how BH might have interpreted Euro-American fighting from a Sauk perspective.

108. The Lance, or Shamaga, was a Sauk chief from the Missouri band. American officials persuaded fifteen hundred Sauks and Foxes to move away from their anti-American neighbors and resettle along the Missouri River in the autumn of 1813, west of the Republic's stronghold at St. Louis (near modern Jefferson City, Missouri, and upriver of Cote

Sans Dessein), because the white population feared that the aboriginal people otherwise might take up arms against them. The move made sense for these natives (most of whom were willing to adopt a neutralist stance) because it offered them protection against retribution from pro-British people and because they could receive material support from the Americans to replace British presents and supplies they would lose by retiring to a safer location. Some of the people who traveled south, however, either were hostile to the Republic or reconsidered their alliance and engaged in offensive actions against settlers. With escalating tensions in 1814, half of the group returned to Saukenuk, although many individuals went home for trade or personal reasons rather than because they held militant views. On their way, some of them robbed settlements.

109. Keokuk, or Watchful Fox, became BH's principal rival in the Sauk nation after his rise to leadership during the War of 1812. As the leading accommodationist once peace had returned, he solidified his power by gaining control over the annuities the American government paid to the natives and by being affirmed by white officials in his role of chief of the Sauks (and Foxes).

110. Wacome may have been a chief known as Waukkummee.

111. Between August and October 1813, thirteen hundred Americans from St. Louis moved north to destroy native villages along the Illinois River Valley, build Fort Clark at Peoria to serve as a barrier to southbound war parties from northern Illinois, and project American power to the north of their main areas of settlement. Some Sauks fought against the white force during this campaign. A detachment of one hundred soldiers rode off to patrol in the direction of the Rock River. Although it never moved closer than forty-five miles from Saukenuk, it frightened the people there, who expected to be attacked at a time when a large proportion of their men were away with BH. As it was, other native people had abandoned their homes elsewhere in the face of this patrol (Hurt, *Nathan Boone*, 96–97).

BH pointed out that Keokuk became a military leader without having met the normal requirement of performing well in combat, perhaps to make the point that his own standing as a leader was more legitimate, despite saying he was satisfied with the story he had been told in the next sentence. Yet without seeing action, according to BH, Keokuk had offered to defend his people in fulfillment of the warrior's primary role in Sauk society while BH had not done so in 1813, at least not directly, because he was away on the Detroit front. In contrast to BH's words, a source published shortly after BH's autobiography claimed that Keokuk in fact had killed a man in battle beforehand but said that he had been excluded from the council due to his youth (McKenny and Hall, *Indian Tribes*, 2:127–28). Keokuk, however, had been born in the 1780s (Colbert, "Hinge on Which All Affairs," 55); thus, Keokuk was old enough to participate in the deliberations. While BH sometimes was inaccurate, it is difficult to know which claim is correct, and it is possible that McKenny and Hall wanted to undermine BH in favor of a pro-American chief in the wake of the Black Hawk War. Whatever the factors for Keokuk's exclusion from the council, a third source agreed with these two that it was his behavior at the council that had led to his rise to leadership (Morrell Marston to Jedidiah Morse, November 1820, Blair, *Indian Tribes*, 2:157).

BH may have placed his account of Keokuk's rise between the two halves of the narrative about avenging the death of his friend's son as a way of undermining the legitimacy of his rival's status as a war leader in contrast to his own role in discharging another of the core traditional military obligations of Sauk males. Furthermore, Keokuk's words on how the Sauks ought to protect their homes aligns with what BH did in 1832 but contradicts

Keokuk's accommodationist stance at that time, which BH perhaps hoped readers would recognize.

112. This sentence makes the skirmish at the Sinkhole and Fort Howard sound like it occurred in 1814 rather than in 1815.

113. Two challenges with BH's statement on his personal motivations that led to the confrontation at the Sinkhole are that it differs from the views he expressed to British officials on the eve of the event and may have conflicted with Sauk customs related to avenging deaths. In 1815, he stated that he wanted to continue protecting Sauk independence fundamentally through national rather than private war: "I have fought the big knives [Americans], and will continue to fight them until they retire from our lands. Till then, my father, your red children cannot be happy" (BH Speech, April 18, 1815, "Prairie du Chien Documents," 278, reproduced in section 6 of BH's texts in this book). As well, other Sauk war parties took to the field at about the same time, indicating that his efforts likely were part of a larger decision to continue fighting. Furthermore, the Americans had provided gifts to the victim's family in conformity to indigenous custom, which normally people accepted as a substitute for the need to avenge a death (Ferguson, *Illinois in the War of 1812*, 117). It is possible, however, that BH may have felt the presents failed to meet the appropriate First Nations standard, such as because they had been delayed. It also is possible that his memoirs from the 1830s interpreted the Sinkhole skirmish within the context of a justifiable private act of war rather than a community initiative in order to defend behavior that in retrospect hurt his tribe's desire for autonomy because the Americans were harsh toward the Sauks in its wake as the encounter had occurred after the end of the War of 1812. Alternatively, what he told the British in 1815 may not have been the whole story because council speeches were diplomatic acts meant to achieve predetermined community goals and thus often did not address all of the complexities behind a decision. As well, the division between private and national war among the First Nations, while important, was not hard and fast, and there is no reason why his decision to lead a war party in 1815 could not have combined more than one objective.

114. The Americans burned and evacuated Fort Madison in the autumn of 1813 after a summer of aboriginal harassment.

115. During the period covered by this sentence, a war party, which may have been BH's, killed a family of settlers by the name of Ramsay (Ferguson, *Illinois in the War of 1812*, 194).

116. Cap au Gris was a rocky prominence on the east bank of the Mississippi, twelve miles north of the mouth of the Cuivre River. The post BH mentioned was Fort Howard, built to protect American settlements in 1812 (and not to be confused with Fort Howard on Green Bay, established in 1818, or Fort Independence, which had been constructed nearby but was flooded by the Mississippi in 1815). Other men in BH's party opened fire on some soldiers outside the fort, and a general skirmish ensued at the start of the "Battle" of the Sinkhole of May 24, 1815, as men in the garrison came out to participate in the fighting.

117. The person who hit BH seems to have been Frederick Dixon (Mudd, "History of Lincoln County," 10).

118. The scalped man was Roswell Durgee (ibid.). An individual could survive a scalping if his or her skull received no serious damage when the hair and skin of the scalp were cut off.

119. One of the boys was Chauncy Durgee, who later recalled that he thought BH had

made eye contact with him when he peered out from his hiding place. Local memory within the white community suggests that there were three children present, with the others being John Ewing and John McLane (ibid.). Killing one man to put him out of his misery and sparing the lives of the man who had helped the Sauks and of the helpless boys could be interpreted as an affirmation of BH's decency, in contrast to the people who murdered his friend's son, which had led him to this encounter, although we do not know if BH intended to make that point.

120. The mounted party numbered twenty-five men from Fort Howard, who later were reinforced by another twenty soldiers. The man killed was a Missouri Ranger, Captain Peter Craig, the post's commandant. Another source says the men dismounted to fire at the natives and indicates that Craig may have been on foot when shot (Shaw, "Personal Narrative," 214).

121. Part of BH's party sought refuge in the sinkhole, while others withdrew elsewhere before returning to Fort Howard to fire on the post. Located half a mile from the fort, the sinkhole was roughly sixty feet long, fifteen across, and twelve deep. There was a sheltered rocky surface underneath one of its banks where the warriors took cover (ibid., 214–15).

122. By "singing their death songs" BH meant that his followers did not expect to survive.

123. The "battery" was a farm cart the Americans strengthened with heavy planks to use as a mobile shield to get into position and direct small-arms fire into the sinkhole (Shaw, "Personal Narrative," 216).

124. After several hours of fighting, BH's enemies retired from the sinkhole to strengthen Fort Howard, which they feared would be assaulted when they heard other men in the war party firing at the post. The dead American was Lieutenant Edward Spears (or Spear), a Missouri Ranger, but the warrior's identity has been lost to us. BH's band suffered five killed and some wounded; the Americans lost eleven or more killed and a number of wounded in the various skirmishes around Fort Howard that day. Fifty warriors and sixty soldiers had engaged in these events, exclusive of the Americans who remained inside the fort.

125. Assuming BH remembered the events accurately, the hunt occurred in June and/or July 1815 because he met with British officials at Prairie du Chien at the beginning of August (BH Speech, August 3, 1815, British Military Records 258:285–87).

126. Washeown's identity is uncertain, although he seems to have been a Kickapoo (Ferguson, *Illinois in the War of 1812*, 158).

127. This was Fort Clark, built in 1813 at Peoria. The Sangamon River is sixty miles south of the town.

128. The "defeat" refers to the Battles of Lake Erie and Moraviantown in September and October 1813. Malden became the common post-1815 name for the British fort at Amherstburg near Detroit in Upper Canada, although it was used at the time of the war too (e.g., Smith, *Geographical View of the Province of Upper Canada*, 48).

129. Washeown is the speaker.

130. Gomo's story relates to a larger peacemaking effort by some Potawatomis which occurred after the British and aboriginal defeat at Moraviantown in 1813 and took place during a winter of shortages, which made the natives more vulnerable, especially because American actions in the Peoria area impaired access to the winter hunting grounds in the south. BH's dismissal of Washeown's words might be understood as a general censure

of native people who spoke well of the Americans in light of negative indigenous experiences with them.

131. Despite the name, the peace party included people who were hostile to the United States. The mention of scalps taken on the Cuivre seems to be a chronologically unfeasible link to the Sinkhole skirmish that occurred later, but might refer to a now-unrecorded event. We do not know why BH recommended that they return to the Missouri, although the text suggests that it was a reaction to the Potawatomi decision to make peace (and presumably a sense that the British no longer were powerful in light of their defeats on the Detroit front).

132. The identities of Sanatuwa and Tatapuckey are uncertain, although they probably were the "two chiefs" mentioned earlier in the section in relation to Potawatomi-American peace negotiations.

133. These individuals may have been offered as hostages, which sometimes occurred in white-native and intertribal diplomacy as a sign and encouragement of peaceful relations.

134. The murder near Fort Clark at Peoria confirmed BH's view of Washeown's naivety and represented another instance of betrayal that dominated much of the autobiography.

135. Perhaps BH used his ability to appear anonymously at Fort Clark to assess his enemy's strength while providing carefully constructed answers about the Sauks in return.

136. The Americans sailed up the Mississippi River from St. Louis in May 1814 and persuaded the tribes along its banks to agree to restore peace. They then entered Prairie du Chien unopposed on June 2 after the handful of local militiamen withdrew without engaging their opponents (although the Americans captured a number of people—mainly Winnebagos—some of whom they killed when they tried to escape, and may have murdered others). The soldiers next constructed Fort Shelby in the community, planning to use large keelboats to keep it supplied from St. Louis and thereby prevent the British from using Prairie du Chien as a base for operations directed against more southerly regions.

137. Despite BH's affirmation of the friendliness of the Americans, the white force of 260 men took prisoners and made other threatening gestures to coerce the Sauks (some of whom had fired on the Americans) to enter into peace negotiations and agree to fight the still-hostile Winnebagos. The white commander was William Clark, the governor of the Missouri Territory, an Indian agent, and a fur trader, who competed against British traders along the Mississippi (and who, with Meriwether Lewis, had led the famous Corps of Discovery that explored the American West in 1804–6). After the capture of Prairie du Chien, Clark turned command over to Lieutenant Joseph Perkins of the 24th Regiment of Infantry and returned downriver with part of the contingent. Subsequent actions described by BH suggest that the Sauks had negotiated a settlement because of the immediate threat to their well-being (and perhaps out of pessimism over how the war was unfolding) but without any real commitment to maintain good relations should the course of events shift against the Americans. Yet the situation was tense and uncertain enough that the leading British official in the region, Robert Dickson, sent word to the Sauks that he would set other tribes on them if they did not support the British, as he had threatened to do earlier in the conflict. In addition to advancing the British cause, Dickson may have been concerned about the security of the Winnebagos, as it was one of the tribes that he favored along with the Sioux and Menominees, but the Winnebagos sometimes fought against the Sauks and Foxes (Robert McDouall to Frederick Robinson, September 22, 1815, British Military Records, 258:274–75).

138. The peace establishment comprised the Sauks along the Missouri River.

139. This meeting between the Americans and Sauks took place on July 19 or 20, 1814. The commanding officer was Captain John Campbell of the 1st Regiment of Infantry (mentioned in an earlier citation when he was a lieutenant). He had been dispatched from Cap au Gris to transport supplies and reinforcements to Fort Shelby at Prairie du Chien. He reminded the Sauks of their promise to fight the Winnebagos, but they put him off by telling him that they would not do so unless they were supplied with ammunition.

140. The British, fearing that the Americans at Fort Shelby in Prairie du Chien could drive the region's tribes out of the war, organized a mixed aboriginal-white expedition from Mackinac to expel their enemies. The sixty-five Americans in the fort capitulated to 650 attackers on July 20, 1814, after the siege of July 17–19, while the forty Americans on board the gunboat *Governor Clark* at the village withdrew downriver after suffering damage and casualties from a small British artillery piece. (Mississippi River gunboats at the time were fortified barges propelled by sails and oars and equipped with small artillery pieces.) The victors paroled the prisoners, sent them south, and renamed the captured post Fort McKay after William McKay, a fur trader, Indian Department official, and military officer who commanded the British at the siege. This event shifted the balance of power along the upper Mississippi and thereby ended the short peace between the Americans and the people of Saukenuk. The British delegation that went to Saukenuk, mentioned by BH, asked the natives to intercept the armed vessels that had escaped from Prairie du Chien, unaware, at least when they left the fur trade community, that Captain Campbell's flotilla mentioned in the previous note had just sailed north past the mouth of the Rock River (while Campbell likewise was unaware of the recent British victory to the north).

141. The Battle of Campbell's Island (on the Mississippi, ten miles north of the mouth of the Rock River) took place over about three hours between four hundred or more Sauks, Foxes, Kickapoos, and other natives against John Campbell's 125 soldiers and some dependents on five boats, three of them being gunboats, on July 21, 1814. The wounded "war chief" may have been Campbell, who was one of the officers shot during the battle. The boat commander who impressed BH was Lieutenant Jonathan Riggs, a ranger from Missouri. American casualties numbered thirty-seven killed and wounded; BH spoke of losing two men, and we know a woman died participating in the attack, while the Americans thought native losses were higher (see William McKay to Robert McDouall, July 27, 1814; Wood, *Select British Documents*, 3, part 1: 264; Ferguson, *Illinois in the War of 1812*, 167–70).

142. A skiff was a small, light boat, usually equipped for sailing or rowing. The men came from the crew of the *Governor Clark*, still upriver of Saukenuk, who had been sent to reconnoiter (Ferguson, *Illinois in the War of 1812*, 170).

143. Perhaps the negative comment about the medicine was an attempt by J. B. Patterson to add some naive color to the narrative and affirm his view that BH did not understand the complexities of white civilization, although one could read it simply as an ironic affirmation by BH of the superiority of Sauk medicine over Euro-American treatments. The text surrounding these river battles suggests that the translation may have been somewhat freer than elsewhere in the autobiography because it seems doubtful that BH knew such nautical terms as "dropped anchor" or spoke of boats in the feminine, as was normal in English.

144. The "cloth lodges" were tents. Distributing spoils to followers was a mark of generosity expected of war leaders.

145. The village was Wapello, near Saukenuk in today's Rock Island, Illinois.

146. The vessels were the two unarmed boats that earlier had accompanied John Campbell and his gunboats but which had not participated in the Battle of Campbell's Island, as well as the *Governor Clark*, which had escaped from the British attack on Prairie du Chien. They later arrived at St. Louis after suffering seven casualties from native fire directed at them along a fifteen-mile stretch of the river where the Sauks had concentrated their efforts to stop the Americans (Ferguson, *Illinois in the War of 1812*, 170).

147. The British from Prairie du Chien arrived with their artillery about six weeks after the events of the previous paragraph of BH's autobiography when they learned that an American expedition was heading north from St. Louis. The "big gun" was a modest three-pounder. The British also brought two small swivel guns with them, which were the lightest artillery pieces used in the war.

148. While BH smashed the kegs of whiskey the Americans had on their boats, he accepted British spirits, which could be symbolic of his opinion of the two sides (or simply a contradiction), although whiskey from the Americans was associated with the use of alcohol to exploit native people, sometimes was made improperly and thus was poisonous, and was understood by both natives and newcomers to be the source of much of the social challenge and population decline faced by aboriginal peoples.

149. In late August 1814, Major Zachary Taylor of the 7th Regiment of Infantry (and future American president) led 430 men north from Fort Independence at Cap au Gris in eight gunboats with the objective of destroying native settlements, including Saukenuk, and building a fort to regain control of the upper Mississippi, but without challenging the British at Prairie du Chien (although the British concentrated most of their local force there, thinking the post was Taylor's objective). On his way, unusually strong winds drove him to shelter at a small willow island just upriver of Credit Island near the mouth of the Rock River, close to Saukenuk, on September 4 to prevent his boats from being blown onto sandbars. Seeing large numbers of natives on shore, Taylor raised a white flag, apparently to trick them to come to a council where he could retaliate for their earlier hostilities, but without success, while an aboriginal attempt to induce him to come ashore and fight also failed. At daylight on September 5, over one thousand Sauk, Fox, Winnebago, Sioux, and other warriors, along with thirty-two white men, attacked from both banks of the Mississippi and from Credit Island. With losses of fourteen or fifteen casualties after fighting on the island and from his boats in the Battle of Credit Island (or Rock Island Rapids), the Americans withdrew downriver and built Fort Johnson on a bluff on the east bank of the Mississippi overlooking the mouth of the Des Moines River near modern Warsaw, Illinois. Native losses are not known but almost certainly were light.

150. This was Fort Johnson, mentioned in the previous note, although some historians have assumed it was Fort Mason. The Two River country was a hunting ground southwest of Fort Madison (in today's northeastern Missouri).

151. BH's actions were part of a British and aboriginal campaign to harass their enemy, which, combined with supply shortages among their opponents, led the Americans to burn Fort Johnson and withdraw to St. Louis in October 1814. The Americans made no further attempts against the Rock River settlements or Prairie du Chien, leaving the British and natives in control of the upper Mississippi for the rest of the war. The following spring, BH went on his expedition that led to the skirmish at the Sinkhole.

152. Portage des Sioux was a francophone village on the Mississippi, six miles above the mouth of the Missouri River, which the Americans had used as a base to patrol the

region during the war. It was a good site for treaty councils for various First Nations be-cause it was accessible via the Mississippi, Missouri, and Illinois Rivers. The Americans, headed by Governor William Clark of the Missouri Territory, Governor Ninian Edwards of the Illinois Territory, and prominent trader Auguste Chouteau, convened councils in July, September, and October 1815 to negotiate peace. Some Sauks went to the July meeting for preliminary discussions, where government officials threatened them with violence if they did not send some important chiefs, as well as BH, or otherwise failed to comply with American requirements. Ominously, some tribes indicated that they might offer military support to the whites if the Sauks remained hostile.

These events unfolded under a cloud associated with ongoing Sauk hostility, such as BH's participation in the skirmish at the Sinkhole in May 1815 after the Anglo-American conflict had ended. News of the peace came to Saukenuk from the Americans at St. Louis just before the British commandant at Prairie du Chien heard it from the same source on April 16, 1815. Some people on the rumor-infested frontier, both white and native, sug-gested that the report was untrue, thinking it may have been a ruse to put them off their guard, before the Americans either launched a strike against them or lured them south into a trap. Wartime passions also ran high, and BH and other Sauks (and Foxes) were unwilling to abandon belligerency despite the wider peace. Hence, BH led his war party south, while some others engaged in continued campaigning on a small scale. For their part, the British did not have the physical ability or the moral right to insist that their First Nations allies stop fighting against their wishes, although they encouraged them to do so and recalled war parties willing to cooperate with them. In fact, as it became increasingly clear that the war had ended, even though the British at Prairie du Chien had not heard the news from their superiors, the king's soldiers believed the warriors might attack them in anger because the Treaty of Ghent had not secured territorial independence for the indigenous people but only restored aboriginal rights to their prewar status. (See Taylor Berry to the Commanding Officer of His Britannic Majesty's Forces at Prairie du Chien, April 10, 1815, and Andrew Bulger to Robert McDouall, June 19, 1815, Thwaites, "Bulger Papers," 130, 150; Thomas Forsyth to the Secretary of War, April 15 and 30, 1815, Thwaites, "Letter Book of Thomas Forsyth," 337–38; Bulger to William Clark, May 23, 1815, Brymner, "Capture of Fort M'Kay," 259; Bulger, *Autobiographical Sketch*, 21–22; Ninian Edwards to the Secretary of War, May 22, 1815, Gregg, "War of 1812," 344–45; Ferguson, *Illinois in the War of 1812*, 184–207.)

Although the British in Prairie du Chien heard that the war had ended from American sources in April, they did not receive official word of peace from their superiors until May 22, 1815, partly because of isolation and bad weather, but mainly because of the personal irresponsibility of the messenger charged with delivering the news. The latter date was important in the immediate postwar interactions between Great Britain and the United States because Crown officers used it to affirm that no war parties had gone on campaign after officially hearing of the end of hostilities (which included BH's followers) and thus claimed that the natives should not be subject to retribution by the Americans. In contrast, the Republic's officials tried to use the late skirmishes to assert their authority on the upper Mississippi with an aggressiveness that violated at least the spirit, if not also the article, of the treaty that restored indigenous rights in the United States. As it was, the Ameri-cans knew that at least a portion of the Sauks and Foxes had decided to continue fighting after learning about the return of peace in April 1815, which helped to harden their anti-aboriginal views. (See Robert McDouall to Frederick Robinson, August 3 and 19, 1815, and Extract from Proceedings of a Court of Inquiry, October 6 and 10, 1815, British Military Records, 258:210–17, 324–54; Thomas Forsyth to the Secretary of War, April 30, 1815, Thwaites, "Letter Book of Thomas Forsyth," 338.) Even the title assigned to BH's April 18, 1815, speech suggests that he had no *official* knowledge of the war's end as it included the phrase, "Delivered before Peace was Known, at Prairie du Chien" ("Prairie du Chien Documents," 278; see also Gregg, "War of 1812," 344–47).

153. In addition to debate within the Sauk community mentioned by BH, British officials returned to Prairie du Chien and held a council in August 1815 with the tribe and other First Nations. They encouraged the natives to make peace and clarified how aboriginal rights that had existed in 1811 had been restored in the Treaty of Ghent despite strong insinuations from the Americans to the contrary. BH attended that council and understood the provisions of the peace as they affected the Sauks but was despondent that more had not been gained. He also said he was pleased with the quantity of presents the king's representatives gave his people to help them through the coming winter; however, he tried to shame his allies by reminding them that the Sauks had been reluctant to take up arms until threatened by Robert Dickson, and he recalled his understanding that the British had told the Sauks they would not make peace "until the Americans were entirely driven off our lands and those of our ancestors" before concluding with statements that indicated that he might continue fighting despite the appeal to stop (BH Speech, August 3, 1815, British Military Records, 258:285–87, reproduced in section 6 of BH's texts in this book).

154. Namoitte (or Nomite or LaMoite) had moved to the Missouri River during the war to settle with the neutralist party but flew a Union Jack over his lodge on occasion and otherwise expressed contempt for Americans. The Sauks were unsure what to do because ongoing anti-American militancy seems to have been stronger among a larger portion of them than within other tribes in 1815.

155. BH's text might be read to mean that the chief who died was Namoitte, but it distinguishes between him as a "principal chief" and "our chief," who might have been someone else, whose identity is uncertain, as is his successor's, although BH then called the new person a "principal chief." BH's band did not participate in the peace treaties arranged on September 13–14, 1815, at Portage des Sioux, which were signed by the Sauks of the Missouri and by the Foxes. While BH gave the chief's death as the reason for being absent from negotiations, other records suggest that he and the people associated with him maintained a belligerent attitude toward the Americans. Namoitte and BH told British officials at Prairie du Chien in the summer of 1815 that Missouri governor William Clark had seized hostages and had threatened to kill them if BH and Namoitte did not negotiate with him within a short period of time, and they stated how the Sauks had been mistreated in council with the Americans and how officials had made claims against the tribes that contradicted their understanding of the Treaty of Ghent, which undoubtedly offended their sense of diplomatic decency. (See Jackson, note 61, *BHA*, 83; "Indian Documents," June– August 1815, 192–96. BH's speeches at Prairie du Chien [often incorrectly assumed to have occurred at Mackinac] on August 3, 1815, are presented in section 6 of BH's texts in this book. The treaties from this period are printed in Kappler, *Indian Affairs*, 2:passim. For a document confirming that American officials had seized "five principal chiefs of the Sauks and Foxes . . . as hostages" to force the "hostile tribes" to treat with the Republic, see John McDonald to Edward Tiffin, October 29, 1815, Carter, *Territorial Papers*, 17:234.)

156. The Americans made preparations to undertake offensive operations against the Sauks and Foxes if the tribes did not sign a treaty that also would confirm the 1804 land cession (Richard Graham to George Graham, April 29, 1816, Carter, *Territorial Papers*, 17:328).

157. The Americans established Cantonment Davis near the abandoned Fort Johnson late in 1815 and built Fort Edwards the next year on the east side of the Mississippi opposite the mouth of the Des Moines River. The commanding officer, on one of two gunboats at the site, may have been Colonel Robert Nicholas of the 8th Regiment of Infantry.

158. The word "squaw" is problematic because it is very rude. We might presume this was a translator's or editor's choice because it was used commonly as a substitute for "woman" in English at the time, often by people who did not realize how pejorative it is.

159. One benefit of inserting an out-of-sequence story of the murder of a group of Potawatomis by a group of rangers in 1814 as a division between the two sections on Sauk treaty negotiations in 1815 is that it strengthened BH's assertions that the Americans could not be trusted and represented a grave threat to aboriginal peoples.

160. The commandant was Captain Joseph Philips of the Corps of Artillery. Gomo's story took place in November 1814. Gomo had made peace with the Americans following the 1813 Battle of Moraviantown.

161. The cattle were meant to supply Fort Clark, which nearly had run out of food, which had necessitated engaging Gomo's people to hunt for the garrison.

162. In mid-November 1814, seventy rangers under Captain James Moore killed five Potawatomis (three men, a woman, and a boy), took a woman and child prisoner, and then retreated toward Camp Russell (in today's Madison County, Illinois). Five other natives seem to have escaped from the soldiers. In the spring of 1815, American officials "covered the graves" of the victims through offering presents and condolences, although Moore was exonerated, in part because a court of inquiry decided that the Potawatomis were "hostile." The charge that the natives were enemies does not sound convincing: even after the rangers killed people, their relatives did not attempt to avenge the deaths although they had a number of opportunities to do so; yet it is possible that they may have taken up arms against the Americans earlier in the war before reestablishing peace following the Battle of Moraviantown. (See Ninian Edwards to the Secretary of War, May 3, 1815, Carter, *Territorial Papers*, 17:171–72; Thomas Forsyth to the Secretary of War, April 13, 1815, Thwaites, "Letter Book of Thomas Forsyth," 336–37; Ferguson, *Illinois in the War of 1812*, 181–83, 189–90, 299–300.)

163. The great chief at St. Louis was Missouri governor William Clark.

164. During the treaty negotiations, William Clark said that the United States had driven Great Britain from the upper Mississippi and that the natives would not be able to deal with British traders in future. This angered the Sauks, who had heard a different and more accurate interpretation of the Treaty of Ghent from the king's representatives, who stated that the peace restored native rights to their prewar standing. Clark's statement thus led the tribespeople to reply that the Americans were deceitful, which caused him to break off negotiations. Influenced in part by a military show of strength at the council, the Sauks apologized and asked to resume the council. BH later told the British about this meeting (or possibly a similar one) in which he had been treated with disrespect by the Americans, who he believed had expressed outrageous views (BH Speech, August 7, 1817, Indian Affairs Records, 32:19162–68, reproduced in section 6 of BH's texts in this book).

165. The treaty signed on May 13, 1816, included confirmation of the 1804 treaty by the

Sauks of Rock River, as did an 1815 treaty with the Missouri Sauks and Foxes. (It is printed in Kappler, *Indian Affairs*, 2:126–28; see ibid., passim, for related Sauk and other treaties; see also Ferguson, *Illinois in the War of 1812*, 202–7.) The Sauks had little choice but to sign because continued hostilities were not viable in the face of the wider return to peace and the potential loss of alternative trade opportunities associated with the general British withdrawal from the region. By 1818, however, BH and other Sauks began refusing government annuities when they realized that they were payments for the 1804 land surrender. In 1829, Thomas Forsyth held a council at which BH was present and noted, "I also reminded the Black Hawk of the treaty of 1816, when the commissioners refused to smoke with him and the other Sauk chiefs who accompanied him down to St. Louis to make peace until they signed the treaty. The Black Hawk denied that any mention was made to him about land in making the treaty of 1816, but that the commander must have inserted in the treaty what was not explained to him and [his] friends" (Forsyth to William Clark, May 17, 1829, A. Wallace, "Prelude to Disaster," 271). At another meeting, Forsyth recorded that either BH or one of his supporters had said that the land was theirs, in part because they had defended it successfully in the War of 1812 (Forsyth to Clark, June 7, 1829, ibid., 31). This is a remarkable comment because the war could be interpreted as abrogating the original treaty, which presumably would not have come back into effect legally if its provisions had been incorporated in the 1815 and 1816 treaties without the knowledge of the Sauks and Foxes. For his part, BH told British officials that he had refused to sign a treaty surrendering land (BH Speech, August 3, 1815, Indian Affairs Records, 31:19162–68, reproduced in section 6 of BH's texts in this book).

166. This was Fort Armstrong, constructed on Rock (or Arsenal) Island near the mouth of the Rock River. Its garrison arrived when the chiefs were in St. Louis negotiating peace with the government, justifying the action on the grounds that the Rock River Sauks had not signed a peace treaty yet. The army built this post, along with Fort Crawford at Prairie du Chien and Fort Howard at Green Bay, as well as reoccupied Detroit, Mackinac, and Fort Dearborn in the postwar years. Additionally, the Americans banned British traders from this area and took other actions to secure their dominance and pave the way to remove native populations and open their lands for white settlement. The government also established the Indian agency for the Sauks and Foxes at Rock Island to exercise increased influence in tribal affairs. Part of this plan included promoting Keokuk's accommodationist leadership. When BH said that his people did not "object" to the construction of Fort Armstrong, he may have meant they did not use force against the post; however, American sources claimed that the Sauks and Foxes contemplated an attack due to their distress over the treaties of 1815 and 1816, the establishment of the fort, and its proximity to Saukenuk. At the time the natives asked neighboring tribespeople to join them but did not receive any support for renewed warfare (Richard Graham to the Secretary of War, July 8, 1816, and William Clark, Ninian Edwards, and Auguste Chouteau to the Secretary of War, July 15, 1816, Carter, *Territorial Papers*, 17:360, 362).

167. In addition to a supreme but distant god, traditionalists in the native world of the Great Lakes and upper Mississippi regions believed in a profusion of spiritual beings of greater or lesser powers, of similar or different attributes compared to humans, and of good and bad characteristics. People saw these beings playing active roles in their lives and needed to respect and propitiate them and harness their powers for the protection and good they could offer (or to prevent the evil they might inflict). The loss of the swan

spirit logically would be interpreted by Sauks as a heartbreaking event in itself, but also one that heralded a diminution of their access to the supernatural realm and a misbalancing of the human-spiritual relationship. That the Americans were responsible presumably affirmed Sauk understanding of the ignorance of the newcomers as they blundered onto the landscape, and it spoke to the larger destruction outsiders wreaked beyond the temporal damages they caused. As well, the loss of the island was sad because of the impact it had on how people enjoyed themselves and how they supplemented their diet on a seasonal round in a society where a mix of ecological zones provided a diversity of subsistence opportunities that enhanced the quality of life and helped insure people from periodic shortages that often occurred in other environmental areas due to such causes as the weather.

168. BH Speech, April 18, 1815, "Prairie du Chien Documents," 278.

169. The great father at Quebec was Sir George Prevost, governor in chief of British North America. Prevost's words almost certainly came to BH through an intermediary because there is no evidence that they ever met face to face. (For example, BH was not listed in the document "Names of the Chiefs of the Western Tribes who go to Quebec," n.d., British Military Records, 257:219.)

170. The "Red Head" was Robert Dickson, named after the color of his hair.

171. British officials gave BH some presents the day after this speech.

172. BH Speech, August 3, 1815, British Military Records, 258:140–41.

173. Namoitte's speech included the statement that "I am highly pleased to hear that our great father has made peace, but I will be better pleased when I see the Americans withdraw from where they are." It also incorporated a veiled threat that he might make peace with the United States at the expense of British interests (presumably from a sense of betrayal, as well as to encourage the Crown's representatives to address Sauk concerns more diligently since such threats were common in aboriginal diplomacy in order to force white powers to attend to native issues). He also complained that it "is a misfortune for me, after having reinforced my village . . . that I should . . . be obliged to bury the war club" (Speech from the Sauk Chief, August 3, 1815, British Military Records, 258:139–40; see other Namoitte speeches, August 3, 1815, ibid., 258:179–83). At the same time, the Sauks informed the British that they might continue fighting, as one document noted that some chiefs had stated that "no American fort should be established on their lands and they would defend their country like men" (Robert McDouall to Frederick Robinson, September 22, 1815, ibid., 258:273; see also Extract from Proceedings of a Court of Inquiry, October 6 and 10, 1815, ibid., 324–54).

174. BH Speech, August 3, 1815, ibid., 258:285–87. The speech was made in reply to one by Brevet Lieutenant Colonel Robert McDouall of the Glengarry Light Infantry, the senior British officer on the upper Great Lakes–Mississippi front, but McDouall was not present at Prairie du Chien; instead, Thomas Anderson of the Indian Department relayed his words at the council. This has generated some confusion because McDouall's presentation is dated Mackinac, June 28, 1815 (ibid., 258:276–79), which has led some historians to think that the meeting between BH and the British occurred at that location on that date; however, BH spoke at Prairie du Chien as indicated in a closely related document (Address to, and translated by, Captain Thomas Anderson at Prairie du Chien, August 3, 1815, ibid., 258:284).

175. The British distributed large quantities of presents at this council.

176. One Crown official, in reference to BH's accusation directed at Dickson, com-

mented that the speech of "Black Hawk (perhaps the ablest and bravest since the death of Tecumseh), is strictly true. Mr. Dickson in May 1814, prior to my arrival at Mackinac, sent the threatening speech to which he alludes, and which the Sauks did not act on till the recapture of Prairie du Chien by Lieutenant Colonel McKay in July, who sent them a supply of powder, and the very next day they attacked and completely defeated a strong detachment of the Americans destined to reinforce their garrison at La Prairie [at the Battle of Campbell Island]. They were commanded by the Black Hawk, who is famous for his exploits on the Mississippi" (Robert McDouall to Frederick Robinson, September 22, 1815, British Military Records, 258:274–75).

177. Many native people wanted the Ohio River to be the boundary between their lands to the north and west and those of the United States to the south and east. It not only represented an agreed border established in 1768 before the American Revolution, when Britain asserted sovereignty over the territory that later became part of the United States, but reflected the military situation when Britain acknowledged American independence in 1783 because Crown and indigenous forces controlled the country north of the river, even though diplomats agreed to establish the British-American border farther north through the Great Lakes. The Americans, however, had conquered much of modern Ohio from the First Nations during the 1790s, so logically a border, in the best of circumstances had a native homeland been created, would have been located somewhat north and west of the Ohio River in the Old Northwest.

178. BH meant that he would visit the British, although he was unsure whether they would retain Mackinac Island in the larger Michilimackinac region or establish another post elsewhere (which the British did on Drummond Island in Lake Huron for a time, although the Sauks also visited them at Amherstburg on the Detroit River).

179. BH meant that while he was willing to follow British advice to maintain the peace, the hostility he felt for the Americans made it difficult to do so.

180. BH Speech, August 7, 1817, Indian Affairs Records, 32:19162–68.

181. Marginal note in the original (henceforth MN) associated with "black cloud": "Americans."

182. MN for "smoked the pipe": "made peace."

183. MN for "your neighbors": "traveled in fear at Michilimackinac" (restored to American control after the war as part of the requirement that both powers return captured territory to their former enemy).

184. MN for "paukumangin": "war club"; MN for "brethren": "allies."

185. MN for "Red Head": "Mr. [Robert] Dickson"; MN for "agent at Amherstburg": "Colonel [William] Caldwell" (Indian Department superintendent in the Western District, militia officer, and prominent Upper Canadian).

186. MN for "Michnenany": "pointing to a principal warrior." The "great warrior" was Sir George Prevost, who oversaw the defense of British North America during the war.

187. MN for "a great man": "nation."

188. MN for "parole": "the foregoing speech."

189. William McKay was the senior Crown official present to hear BH's words. The incident referred to events associated with the British capture of Prairie du Chien in July 1814.

190. MN for "large canoes": "gun boats" at the Battle of Campbell's Island in July 1814.

191. MN for "hair off from a great many big knives' heads": "scalps"; MN for "slaves": "prisoners"; MN for "Tebisauque": "Fort McKay, Prairie du Chien."

192. MN for "the river": "Mississippi"; MN for "full of warriors": "six hundred men"; MN for "great guns": "eight gunboats, twelve guns each." The officer mentioned was Captain Thomas Anderson.

193. The event was the Battle of Credit Island in September 1814.

194. MN for "great tomahawk": "war belt with twelve tribes of Indians marked upon it" (made with wampum).

195. MN for "creditors": "Americans." Why BH called them creditors is unclear.

196. MN for "their hair": "scalps."

197. MN for "hair and slaves": "thirty-four scalps and three prisoners"; MN for "be charitable to them": "restore the prisoners [to their own people] and buy the scalps" (or, more precisely, present gifts in recognition of native achievements because the British did not buy scalps).

198. MN for "yesterday": "last year"; MN for "black cloud": "the Americans."

199. MN for "the big knives below our village": "at St. Louis."

200. MN for "American chiefs": "officers."

201. MN for "men ready to light them": "gunners with matches in their hands"; MN for "lances": "bayonets."

202. MN for "under the shadow": "protection." The great American father was President James Madison.

203. MN for "yesterday": "last year."

204. MN for "scalp song": "song used after battle."

205. BH Speech, August 9, 1817, Indian Affairs Records, 32:19169–70. In reply to BH's previous speech of August 7, the British acknowledged the difficulties the natives faced and promised to communicate their concerns to their superiors. On August 8 they distributed presents to the aboriginal delegates; then BH gave this speech the next day.

206. MN for "the key": "[Saukenuk at] Rock River" (located astride the Mississippi River route between the strategic communities of St. Louis and Prairie du Chien).

207. MN for "the pipe": "pipe of friendship." The Mesquakies are the Foxes, and the Moovavantics are the Eastern Sioux or Santee, a branch of the Dakotas.

208. MN for "like thunder": "inviolable."

209. MN for "hearts are still bloody": "mourn."

210. MN for "our hatchet was still red with blood": "immediately after the peace" (at Prairie du Chien in August 1815).

211. MN for "charitable chief": "[Brevet Lieutenant] Colonel [Robert] McDouall" (who commanded at Mackinac during the later period of the British occupation of the post in the war, and who sent the supplies from there to Prairie du Chien).

212. The speaker was William McKay.

213. MN for "nights": "years."

214. MN for "tomorrow": "next year." The statement "cross the great salt lake and beg the assistance of our great father" indicated that he would cross the Atlantic to see King George III and plead his case at the highest political level possible.

WILLAIM APESS (PEQUOT)

1. The family name was spelled "Apes," although William Apess (henceforth WA) used "Apess" later in life, such as after publishing his memoirs, perhaps to clarify pronunciation

and reduce opportunities to insult him. While that spelling does not seem to have been used at the time of the War of 1812, the current scholarly consensus favors it over "Apes," and generally I use it in this book except where the other spelling is more appropriate. For WA's publications accompanied by an extensive introduction and annotations, see WA, *On Our Own Ground* (henceforth *OG*), although its editor, who deserves considerable credit for reintroducing WA to us, does not provide the level of detail related to WA's 1812–era memoirs (and a few other aspects of his life) that this book does. Other important texts include O'Connell, "Apess, William," 1:555–57; O'Connell, "'Once More let us Consider,'" 162–77; McQuaid, "William Apes."

2. Someone named William Apes served in Seldon's Regiment from Connecticut, which fought against the Crown during the American Revolution (Compiled Service Records, 1775–83). It also is possible that this person served in the Seven Years' War (Brown and Rose, *Black Roots*, 9–11). Alternatively, this limited information may indicate that one or more relatives of WA had enlisted in white military forces in the eighteenth century.

3. WA gave two different birthdays, January 30 and 31 (*Son of the Forest* and *Experiences of Five Christian Indians*, *OG*, 3, 120). See also O'Connell, "Introduction," *OG*, xxvii–xxx; O'Connell, "Introduction," WA, *Son of the Forest and Other Writings*, xi.

4. For details on WA's family, see O'Connell, "Introduction," *OG*, xxvii–xxx; WA, *Son of the Forest* and *Experiences of Five Christian Indians*, *OG*, 3–5, 119–20; O'Connell, "Apess, William," 1:555; Brown and Rose, *Black Roots*, 9–11. Interestingly, the 1834 Mashpee census listed WA as being native and white, although his possible black origins may not have been noted by the census taker, who recorded WA's age incorrectly (Communication from Rosemary Burns at the Mashpee Historical Commission and Archives, June 14, 2012). For native indentured servants, see Silverman, "Impact of Indentured Servitude." For the black presence within aboriginal society in the region, see Mandell, "Shifting Boundaries of Race and Ethnicity"; J. Sweet, *Bodies Politic*.

5. O'Connell, "'Once More let us Consider,'" 173.

6. Brown and Rose, *Black Roots*, 11. The number of children implied by WA's *Son of the Forest*, *OG*, 5, was greater than the number listed in *Black Roots*.

7. WA, *Son of the Forest*, *OG*, 6–7; see also Brown and Rose, *Black Roots*, 11. The woman described in the 1831 edition as WA's grandmother may not have been a blood relation because the 1829 edition of *Son* described her as his grandfather's "companion" (O'Connell, "Textual Afterword," *OG*, 315).

8. O'Connell, "Introduction," *OG*, xlviii.

9. WA, *Son of the Forest*, *OG*, 11.

10. For discussion of indentured servitude and maintaining family ties in the native world, see Herndon and Sekatau, "Colonizing the Children." Beyond the personal descriptions of his problems as an indentured servant in this book, WA also spoke about his sister, who "was slavishly used and half starved," while also recording that "I have not forgotten, nor can I ever forget, the abuse I received myself," and noted that white masters also kept native children at home to perform work "unbefitting the Sabbath" rather than let them go to church (WA, *Indian Nullification*, *OG*, 187).

11. WA, *Son of the Forest*, *OG*, 6–7.

12. WA, *Experiences of Five Christian Indians*, *OG*, 148–51 (quote on 150); Brooks, *Common Pot*, 228. For more on Sally George, see WA, *Son of the Forest*, *OG*, 40.

13. WA, *Son of the Forest*, *OG*, 41. The Lamb (of God), of course, is Jesus Christ.

14. Ibid., 42.

15. Ibid., 44; see also 51.

16. Ibid., 46.

17. Ibid.; O'Connell, "Introduction," *OG*, xxxiv; O'Connell, note 45, WA, *Son of the Forest and Other Writings*, 46. The 1834 Mashpee census, mentioned above as of limited veracity, listed Mary Apess as a mulatto (Communication from Rosemary Burns at the Mashpee Historical Commission and Archives, June 14, 2012).

18. Mary Wood's autobiography forms part of WA, *Experiences of Five Christian Indians*, *OG*, 133–44.

19. WA's 1831 edition of his autobiography did not include discussion of his change in ecclesiastical allegiance, but it may be examined in the 1829 edition in O'Connell, "Textual Afterword," *OG*, 321–24. WA's status within the Methodist Protestant Church is unclear. As someone with a preaching license who worked as a missionary, he almost certainly was a layperson rather than an ordained minister, although he did imply he had been ordained when he wrote in 1833 that he had been with the Methodist Protestant Church "something like four years, as a preacher of the Gospel; and in that time have received holy orders as an authorized minister of Christ, to attend to the duties of a pastor" (WA, *Experiences*, *OG*, 133). The terms "holy orders," "minister," and "pastor," however, can be used with enough fluidity to incorporate lay individuals fulfilling a role in a church, although most people naturally would read these words to mean that someone was an ordained clergyman, and WA may have intended to claim a status he did not possess. A lawyer, Benjamin F. Hallett, who wrote a foreword to one of WA's publications, described him as a "regularly ordained minister," and various documents included in the booklet describe him as "the Reverend William Apes" (WA, *Indian Nullification*, *OG*, 167 et passim). Nevertheless, there remains enough mutability in "regularly ordained" to allow someone to imply a standing in the church other than the post actually held while avoiding a charge of outright falsehood, while Hallett may have been mistaken or misled. Newspapers that implied or assumed ordination by using the term "the reverend" include the *Salem Gazette*, October 1, 1830; *Liberator*, August 11, 1832; *Norfolk Advertiser and Independent Politician*, March 23, 1833; *Eastern Argus*, June 11, 1834; and *Massachusetts Spy*, June 17, 1835, but we have no reason to think they did so for reasons other than that they had been led to believe WA was a minister without questioning his status. WA did call himself "the reverend," such as on the title page of his *Eulogy on King Philip* in 1836. We also need to remember that "reverend" is an adjective, not a noun, which again allows for some flexibility in meaning, even though it is a term primarily meant for ordained people. Indications that WA was not ordained in the sense most people would assume to be the case exist in a notice in the *New York Evangelist* of July 26, 1830, which only recorded WA's receipt of a preaching license (Miller, "Mouth of God," 228–29), and a notice WA placed in a paper announcing a camp meeting where he described himself only as "Preacher in Charge" (*Nantucket Inquirer*, July 23, 1836), both of which suggest he fulfilled a lay leadership role. One paper presented WA as a licensed preacher rather than an ordained minister (*Norwich Courier*, January 9, 1833), and a notice of his death described him as "William Apes, otherwise known about the country as 'Apes the Missionary Preacher,'" again implying that he may not have been ordained formally as a clergyman, and hence was ineligible, for instance, to celebrate the Lord's Supper or solemnize marriages (*North American*, April 12, 1839). In 1833, when charged with committing

crimes in association with the Mashpee Revolt, the court record listed WA's occupation as "clerk" (*Commonwealth of Massachusetts v. William Apes et al.*, Court of Common Pleas, Barnstable, September Term, 1833). Technically, the term can be used for a clergyman, as in "clerk in holy orders," but that was most unusual at the time and generally was restricted to governmentally established churches, not denominations like the Methodists. If the court document used the term "clerk" to indicate a church position as opposed to a secular one, it would make more sense to interpret the designation as a parish clerk of the kind who assisted in worship, such as in leading the people's parts of liturgically based services, as commonly occurred in some churches, although this role largely became extinct later in the nineteenth century and is unfamiliar to us today. There also is a letter from a knowledgeable church official that suggests that WA was not ordained to the ministry. Written in support of WA's integrity by the president of the Protestant Methodist Conference in Massachusetts in the 1830s, it describes WA only as "the preacher to the Marshpee Indians," while another person in the letter was designated as an ordained minister through use of the term "the reverend," with the distinction between the two men logically being read to mean that WA was a lay preacher (Thomas F. Norris to whom it may concern, May 7, 1835, reproduced in *Indian Nullification, OG*, 247). Most scholars seem to have accepted WA's status as an ordained clergyman from his own assertions or from people who reported his words without confirming the claim independently, although at least one researcher thought WA only was a licensed preacher and not ordained because he could find no record of ordination in archival sources (Dexter, "Foreword" and "Introduction," Apes, *Eulogy*, iv, x). A search for independent and authoritative confirmation of ordination undertaken for this book failed to find evidence to support ordained status. Therefore, unless other evidence comes to light, it seems that WA only was a lay preacher.

20. Konkle, *Writing Indian Nations*, 100.

21. Phineas Fish to Josiah Quincy, November 25, 1833, Nielsen, "Mashpee Indian Revolt," 404.

22. Petition to Harvard College, May 21, 1833, and Proclamation, June 25, 1833, WA, *Indian Nullification, OG*, 175–77, 179–80 (quote on 179).

23. *Commonwealth of Massachusetts v. William Apes et al.*, Court of Common Pleas, Barnstable, September Term, 1833.

24. McQuaid, "William Apes," 612–22. The timing of WA's departure is uncertain, but he wrote that he knew the Mashpees for eighteen months after arriving among them in May 1833 (WA, *Indian Nullification, OG*, 190).

25. Konkle, *Writing Indian Nations*, 147–48, 156. A charge of misusing funds also dates to the period just before WA went to the Mashpees when one newspaper expressed concern over his intentions in soliciting money to build a church for the Pequots, based on information received from a Pequot woman and a white man (*Norwich Courier*, January 9, 1833). In another instance, a Methodist minister and others accused him of being "a colored man, professing to be a minister" and a "deceiver and an imposter" who bought "lottery tickets" and misappropriated "money collected by him from religious persons for charitable purposes" (*Newburyport Herald*, October 9, 1832). In that instance, however, WA challenged these claims in court and forced his accusers to retract their statements even though they probably were correct in indicating that he was not ordained (WA, *Indian Nullification, OG* [which includes third-party documents affirming the retraction], 242–47).

26. A good study of the *Eulogy on King Philip* within the social context of 1830s Boston is Vogel, "Staging Race and Sabotaging Whiteness," 55–95. See also O'Connell, "Introduction," *OG*, xiii–xxiv; Brooks, *Common Pot*, 198–218.

27. Report from Washington in the *Sun* (New York), December 4, 1837.

28. One scholar, Maureen Konkle, supports the idea that WA's first wife died, while another, Robert Warrior, thinks the limited evidence suggests that WA left his wife (Konkle, *Writing Indian Nations*, 147, 152–56; Warrior, *People and the Word*, 40–41).

29. *Albany Evening Journal*, April 13, 1839.

30. Konkle, *Writing Indian Nations*, 147, 152–56; quotations are from the coroner's inquest, April 10, 1839, ibid., 154–55. Alcohol may have been a fundamental factor in WA's death (Warrior, *People and the Word*, 40–41).

31. Tiro, "Denominated 'Savage.'" See the bibliography for a selection of recent historical and literary scholarship on WA.

32. E.g., P. Jones, *History of the Ojebway Indians*; Copway, *Traditional History and Characteristic Sketches*; Williams, *Life of Te-ho-ra-gwa-ne-gen*. See also Peyer, *Tutor'd Mind*.

33. Seaver, *Narrative of the Life of Mrs. Mary Jemison*; R. Anderson, *Memoir of Catharine Brown*.

34. Scholarship on these forms of literature is extensive, and one text of particular relevance to the use of captivity stories (actual and fictional) in the War of 1812 is Eustace, *1812*, 118–67.

35. The appendix derived from Elias Boudinot is in WA, *Son of the Forest*, *OG*, 52–97. For discussions on WA's authorship, see O'Connell, "Introduction," *OG*, xl–xlv, 165; O'Connell, "Introduction," WA, *Son of the Forest and Other Writings*, xvi–xix; Konkle, *Writing Indian Nations*, 148–54. O'Connell suggests that there is a hint in the first edition of *Son* that WA may have dictated some or all of that version of his life story because the book refers to him in the third person in one instance (O'Connell, "Textual Afterword," *OG*, 315), but the bulk of the internal evidence, such as consistency of voice over several publications, suggests that he wrote his own works, at least for the most part.

36. The wicked one was Satan.

37. William Hillhouse of Montville near New London was a judge and political figure from a prominent family. He had been elected to the Continental Congress in the 1770s, although he did not attend, but had fought against the Crown during the American Revolution as a cavalry officer.

38. It was WA's indenture that had been sold. Years later, he may have alluded to the pain of this incident when he noted that during King Philip's War in 1676, settlers sold the ten-year-old son of the native chief into slavery, which he described as a "horrid act," and exclaimed, "I can hardly restrain my feelings, to think a people calling themselves Christians should conduct so scandalous, so outrageous" an act, "making themselves appear so despicable in the eyes of the Indians" (*Eulogy on King Philip*, *OG*, 301).

39. The Furmans' decision to sell the indenture seems harsh, but there are indications elsewhere in the autobiography that WA may have been uncontrollable. William Hillhouse was in his early eighties; he died in 1816.

40. "Presbyterian" here and elsewhere in fact referred to the Congregationalist Church. WA, like many other contemporary evangelicals, favored spontaneous prayers and demonstrative expressions of faith, condemning written prayers and liturgical worship.

41. Presumably WA meant Baptist or other evangelical religious services while living in the Furman household.

42. The evening meetings were religious services or events, possibly within a Baptist church with which WA was familiar from his life with the Furmans.

43. Note how the injustice of selling WA's indenture without his consent was made worse in his eyes because it was done by a people possessing a history of abusing and exploiting native people (see Wyss, "Captivity and Conversion," 75).

44. Like William Hillhouse, William Williams III came from a prominent family and was a judge. He also served as overseer of the Mashantucket Pequots at a later date.

45. The judge was William Hillhouse, who presumably had warned William Williams about WA's rebelliousness.

46. By not professing religion, WA meant that he had not formally joined a church through baptism, which was logical given his young age and the evangelical practice of waiting until people had reached a level of maturity to understand their faith before being baptized, unlike other churches that baptized infants. (He was baptized in 1818.) The "Christians" seem to have been an evangelical sect with whom he was familiar, possibly a group called the "Christian Church" (WA, *Son of the Forest*, OG, 12, and O'Connell, note 6).

47. WA's allusion is to the hymn *Love* by Isaac Watts (1674–1748), which derived from 1 Corinthians 13:1. His autobiography is full of quotations from and references to the Bible and devotional texts, but citations to them in this book have been confined mainly to those he emphasized through quotation marks, italics, or exclamation points in his 1831 publication and which have been regularized here with quotation marks.

48. The "two or three years" included time covered in the previous section. The date at which the Methodists arrived in his community is uncertain, although it seems logical that it was in 1812, judging from the way WA covered his story. The "Pharisee and the worldling" represented an unholy union of people from mainline churches and individuals indifferent or hostile to religion.

49. "Noisy" described aspects of Methodist services, marked by shouts of praise and other exuberances during the years before the church moved to more restrained forms of worship.

50. WA's other autobiography, *Experiences of Five Christian Indians* (OG, 125), also notes that this was the first time WA attended a Methodist meeting, although he clearly had been exposed to evangelical worship before with other Christians.

51. Presumably "cementing the brethren" included WA's incorporation into the congregation, as he likely enjoyed a sense of belonging among his coreligionists in contrast to the general alienation that marked his indentured life and, to some extent, mirrored his sense of estrangement from the dominant society because of his aboriginal status (Tiro, "Denominated 'Savage,'" 658–59).

52. Brother Hill, whose identity is uncertain, appeared as a preacher in *Experiences of Five Christian Indians* (OG, 127) and seems to have made a significant impression on WA. The biblical allusion is to John 1:29.

53. The quotation derives from Numbers 10:29.

54. "Awful place" indicated hell, while "another place" referred to an afterlife in heaven. These allusions and descriptions in WA's text likely captured some of the characteristics of the preaching he heard among the Methodists.

55. WA's allusion to brass is to God's curse for obstinacy in sin, as in Deuteronomy 28:22–23.

56. While not biblical, this phrase was common in religious discourse, although its sense is captured in Philippians 3:21.

57. "Perfect freedom" does not appear in the Bible but in other texts, most famously in the Collect for Peace in the Anglican (or Episcopal) Book of Common Prayer. There is a modest irony in WA's use of a text from this liturgically centered denomination, given his stated opposition to written prayers. He owned Anglican literature (Konkle, *Writing Indian Nations*, 153).

58. This phrase that captured WA's epiphany incorporates the language of various texts, such as Luke 7:47, John 5:8, 5:14, and 8:10–11.

59. The quotation is from Luke 2:13–14.

60. Presumably the "children of God" were fellow members of WA's Methodist congregation rather than Christians as a whole, who, of course, formed the vast majority of people in Connecticut at the time. As written, the text does not indicate that he favored one kind of person over another in his faith based on racialized differences.

61. Given that his conversion occurred on March 15, 1813, and that he ran away from the Williams household on March 25 (as indicated in his memoirs), the intervening text between the conversion and escape makes better sense if read to include the period leading up to that moment as well as the ten days that followed, which perhaps covered a period from some point in 1812 to March 1813, and which also suggests that while his conversion can be dated precisely it actually occurred as a process over a period of time rather than as a sudden event.

62. The classes were meetings that occurred on days other than Sundays, such as worship services that included Bible or catechism lessons, and which may have included instruction in reading and writing, as was not uncommon.

63. Before St. Paul experienced his conversion to Christianity on the road to Damascus in c. AD 33–36, he was Saul, the aggressive oppressor of the emerging church. The analogy to WA's condition is remarkably overstated.

64. John Miner was the other boy (O'Connell, "Introduction," *OG*, 22). It is possible that Miner was another servant of William Williams but probably was not indentured like WA because Williams did not take out a newspaper advertisement for his return as he did for WA's (*Connecticut Gazette*, April 21, 1813).

65. In fall and redemption literature, the first incident toward a collapse into a life of sin typically is a small one such as WA's minor fraud.

66. They ran away on March 25, 1813 (*Connecticut Gazette*, April 21, 1813).

67. Privateers were privately owned ships and schooners that preyed upon enemy vessels in wartime as a kind of state-sanctioned piracy. Both sides licensed privateers during the War of 1812.

68. A great variety of coinage from different countries circulated in nineteenth-century North America, such as WA's British shillings, although the most common silver coins were Spanish-American dollars and fractions of dollars. WA may have used the term here (and below) to refer to money generically rather than specifically to coins from the United Kingdom.

69. A brig was a two-masted, square-rigged small ship.

70. Britain and America "exchanged" or traded prisoners of war from time to time during the conflict.

71. Presumably this was the Kingsbridge in today's Bronx, New York.

72. Hurl Gate was a dangerous strait connecting Long Island Sound to the East River, not far from New York City. This boat trip was a short one.

73. Actually, WA did not lie: William Williams offered a perversely small reward of one cent, perhaps because he did not want the troublesome boy back, although by advertising the fact that WA had run away, Williams may have wanted to express his anger and prevent WA from finding work or comfort. The notice read, "Ran away from the subscriber, twenty-fifth ultimo, an Indian boy, named William Apes, aged fifteen years. All persons are forbid harboring or trusting him on penalty of the law. One cent reward will be given to any person who will apprehend and return him to me" (*Connecticut Gazette*, April 21, 1813).

74. Why the captain wanted payment is unclear, given that the two boys worked on the vessel to pay for their passage, although he simply may have seen an opportunity to profit from their vulnerability.

75. A packet was a mail boat or passenger vessel.

76. WA may not have been able to find work on an ordinary commercial vessel because the Royal Navy began to blockade New York in March 1813 as part of its growing presence off the Atlantic Seaboard and its efforts to seize American ships at the same time that privateers from Britain and its colonies also tried to capture merchant vessels. In contrast, his companion, John Miner, may have joined a privateer easily because their captains generally needed larger crews to engage in, or threaten, combat when approaching vulnerable targets.

77. WA's five-year enlistment occurred less than a month after he had run away, on April 19, 1813. At fifteen, he was not old enough to be recruited, but the military, having difficulty obtaining soldiers, falsified his record by stating that he was seventeen. Aside from being too young, WA was not white, and therefore legally should not have been able to join the army, but the regiment did take in some nonwhites, in part because of the problems it faced filling its ranks. WA served in the regular army, originally in the 3rd Regiment of Artillery, and then in the Corps of Artillery created as part of a reorganization of the military in 1814 (see O'Connell, "Introduction" and note 14, *OG*, xxxii, 25; Barbuto, *Long Range Guns*, 17, 19). This paragraph implies that WA may have been duped into joining, although his other autobiography suggests he chose to enlist (WA, *Experiences of Five Christian Indians*, *OG*, 130, reproduced in this book in section 5 of WA's texts). Presumably his thoughts on the mistake in joining the military came to him after he sobered up from his recruitment and began to experience the realities of army life, although he also expressed patriotic sentiments about being an American elsewhere in his autobiography.

78. Governors Island, off the southern tip of Manhattan, was the site of two defensive works, Fort Columbus (or Jay) and Castle Williams.

79. This is a reference to St. Paul's conversion to Christianity, like one WA made earlier. As also noted, his statement that he had "made no profession of religion" meant that he had not been baptized, but his assertions of being a Christian referred to the fact that he nevertheless was a believer.

80. Armies used various tunes and drumbeats to communicate orders and information around camps, garrisons, and in the field as well as to add spirit to military events,

boost morale, inspire people to enlist, maintain good relations with civilian society, and affirm traditions and values.

81. There were several fortified positions on Staten Island south of Manhattan to guard the entrance to the Hudson River and the approaches to New York Harbor.

82. A sloop was a one-masted, fore-and-aft-rigged vessel. WA traveled up the Hudson River to Greenbush near Albany, the site of a military camp and headquarters of the army's Northern Division.

83. WA was a fairly short fifteen-year-old; his enlistment record stated that he was five feet two inches tall, a height that, for instance, would have made him ineligible for recruitment in Britain's Royal Artillery, which recognized the strength men needed to operate guns and other ordnance properly. The record also said he had hazel eyes, black hair, and a dark complexion (O'Connell, "Introduction," *OG*, xxxii).

84. It seems odd that WA was so naive about army regulations regarding desertion, although he may have been told he only would serve as a drummer, as was common for underage recruits, but the enlistment form seems to have been intended to overcome that obstacle by falsifying his age as seventeen.

85. The context of this threat is unclear, although it may have related to his desertion. The racist character of the abuse is noteworthy and resonates with other examples of the prejudice WA suffered because of his origins, although he was punished very lightly (unless he chose not to mention being flogged or otherwise disciplined bodily, as was normal for deserting).

86. In the autumn of 1813 Major General Wade Hampton led four thousand soldiers north toward Montreal while another American army moved east along the St. Lawrence River against the city.

87. American soldiers regularly found themselves short of food, clothing, and equipment owing to a number of factors centered on an inadequate logistical system, as well as incompetence and corruption in the army's command and administration.

88. WA seems to have arrived at Four Corners, New York, near the border with Lower Canada in October 1813; the army left there on October 21.

89. An infantry battalion typically had a pioneer platoon, consisting of soldiers equipped with axes and other tools to clear roads, build bridges, and erect field fortifications. British forces had cut trees across the aready poor roads and otherwise had obstructed the approaches to Montreal.

90. Two dollars was a significant sum; for comparison's sake, a private in the American army earned eight dollars per month.

91. The Battle of Châteauguay in Lower Canada occurred on October 26, 1813, about thirty miles southwest of Montreal near the border (in a different location from the town of the same name). The defenders, under the command of Lieutenant Colonel Charles de Salaberry of the Canadian Voltigeurs, took up strong positions behind field fortifications and destroyed bridges and put up obstacles in an area where the terrain was difficult for the Americans to maneuver. They also tried to frighten the invaders into thinking they had a large force by making considerable noise through aboriginal war cries, bugle calls, and other means on the invaders' flanks, although the American commander, Wade Hampton, knew he possessed overwhelming numerical superiority. In the ensuing confrontation, 3,560 Americans fought four hundred opponents (mainly Canadians), with Hampton suffering between forty and eighty killed and wounded plus two dozen captured, to de

Salaberry's eighteen casualties and four men taken prisoner. After five hours of action, the Americans withdrew from the field, although they continued to suffer from Abenaki and Nipissing warriors who shadowed their retirement, harassed them the following night, and followed Hampton's army as it returned to the United States.

92. The American army endured severe privations over the winter of 1813–14 for want of shelter and other necessities (which forced many soldiers to pass the frigid months in tents), with the result that it lost many men to sickness and desertion.

93. There were three forts at Plattsburgh (Brown, Moreau, and Scott), as well as other military works. Although WA noted their construction here in his memoirs, work on these defenses occurred after the Battle of Lacolle Mill (or Odelltown), which he described next.

94. "Montreal in our view" was meant to be understood metaphorically, as Odelltown was about forty miles from the city. Major General James Wilkinson marched four thousand men into Lower Canada and occupied the village. He planned to drive the British from Lacolle just to the north of Odelltown, but it is unclear what the enigmatic general hoped to do afterward. While the fort at Île-aux-Noix in the Richelieu River five miles to the north and/or strategically located Montreal may have been targets, it also is possible that he only planned to hold a strong position on the Lacolle River in anticipation of further operations later in the year. "Heads up and eyes right" (as opposed to "forward") was a practice in the linear tactics of the period where soldiers looked slightly to the right when marching in order to align their movements to the man on their right and thereby keep their lines straight for firing and maneuvering. The phrase likely expressed the professional confidence that the soldiers felt at the beginning of the March 30, 1814, Battle of Lacolle Mill.

95. "John Bull" is a personification of England (while the British personified Americans as "Jonathan"). The "picked troop" comprised about forty men of the Frontier Light Infantry, including recent drafts from the militia, and did not constitute either an elite or a formidable force.

96. Although General James Wilkinson was an incompetent general and a notorious schemer, the pejorative statements here seem unfair. He was conspicuously active during the battle, and the "nightcap" and "dishcloth" likely were a winter hat and cape of a design worn by some American officers. (I thank Robert Henderson, whose communications of December 15 and 16, 2012, provided valuable insights into the battle.)

97. WA almost certainly used the word "fort" as a synonym for the mill rather than a separate structure, although it had some outerworks and there were other defenses in the area. There were no guns at the mill, however, and the shot came from a British flotilla on the Lacolle River that WA probably could not see. The position of the boats was such that a portion of their shot hit the top reaches of the trees.

98. A twelve-pounder was a medium artillery piece or gun, which fired solid shot as well as grape, case, and other projectiles.

99. The whistling sound indicates that some of the British shot consisted of spherical case, or shrapnel. That projectile consisted of a hollow iron ball filled with gunpowder and small balls, and which operated as an anti-personnel device like case or grape shot (although it was fired on an angled rather than a straight trajectory and was designed to explode over the heads of the enemy and had a much longer range than case or grape). WA was indeed lucky to survive the fighting that day, given his position on the twelve-pounder. At first the gun had been managed by men from the Regiment of Light Artillery, who fell as casualties; WA was part of a group from the 3rd Regiment of Artillery ordered to replace

them, but most his compatriots also fell, and the twelve-pounder had to be operated mainly by infantrymen toward the end of the battle.

100. The American army camped at Odelltown the evening after the battle, largely expecting to renew the fight the next day, but heavy rains through the night and following day made maneuvering even more difficult than it already had been. Therefore, Major General James Wilkinson returned to the United States, with the victory going to the much smaller opposing British force of less than a thousand defenders. The Americans suffered 150 casualties compared to sixty on the other side.

101. British forces raided Washington on August 24–25, 1814, and burned various federal buildings, including the White House, Congress, and the offices of the State, Navy, and War Departments, largely to retaliate for American misbehavior in Canada in 1813.

102. Lieutenant General Sir George Prevost, governor in chief of British North America, crossed the border on September 1, 1814. With 10,350 soldiers under his command, his objective was to occupy parts of the American border region and capture Plattsburgh in order to improve Lower Canada's defensibility and give the British an additional advantage in peace negotiations. He was able to take offensive action for the first time in the war after receiving reinforcement from Europe once Britain had defeated Napoleon. On Lake Champlain, the Royal Navy squadron supported Prevost, although some of its vessels still were under construction as it sailed into battle, and its crews had not been together long enough to train effectively.

103. At Plattsburgh, Brigadier General Alexander Macomb commanded 3,400 men, along with a United States Navy squadron on Lake Champlain. Additional militia and volunteers reinforced him as the British advanced.

104. Congreve rockets fired artillery projectiles across fairly long ranges. Their main advantage was their extreme lightness compared with artillery, but they suffered from problems of accuracy. WA's "bombshells" probably were exploding shot, made of hollow iron balls filled with gunpowder. When fired, a fuse lit so that the shell would blow up at or above the target. Exploding shot normally was not fired from standard guns or cannon that fired more or less along a straight trajectory (with elevations being five or fewer degrees), but from howitzers and mortars, which fired on higher trajectories. It also is possible that some of the shot fired consisted of spherical case (or shrapnel), such as WA endured at the Battle of Lacolle Mill.

105. Artillery batteries typically had small, often buried, expense magazines to secure gunpowder from danger. It also is possible that WA's magazine was a wooden box (perhaps mounted on a limber or cart) of the kind that mobile artillery used to transport their munitions. Being in "charge" of a magazine—a simple job—might have reflected WA's youth, lack of physical strength, or limited skill as a gunner despite his combat experience at Lacolle Mill.

106. Master Commandant Thomas Macdonough, USN, emerged as the hero of the Battle of Plattsburgh (also called, perhaps more accurately, the Battle of Lake Champlain).

107. The Green Mountain Boys were volunteers from Vermont who reinforced the garrison at Plattsburgh against the British. The name recalled the exploits of their famous predecessors in the American Revolution.

108. As Lieutenant General Sir George Prevost's troops advanced after crossing the border, they engaged in light skirmishing with the Americans. On September 6, a force of 8,100 men entered the north side of Plattsburgh while the Americans withdrew across

the Saranac River to the south side. The British erected batteries and exchanged artillery fire with the defenders while infantry on both sides harassed each other's positions. Yet before engaging in a serious land assault against the Americans, Prevost wanted his Lake Champlain squadron to defeat the opposing naval force so that his rear would not be threatened. On September 11, 1814, the ten gunboats and four larger vessels of the American squadron defeated the eleven gunboats and four larger craft of the Royal Navy (and captured four vessels). Sir George was unwilling to continue with the USN triumphant and capable of supporting the defense of Plattsburgh, threatening his communications, and even nullifying the strategic value of a victory on land in the overall negotiations to end the war (while also being concerned to prevent unnecessary casualties). He therefore cancelled the landward attack and withdrew back to Canada. Losses over the campaign were 220 killed and wounded on the British side and 210 on the American. The British also lost five hundred men taken prisoner (largely on the naval squadron), whereas the number of Americans captured, although uncertain, was a fraction of that figure.

109. The quote derives from Master Commandant Oliver Hazard Perry's report made after his naval squadron defeated the British on Lake Erie in September 1813: "We have met the enemy and they are ours: two ships, two brigs, one schooner, and one sloop" (Benn, *War of 1812*, 46).

110. The statement about men falling in defense of their country may have been meant as a straightforward and heartfelt statement, although it also is possible that WA thought of the sacrifices of these (mainly) ordinary people in contrast to the antiwar sentiments of leading New England Federalists, such as the Hillhouse family to which he had been indentured. For example, his master's son, James, was a Federalist who attended the Hartford Convention in 1814, which had been suspected of disloyal attitudes, while some people also expressed fears that the Federalists might make a separate peace with Britain and pull New England out of the American union. (See Banner, "Hillhouse, James," 814.)

111. WA heard of the end of hostilities in February 1815, about the same moment that the government of the United States formally ratified the Treaty of Ghent, bringing the war to its official close.

112. Army records noted that WA deserted on September 14, 1815, although he may have left earlier, in March or April (O'Connell, "Introduction," *OG*, xxxii). As a deserter, he would have been ineligible for a bounty and land grant, which undermines the power of his statement if we can assume that the army records are accurate, in which case his words "obtained my release" would be misleading.

113. Normally only white males possessed the franchise in this period. For example, the 1818 constitution of WA's home state of Connecticut restricted voting rights to white male citizens above the age of twenty-one who possessed a minimum amount of property or other claim to social standing. The constitution postdated the War of 1812, but WA wrote his autobiography years later when it was in place.

114. WA may have gone to Lower Canada at this point and stayed with the Iroquois (or Haudenosaunee) at Kahnawake outside Montreal or in one of the other aboriginal communities along the St. Lawrence River. Alternatively, he may have visited with natives in the northern United States before crossing the border.

115. Presumably the farmer also housed and fed WA because the salary was small by the period's standards, as are most of the other rates of pay WA mentioned receiving, which might reflect some combination of his vulnerability and racialized status. His army

pay, at eight dollars per month, was higher than the amount the farmer gave him in this instance, and military salaries were very low in comparison to even day laborers' wages.

116. By period standards, this was a generous but not unusual amount of rum to consume in a day.

117. There were both Algonquian Mississaugas and Iroquois Mohawks in this part of Upper Canada, although the Mohawk community of Tyendinaga actually was on the Bay of Quinte, on the north shore of Lake Ontario, west of Kingston near modern Belleville, Ontario.

118. Lake on the Mountain sits two hundred feet above the Bay of Quinte and remains a visitor attraction in today's Prince Edward County, Ontario.

119. This is below Lake on the Mountain, where the springtime overflow drilled the hole before modern changes were made to the lake's drainage. While the rock exists today, it is in an overgrown area.

120. The first quote derives from Mathew 22:37–40; the second is written in Micah 7:8.

121. This is derived from Matthew 7:15.

122. WA meant that he relapsed into a state of sinfulness.

123. This differs from the account in *Son of the Forest* in that it suggests he chose to join the army, whereas *Son* implies that he was duped into enlisting.

124. The references are to Brigadier General Alexander Macomb at Plattsburgh (September 1814), Major General Wade Hampton at Châteauguay (October 1813), and Major General James Wilkinson at Lacolle Mill (March 1814).

125. WA presumably made the journey through Upper Canada and over to Fort Niagara, the American army post at the mouth of the Niagara River, while working on the sloop he mentioned in *Son of the Forest*. The Kingston mentioned was the town in Upper Canada, not the one in New York.

126. This five-year period when WA's family apparently had given him up for dead covered the time from his enlistment in 1813 after running away from the household of William Williams to his return to the Pequot reservation at Ledyard and/or to Groton, Connecticut, in the winter of 1817–18.

127. By saying he was "ignorant as to the letter," WA meant that he lacked extensive theological training.

Bibliography

A common variation of the name William Apess is "Apes," although current scholarship prefers the longer spelling, which he adopted toward the end of his life. Books marked with an asterisk are the base texts used to transcribe and edit the autobiographies of Black Hawk and William Apess.

Allen, Robert S. *His Majesty's Indian Allies: British Indian Policy and the Defence of Canada, 1774–1815.* Toronto: Dundurn, 1992.

America's Historical Newspapers. Online through *Readex* via subscribing institutions at www.readex.com/readex/index.cfm?content=96. Papers cited in the notes in this book: *Albany Evening Journal, Connecticut Gazette, Eastern Argus, Liberator, Massachusetts Spy, Nantucket Inquirer, Newburyport Herald, Norfolk Advertiser and Independent Politician, North American, Norwich Courier,* and *Salem Gazette.*

Anderson, Rufus. *Memoir of Catharine Brown, a Christian Indian of the Cherokee Nation.* Boston: S. T. Armstrong, and Croker and Bruster, 1825.

Anderson, Thomas G. "Personal Narrative of Captain Thomas G. Anderson." c. 1870. *Collections of the State Historical Society of Wisconsin* 9 (1882): 136–206.

———. "Captain T.G. Anderson's Journal, 1814." *Collections of the State Historical Society of Wisconsin* 9 (1882): 207–52.

Antal, Sandy. *A Wampum Denied: Procter's War of 1812.* Ottawa: Carleton University Press, 1997.

Apes, William. *A Son of the Forest: The Experiences of William Apes, a Native of the Forest.* New York: Author, 1829.

*———. *A Son of the Forest, The Experience of William Apes, a Native of the Forest.* 2nd ed. New York: Author, 1831. (Copy at the Toronto Public Library.)

*———. *The Experiences of Five Christian Indians of the Pequod Tribe.* Boston: Author, 1833.

———. *Eulogy on King Philip, as Pronounced at the Odeon in Federal Street, Boston, by the Rev. William Apes, An Indian, January 8, 1836.* Facsimile 1836. Edited by Lincoln A. Dexter. Brookfield: Editor, 1985.

———. (Apess). *On Our Own Ground: The Complete Writings of William Apess, a Pequot.* Edited by Barry O'Connell. Amherst: University of Massachusetts Press, 1992. (Cited as *OG*.)

———. (Apess). *A Son of the Forest and Other Writings by William Apess, a Pequot.* Edited by Barry O'Connell. Amherst: University of Massachusetts Press, 1997.

Arthur, Brian. *How Britain Won the War of 1812: The Royal Navy's Blockades of the United States, 1812–1815.* Woodbridge: Boydell Press, 2011.

Artz, Joe Alan, et al. *Investigating the Archaeological Context of the Original Fort Madison*

(13LE10) Battlefield and Black Hawk's Ravine, Lee County, Iowa. Iowa City: Office of the State Archaeologist, 2011.

Ashwill, Gary. "Savagism and Its Discontents: James Fenimore Cooper and His Native American Contemporaries." *American Transcendental Quarterly* 8, no. 3 (1994): 211–27.

Banner, James. "Hillhouse, James." In *American National Biography*. 24 vols. Edited by John A. Garraty and Mark C. Cairnes, 10:813–14. New York: Oxford University Press, 1999.

Barbuto, Richard. *Long Range Guns, Close Quarters Combat: The Third United States Artillery Regiment in the War of 1812.* Youngstown: Old Fort Niagara Association, 2010.

Bayers, Peter L. "William Apess's Manhood and Native Resistance in Jacksonian America." *MELUS* 31, no. 1 (2006): 123–46.

Benn, Carl. *Historic Fort York, 1793–1993.* Toronto: Natural Heritage, 1993.

———. *The Iroquois in the War of 1812.* Toronto: University of Toronto Press, 1998.

———. "Native Military Forces in the Great Lakes Theatre, 1812–15." In *The Incredible War of 1812: A Military History* by J. Mackay Hitsman, 1965; revised by Donald E. Graves, 302–3. Toronto: Robin Brass, 1999.

———. *The War of 1812.* Oxford: Osprey, 2002.

———. "Norton, John." In *Oxford Dictionary of National Biography*. 60 vols. Edited by Colin Matthews et al., 41:177–79. Oxford: Oxford University Press, 2004.

———. *Mohawks on the Nile: Natives among the Canadian Voyageurs in Egypt, 1884–1885.* Toronto: Dundurn, 2009.

———. "Missed Opportunities and the Problem of Mohawk Chief John Norton's Cherokee Ancestry." *Ethnohistory* 59, no. 2 (2012): 261–91.

———. "A Mohawk Memoir from 1812: John Norton / Teyoninhokarawen." Unpublished manuscript.

Bennett, David C. "A New Perspective on the Last Days of Fort Madison," *Journal of the War of 1812* 12, nos. 1–3 (2009): 17–23; 7–15; 14–21.

Bergland, Renée L. *The National Uncanny: Indian Ghosts and American Subjects.* Hanover: Dartmouth College / University Press of New England, 2000.

BHA: see Black Hawk, *Black Hawk: An Autobiography*.

Bizzell, Patricia. "(Native) American Jeremiad: The 'Mixedblood' Rhetoric of William Apess." In *American Indian Rhetorics of Survivance*, edited by Ernest Stromberg, 34–49. Pittsburgh: University of Pittsburgh Press, 2006.

*Black Hawk. *Life of Ma-ka-tai-me-she-kia-kiak or Black Hawk.* Translated by Antoine LeClair; edited by John B. Patterson. Cincinnati: J. B. Patterson, 1833. (Copy at the University of Alberta Library; available at *Early Canadiana Online*, scanned from the Canadian Institute for Historic Microreproduction microfiche 27473, at www.canadiana.ca/en/eco.)

———. *Autobiography of Ma-ka-tai-me-she-kia-kiak or Black Hawk.* 2nd ed. Translated by Antoine LeClair; edited by John B. Patterson. St. Louis: Continental Printing, 1882.

———. *Life of Black Hawk, Ma-ka-tai-me-she-kia-kiak.* Translated by Antoine LeClair; edited by John B. Patterson, with a modern introduction and annotations by Milo Milton Quaife. 1833. Chicago: Lakeside Press, 1916.

———. *Black Hawk: An Autobiography.* Translated by Antoine Leclair; edited by J. B. Patterson, with a modern introduction and annotations by Donald Jackson. 1833/1955. Urbana: University of Illinois Press, 1990. (Cited as *BHA*.)

———. *Black Hawk's Autobiography.* Translated by Antoine Leclair; edited by J. B. Patterson, with a modern introduction and annotations by Roger L. Nichols. 1833. Ames: Iowa State University Press, 1999.

———. *Life of Black Hawk, or Mà-ka-tai-me-she-kià-kiàk, Dictated by Himself.* Translated by Antoine Leclair; edited by J. B. Patterson, with a modern introduction and annotations by J. Gerald Kennedy. 1833. New York: Penguin, 2008.

Blair, Emma Helen, ed. *The Indian Tribes of the Upper Mississippi Valley and Region of the Great Lakes.* 1911–12. Lincoln: University of Nebraska Press, 1996.

Brannan, John, ed. *Official Letters of the Military and Naval Officers of the United States during the War with Great Britain in the Years 1812, 13, 14, and 15.* Washington, DC: Way and Gideon for the Editor, 1823.

British Military Records. Record Group 8. Library and Archives Canada.

Brooks, Lisa. *The Common Pot: The Recovery of Native Space in the Northeast.* Minneapolis: University of Minnesota Press, 2008.

Bross, Kristina, and Hilary E. Wyss, eds. *Early Native Literacies in New England: A Documentary and Critical Anthology.* Amherst: University of New England Press, 2008.

Brown, Barbara W., and James M. Rose, comps. *Black Roots in Southeastern Connecticut, 1650–1900.* Detroit: Gale, 1989.

Brymner, Douglas. "Capture of Fort M'Kay, Prairie du Chien, in 1814." *Collections of the State Historical Society of Wisconsin* 11 (1888): 254–71.

Buckley, Jay H. *William Clark: Indian Diplomat.* Norman: University of Oklahoma Press, 2008.

Bulger, Andrew. *An Autobiographical Sketch of the Services of the Late Captain Andrew Bulger of the Royal Newfoundland Fencible Regiment.* Bangalore: Press of the 2nd Battalion of the 10th Regiment, 1865.

Calloway, Colin G. *Crown and Calumet: British-Indian Relations, 1783–1815.* Norman: University of Oklahoma Press, 1987.

Carter, Edwin Clarence, ed. *The Territorial Papers of the United States.* 28 vols. Washington, DC: United States Government Printing Office, 1934–70.

Chartrand, René. *Forts of the War of 1812.* Illustrated by Donato Spedaliere. Oxford: Osprey, 2012.

Colbert, Thomas Burnell. "'The Hinge on Which All Affairs of the Sauk and Fox Indians Turn': Keokuk and the United States Government." In *Enduring Nations: Native Americans in the Midwest,* edited by R. David Edmunds, 54–71. Urbana and Chicago: University of Illinois Press, 2008.

Commonwealth of Massachusetts v. William Apes et al. Court of Common Pleas, Barnstable. September Term, 1833. Barnstable Superior Court.

Compiled Service Records of Soldiers who Served in the American Army during the Revolutionary War. Record Group 93, M881, roll number 0372 (compiled 1894–c. 1912). National Archives and Records Administration.

Copway, George. *The Traditional History and Characteristic Sketches of the Ojibway Nation.* 1850. Toronto: Coles, 1972.

Cruikshank, Ernest A. "Robert Dickson, the Indian Trader." *Collections of the State Historical Society of Wisconsin* 12 (1892): 133–53.

Davenport, George. Papers. Iowa Historical Society.

Department of State. War of 1812 Papers, Correspondence, 1789–1814, Intercepted during the War of 1812. Microcopy 588. National Archives and Records Administration.

"Dickson and Grignon Papers." *Collections of the State Historical Society of Wisconsin* 11 (1888): 271–315.

Dictionary of Canadian Biography Online at www.biographi.ca/index-e.html.

Donaldson, Laura. "Making a Joyful Noise: William Apess and the Search for Postcolonial Method(ism)." In *Messy Beginnings: Postcoloniality and Early American Studies,* edited by Malini Johar Schueller and Edward Watts, 29–44. New Brunswick: Rutgers University Press, 2003.

Dowd, Gregory Evans. *A Spirited Resistance: The North American Indian Struggle for Unity, 1745–1815.* Baltimore: Johns Hopkins University Press, 1992.

Drake, Benjamin. *The Life and Adventures of Black Hawk.* 7th ed. Cincinnati: G. Conclin, 1849.

Dunnigan, Brian Leigh. *A Picturesque Situation: Mackinac before Photography, 1615–1860.* Detroit: Wayne State University Press, 2008.

Edmunds, R. David. "The Illinois River Potawatomi in the War of 1812." *Journal of the Illinois State Historical Society* 62, no. 4 (1969): 341–62.

Eustace, Nicole. *1812: War and the Passions of Patriotism.* Philadelphia: University of Pennsylvania Press, 2012.

Ferguson, Gillum. *Illinois in the War of 1812.* Urbana: University of Illinois Press, 2012.

Fisher, Linford D. "'It Proved But Temporary, and Short Lived': Pequot Affiliation in the First Great Awakening." *Ethnohistory* 59, no. 3 (2012): 465–88.

Fisher, Robert. "The Treaties of Portage des Sioux." *Mississippi Valley Historical Review* 19, no. 4 (1933): 495–508.

Ford, Thomas. *A History of Illinois: From its Commencement as a State in 1814 to 1847.* Chicago: S. C. Griggs, 1854.

Forsyth, Thomas. Papers. Missouri Historical Society.

Franke, Judith A. *French Peoria and the Illinois Country, 1673–1846.* Springfield: Illinois State Museum Society, 1995.

Fredriksen, John C., comp. *Free Trade and Sailors' Rights: A Bibliography of the War of 1812.* Westport: Greenwood, 1985.

———, comp. *War of 1812 Eyewitness Accounts: An Annotated Bibliography.* Westport: Greenwood, 1997.

Gaul, Theresa Strough. "Dialogue and Public Discourse in William Apess's *Indian Nullification.*" *American Transcendental Quarterly* 15, no. 4 (2001): 275–92.

Gough, Barry. "Michilimackinac and Prairie du Chien: Northern Anchors of British Authority in the War of 1812." *Michigan Historical Review* 38, no. 1 (2012): 83–105.

Graves, Donald. *Field of Glory: The Battle of Crysler's Farm, 1813.* Toronto: Robin Brass, 1999.

Gray, William. *Soldiers of the King: The Upper Canadian Militia, 1812–1815.* Erin: Boston Mills, 1995.

Gregg, Kate L. "The War of 1812 on the Missouri Frontier." *Missouri Historical Review* 33, nos. 1–3 (1938–39): 3–22, 184–202, 326–48.

Gussman, Deborah. "'O Savage, Where art Thou?' Rhetorics of Reform in William Apess's *Eulogy on King Philip.*" *New England Quarterly* 77, no. 3 (2004): 451–77.

Hagan, William T. *The Sac and Fox Indians.* 1958. Norman: University of Oklahoma Press, 1988.

Hallwas, John E. "Black Hawk: A Reassessment." *Annals of Iowa* 45, no. 8 (1981): 599–619.

Hamilton, Martha Wilson. *Silver in the Fur Trade, 1680–1820.* Chelmsford: Author, 1995.

Harrison, William Henry. Papers. Indiana Historical Society.

Hauptman, Laurence M., and James D. Wherry, eds. *The Pequots in Southern New England: The Fall and Rise of an American Indian Nation*. Norman: University of Oklahoma Press, 1990.

Haynes, Carolyn. "'A Mark for Them all to Hiss at': The Formation of Methodist and Pequot Identity in the Conversion Narrative of William Apess." *Early American Literature* 31, no. 1 (1996): 25–44.

Heitman, Francis R., comp. *Historical Register and Dictionary of the United States Army*. 2 vols. Washington, DC: United States Government Printing Office, 1903.

Herndon, Ruth Wallis, and Ella Wilcox Sekatau. "Colonizing the Children: Indian Youngsters in Servitude in Early Rhode Island." In *Reinterpreting New England Indians and the Colonial Experience*, edited by Colin G. Calloway and Neal Salisbury, 137–73. Boston: Colonial Society of Massachusetts, 2003.

Hickey, Donald R. *The War of 1812: A Forgotten Conflict*. Urbana: University of Illinois Press, 1989.

———. "The War of 1812: Still a Forgotten Conflict?" *Journal of Military History* 65, no. 3 (2001): 741–69.

———. *Don't Give up the Ship! Myths of the War of 1812*. Toronto: Dundurn, 2006.

Hickey, Donald R., and Connie D. Clark. *The Rocket's Red Glare: An Illustrated History of the War of 1812*. Baltimore: Johns Hopkins University Press, 2011.

Hitsman, J. Mackay. *The Incredible War of 1812: A Military History*. 1965. Revised by Donald E. Graves. Toronto: Robin Brass, 1999.

Horr, David Agee, ed. *Sac, Fox, and Iowa Indians*. 1958. New York: Garland, 1974.

Horsman, Reginald. "Wisconsin in the War of 1812." *Wisconsin Magazine of History* 46, no. 1 (1962): 3–15.

———. *Expansion and American Indian Policy, 1783–1812*. 1967. Norman: University of Oklahoma Press, 1992.

[Hunt, George?]. "A Personal Narrative." N.d., after 1833. *Report of the Pioneer and Historical Society of the State of Michigan* 8 (1886): 662–69.

Hurt, R. Douglas. *Nathan Boone and the American Frontier*. Columbia: University of Missouri Press, 1998.

Indian Affairs Records. Record Group 10. Library and Archives Canada.

"Indian Documents." *Michigan Historical Collections* 16 (1890): 190–200.

Jefferson, Thomas. Papers. Library of Congress. Online at http://memory.loc.gov/ammem/collections/jefferson_papers/.

Jones, Landon Y. *William Clark and the Shaping of the West*. New York: Hill and Wang, 2004.

Jones, Peter. *History of the Ojebway Indians; with Especial Reference to their Conversion to Christianity*. 1861. Freeport, NY: Books for Libraries, 1970.

Jortner, Adam. *The Gods of Prophetstown: The Battle of Tippecanoe and the Holy War for the American Frontier*. New York: Oxford University Press, 2012.

Jung, Patrick J. "Toward the Black Hawk War: The Sauk and Fox Indians and the War of 1812." *Michigan Historical Review* 38, no. 1 (2012): 27–52.

Kappler, Charles J., comp. *Indian Affairs: Laws and Treaties*. 2nd ed. 2 vols. Washington, DC: United States Government Printing Office, 1904.

Kelsay, Isabel Thompson. *Joseph Brant, 1743–1807: Man of Two Worlds*. Syracuse: Syracuse University Press, 1984.

Konkle, Maureen. *Writing Indian Nations: Native Intellectuals and the Politics of Historiography, 1827–1863*. Chapel Hill: University of North Carolina Press, 2004.

Krupat, Arnold. *For Those Who Came After: A Study of Native American Autobiography*. Berkeley: University of California Press, 1985.

———. *All That Remains: Varieties of Indigenous Expression*. Lincoln: University of Nebraska Press, 2009.

———. "Paterson's *Life*; Black Hawk's Story; Native American Elegy." *American Literary History* 22, no. 3 (2010): 527–52.

Lambert, Andrew. *The Challenge: America, Britain, and the War of 1812*. London: Faber and Faber, 2012.

"Lawe and Grignon Papers, 1794–1821." *Collections of the State Historical Society of Wisconsin* 10 (1888): 90–141.

Lopenzina, Drew. "What to the American Indian Is the Fourth of July? Moving beyond Abolitionist Rhetoric in William Apess's *Eulogy on King Philip*." *American Literature* 82, no. 4 (2010): 674–99.

Malcomson, Robert. *Historical Dictionary of the War of 1812*. Lanham: Scarecrow Press, 2006.

Mancall, Peter C. *Deadly Medicine: Indians and Alcohol in Early America*. Ithaca: Cornell University Press, 1995.

Mandell, Daniel R. "Shifting Boundaries of Race and Ethnicity: Indian-Black Intermarriages in Southern New England, 1760–1880." *Journal of American History* 85, no. 2 (1998): 466–501.

———. *Tribe, Race, History: Native Americans in Southern New England, 1780–1880*. Baltimore: Johns Hopkins University Press, 2008.

Matson, Nehemiah. *French and Indians of Illinois River*. 2nd ed. Princeton, IL: Republican Job Printing, 1874.

McKenney, Thomas L., and James Hall. *The Indian Tribes of North America with Biographical Sketches and Anecdotes of the Principal Chiefs*. 3 vols. Edited by Frederick Webb Hodge. Originally published as *History of the Indian Tribes of North America with Biographical Sketches and Anecdotes of the Principal Chiefs*. 1836–44. Edinburgh: John Grant, 1933–34.

McQuaid, Kim. "William Apes, Pequot: An Indian Reformer in the Jacksonian Era." *New England Quarterly* 50, no. 4 (1977): 605–25.

Melhorn, Jr., Donald F. "'A Splendid Man': Richardson, Fort Meigs and the Story of Metoss." *Northwest Ohio Quarterly* 69, no. 3 (1998): 133–60.

Mielke, Laura L. "'Native to the Question': William Apess, Black Hawk, and the Sentimental Context of Early Native American Autobiography." *American Indian Quarterly* 26, no. 2 (2002): 246–70.

Miller, Mark. "'Mouth of God': Temperate Labor, Race, and Methodist Reform in William Apess's *A Son of the Forest*." *Journal of the Early Republic* 30, no. 2 (2010): 225–52.

Mudd, Joseph A. "A History of Lincoln County, Missouri." In *An Illustrated Historical Atlas of Lincoln County, Missouri*, 9–13. Philadelphia: Edwards Brothers, 1878.

Murray, Laura J. "The Aesthetic of Dispossession: Washington Irving and Ideologies of (De)Colonization in the Early Republic." *American Literary History* 8, no. 2 (1996): 205–31.

Newquist, David LeRoy. "A Reading of Black Hawk's *Autobiography*." PhD diss., University of Iowa, 1980.

Newspapers: see *America's Historical Newspapers*.

Nichols, Roger L. *Black Hawk and the Warrior's Path*. Arlington Heights: H. Davidson, 1992.

Nielsen, Donald M. "The Mashpee Indian Revolt of 1833." *New England Quarterly* 58, no. 3 (1985): 400–420.

Norton, John. *The Journal of Major John Norton, 1816*. Edited by Carl F. Klinck and James T. Talman. 1816/1970. With a new introduction by Carl Benn. Toronto: Champlain Society, 2011.

O'Brien, Jean M. *Firsting and Lasting: Writing Indians out of Existence in New England*. Minneapolis: University of Minnesota Press, 2010.

O'Connell, Barry. "'Once More let us Consider': William Apess in the Writing of New England's Native American History." In *After King Philip's War: Presence and Persistence in Indian New England*, edited by Colin G. Calloway, 162–77. Hanover: University of New England Press, 1997.

———. "Apess, William." In *American National Biography*. 24 vols. Edited by John A. Garraty and Mark C. Cairnes, 1:555–57. New York: Oxford University Press, 1999.

Office of the Adjutant-General. Papers. Record Group 94. United States National Archives and Records Administration.

OG: see Apess, William, *On Our Own Ground*.

"Operations of the Factory System." March 8, 1822. In *American State Papers, Indian Affairs*. Class 2. Edited by Walter Lowrie and Walter S. Franklin, 2:326–64. Washington, DC: Gales and Seaton, 1834.

Owens, Robert M. *Mr. Jefferson's Hammer: William Henry Harrison and the Origins of American Indian Policy*. Norman: University of Oklahoma Press, 2007.

Patterson, J. B. "Black Hawk's Autobiography Vindicated." *Oquawka Spectator*. February 1855. *Collections of the State Historical Society of Wisconsin* 5 (1868): 300–304.

Peyer, Bernd C. *The Tutor'd Mind: Indian Missionary-Writers in Antebellum America*. Amherst: University of Massachusetts Press, 1997.

Powell, William. "Recollections of William Powell." 1877. *Proceedings of the State Historical Society of Wisconsin at its Sixtieth Annual Meeting, held October 24, 1912* (1913): 146–79.

"Prairie du Chien Documents, 1814–15." *Report and Collections of the Wisconsin Historical Society* 9 (1882): 262–81.

Private Collection of War of 1812 Papers (associated with Fort Madison).

Prucha, Francis Paul. *American Indian Treaties: The History of a Political Anomaly*. Berkeley: University of California Press, 1994.

Review of *Life of Black Hawk*. *North American Review* 40, no. 86 (1835): 68–87.

Scheckel, Susan. *The Insistence of the Indian*. Princeton, NJ: Princeton University Press, 1998.

Schmitz, Neil. "Captive Utterance: Black Hawk and Indian Irony." *Arizona Quarterly* 48, no. 4 (1992): 1–18.

Seaver, James. *A Narrative of the Life of Mrs. Mary Jemison*. Canandaigua: J. D. Bemis, 1824.

Shaw, John. "Personal Narrative of Colonel John Shaw, of Marquette County, Wisconsin." *Collections of the State Historical Society of Wisconsin* 2 (1856): 197–232.

Silverman, David J. "The Impact of Indentured Servitude on the Society and Culture of Southern New England Indians, 1680–1810." *New England Quarterly* 74, no. 4 (2001): 622–66.

Smith, M. *A Geographical View of the Province of Upper Canada; and Promiscuous Remarks on the Government.* 3rd ed. Philadelphia: Author, 1813.

Snyder, Charles. "Antoine LeClaire, the First Proprietor of Davenport." *Annals of Iowa* 23, no. 2 (1941–42): 79–117.

Snyder, J. F. "The Burial of Black Hawk." *Magazine of American History* 15 (1886): 494–99.

Stagg, J. C. A. *Mr. Madison's War: Politics, Diplomacy, and Warfare in the Early American Republic.* Princeton, NJ: Princeton University Press, 1983.

———. *The War of 1812: Conflict for a Continent.* New York: Cambridge University Press, 2012.

Strachan, John. Papers. Archives of Ontario.

Sturtevant, William C., ed. *Handbook of North American Indians.* 17 vols. Washington, DC: Smithsonian Institution, 1978–.

Sugden, John. *Tecumseh: A Life.* New York: Henry Holt, 1997.

Sutherland, Stuart, comp. *His Majesty's Gentlemen: A Directory of British Regular Army Officers of the War of 1812.* Toronto: Iser, 2000.

Sweet, John Wood. *Bodies Politic: Negotiating Race in the American North, 1730–1830.* Baltimore: Johns Hopkins University Press, 2003.

Sweet, Timothy. "Masculinity and Self-Performance in the *Life of Black Hawk.*" *American Literature* 65, no. 3 (1993): 475–99.

Tanner, Helen Hornbeck, ed. *Atlas of Great Lakes Indian History.* Norman: University of Oklahoma Press, 1987.

Thwaites, Reuben, ed., "Letter Book of Thomas Forsyth." *Collections of the State Historical Society of Wisconsin* 11 (1888): 316–55.

———, ed. "The Bulger Papers." *Collections of the State Historical Society of Wisconsin* 13 (1895): 1–153.

Tiro, Karim M. "Denominated 'Savage': Methodism, Writing, and Identity in the Works of William Apess, a Pequot." *American Quarterly* 48, no. 4 (1996): 653–79.

Trask, Kerry A. *Black Hawk: The Battle for the Heart of America.* New York: Henry Holt, 2006.

Viola, Herman J. *Diplomats in Buckskins: A History of Indian Delegations in Washington City.* Washington, DC: Smithsonian Institution, 1981.

Vogel, Todd William. "Staging Race and Sabotaging Whiteness: Marginalized Writers Redirect the Mainstream." PhD diss., University of Texas at Austin, 1999.

Walker, Cheryl. *Indian Nation: Native American Literature and Nineteenth-Century Nationalisms.* Durham: Duke University Press, 1997.

Wall, John W. *Uncommon Defense: Indian Allies in the Black Hawk War.* Cambridge, MA: Harvard University Press, 2009.

Wallace, Anthony F. C. "Prelude to Disaster." 1970. *Wisconsin Magazine of History* 65, no. 4 (1982): 247–88.

Wallace, Mark. "Black Hawk's *An Autobiography*: The Production and Use of an 'Indian' Voice." *American Indian Quarterly* 18, no. 4 (1994): 481–94.

Warrior, Robert. *The People and the Word: Reading Native Nonfiction.* Minneapolis: University of Minnesota Press, 2005.

Welburn, Ron. *Roanoke and Wampum: Topics in Native American Heritage and Literature.* New York: Peter Lang, 2001.

White, Richard. *The Middle Ground: Indians, Empires, and Republics in the Great Lakes Region, 1650–1815.* New York: Cambridge University Press, 1991.

Whittaker, William E., ed. *Frontier Forts of Iowa: Indians, Traders, and Soldiers, 1682–1862.* Iowa City: University of Iowa Press, 2009.

Williams, Eleazer. *Life of Te-ho-ra-gwa-ne-gen, Alias Thomas Williams, Chief of the Caughnawaga Tribe of Indians in Canada.* Albany: J. Munsell, 1859.

———. "The Secret Corps of Observation." N.d. *Plattsburgh Republican,* published serially in 1886–87.

Willig, Timothy D. *Restoring the Chain of Friendship: British Policy and the Indians of the Great Lakes, 1783–1815.* Lincoln: University of Nebraska Press, 2008.

Wood, William, ed. *Select British Documents of the Canadian War of 1812.* 3 vols. Toronto: Champlain Society, 1920–28.

Wyss, Hilary E. "Captivity and Conversion: William Apess, Mary Jemison, and Narratives of Racial Identity." *American Indian Quarterly* 23, nos. 3/4 (1999): 63–82.

Index

Black Hawk and William Apess are indicated as BH and WA in subentries. State, territorial, and provincial designations generally are those used in 1812–15, with UC and LC indicating Upper and Lower Canada, respectively. See maps for boundaries, community locations, distribution of First Nations, land alienation, and other information. Gallery illustrations are designated by a **g** and the figure number.